About the author

Described by BBC Radio 3 as 'one of the great British Musical Directors', Kenneth Alwyn is an English conductor, composer and writer. He is a Fellow of the Royal Academy of Music and is married to the actress Mary Law.

This first volume of his memoirs covers the period from his early childhood to conducting the Royal Ballet during the time of Margot Fonteyn.

A BATON IN THE BALLET

and other places

KENNETH ALWYN

Published by FiloBooks
First published 2015

ISBN: 978-0-9931666-0-0

For Mary and our daughters,
Lucina and Timandra

LIVERPOOL HOSPITAL, 1915

On this 100th anniversary of the Great War, *A Baton in the Ballet and Other Places* is dedicated to my father, a soldier in the 2nd Battalion of the Cheshire Regiment. He fought in France, Salonika and Macedonia and miraculously survived being severely wounded and gassed. After eleven years in the Army, he was discharged medically as 'a sergeant of good character'.

His solace was music, and when I was very young, he would play me to sleep with classical music on his wind-up gramophone.

Without him, this book could not have been written.

Under attack at Frezenberg – 2nd Battle of Ypres

Date: 8th May 1915
Regiment: 2nd Battalion, Cheshire Regiment

On 22nd April, the Germans launched the attack that would become officially known as the Second Battle of Ypres. By 8th May, the situation had become critical for the Allied armies. The Cheshires' Regimental History notes that 'behind our gassed and shattered lines, had the Germans only known, lay nothing to prevent their capturing the Channel Ports.'

The section of the front line to be held by the 28th Division, which included the 2nd Battalion (one of the Regiment's two Regular Army Battalions), was about 1.5 miles between Frezenberg at a position known as Mouse Trap Farm. This was 3 miles to the north east of Ypres (now Ieper). The Regimental History notes that 'the line to be held was nothing more effective than narrow trenches three feet deep, hastily constructed, with little wire, no communication trenches and little or no overhead cover. It was not a line in which to meet a heavy attack, yet the Allied plan required it to be held.'

Poison gas had been first used by the Germans on 22nd April. They again used gas in this attack. At that time, there was no practical defence against it. All that was done was to issue each Battalion with 200 cloth bands to be worn across the mouth (it should be noted that a Battalion at full strength would exceed 800).

At dawn on 8th May, the German artillery opened fire from the north, north east and south east with explosive and gas shells. It 'continued till the trenches and troops were battered out of shape and sense. Then the German Infantry came on. They were met by the shell-shocked survivors with the greatest bravery.' For the next few hours, the British troops managed to hold off the attack but, by 10am, the Brigade to the right of the Cheshires was finally forced to give way. This left the 2nd Battalion in a critical position as it meant the Germans could now work round their flank. Reinforcements from the two reserve companies were sent forward but were cut down by shell fire before they could reach the two companies in the front line. The Battalion's War Diary describes the situation at 1pm. 'The positions occupied by Battalion headquarters and No. 1 and No. 4 Companies were surrounded by the enemy and with very few exceptions the whole of the officers and other ranks were killed or taken prisoner.' Only small groups managed to escape. The Diary records that, at this time, known casualties included 17 dead, 200 wounded and 190 missing.

From 'Stockport 1914-1918'
www.stockport1914-1918.co.uk

ACKNOWLEDGEMENTS

I am very grateful to the following for having read that part of these memoirs in which they are mentioned and who have, where my memory has failed or I have got it wrong, very kindly put me straight:

Dame Beryl Grey

Ronald Hynd

Gordon Langford

Geoffrey Lawes

Dame Monica Mason

Diana Murray

Annette Page

Damian Penfold

Jennifer Rignold

Barry Wordsworth

My thanks to Libby Spurrier for abridging what was longer than Tolstoy's *War and Peace*, to Chris Bass for his photo retouching expertise, to Denise Bass for her assistance with proofreading and special thanks to Susie Duffy for her unfailing patience and skill in putting it all together and making it readable.

Kenneth Alwyn
Broadford Bridge
September 2014

CONTENTS

PROLOGUE

NEW YORK, 1958

The intermission was over and the audience at the Metropolitan Opera House, New York were back in their seats. They were excitedly awaiting the last ballet of the evening, a performance of Frederick Ashton's *Birthday Offering* – the *pièce d'occasion* he'd created in 1956 to commemorate the 25th anniversary of the founding of the Sadler's Wells Ballet.

Waiting on stage, was *prima ballerina assoluta* Margot Fonteyn with her *premier danseur étoile*, Michael Somes. Waiting in the wings were six other ballerinas – Beryl Grey, Svetlana Beriosova, Nadia Nerina, Rowena Jackson, Violetta Elvin, Elaine Fifield – and their cavaliers, and in the pit, the orchestra was waiting

But the curtain stayed down.

There are few things in a theatre more calculated to produce a nervous breakdown backstage than when an impatient audience begins the dreaded slow hand-clap. In desperation, the stage director despatched his assistant, Leon Arnold, to hasten an unusually tardy Robert Irving down from his dressing room. But it was empty. Bob had disappeared.

A frantic Leon now pounded the door of the Company's new Musical Director, Hugo Rignold. But having conducted the second ballet, Hugo was, so far as he was concerned, finished for the evening. He was in his underwear, his evening dress was back on its hanger, and he and I were relaxing with cooling gin and tonics.

The slow hand-clap was now joined by voices raised in protest at this interminable delay, and even our usually calm Margot Fonteyn was getting a little edgy.

'Mr Rignold,' gasped Leon (the conductors' dressing rooms were up several flights of stone stairs), 'we can't find Mr Irving, so will you please conduct *Birthday Offering* and *hurry* down?'

'But I'm not down to conduct it,' said Hugo. 'It's Mr Irving's ballet and it's not yet in my repertoire. He must be ill somewhere, or have made a mistake.'

Whatever the reason, it was clear that there was no one to conduct. Would the remainder of the evening have to be cancelled and the audience given their money back?

*Un*like everyone else, I was relaxed and cool in my new grey lightweight suit, purchased that day for twenty-five dollars from Macy's Department Store to combat the stickiness of New York. Unfortunately, whilst playing the piano for the afternoon rehearsals of this very ballet, the red polish from the piano bench had transferred itself to the seat of my trousers, so, from the rear, I was not very presentable and resembled a grey baboon.

Hugo turned to me. 'Do *you* know *Birthday Offering*?'

This was the moment that every performer waits for: the golden opportunity which should be grabbed with both hands, but I decided to play it cool. I murmured that if it were a *real* emergency, I could probably get through the piece, but as I was not down to conduct until a few days later, my evening dress was still in a basket under the stage, so I had nothing to wear.

But the situation was desperate, and so down to the stage I went, wearing Leon's skimpy dinner jacket, my blue shirt, his black bow tie, my grey trousers with the baboon bloom and my brown shoes.

The effect on the dancers of this apparition was relief that someone was at last going to get rid of that demoralising noise from out front, as through the loudspeaker was heard: 'Ladies and gentlemen, the performance is about to commence.'

'*Merde,* Ken!' said Margot, and the others smiled encouragingly.

The orchestra pit at the Met was quite shallow, so as I walked towards the rostrum, my strange garb was illuminated by a spotlight, and there was much laughter from the audience. The musicians, however, were *not* amused, never having seen me before.

Who was this guy in fancy dress?

I smiled reassuringly, shook the limp hand of the leader of the orchestra, a giant of a man who dwarfed his Stradivarius violin, mounted the rostrum and opened the orchestral score.

The house lights dimmed, the laughter died down and the audience at last became silent.

I raised my arms, and in those two or three seconds when bows are raised and long, deep breaths are drawn (a moment which must not be prolonged, lest it passes), every eye was on me. Then down came my baton and the sound of Glazunov's wonderful overture burst into the world from what I later discovered was Toscanini's old orchestra.

It was as though the musicians had given a sigh of relief that they were in safe hands. They played magnificently, and although I conducted them many times afterwards and they always seemed pleased to see me, nothing quite recaptured the magic of our first music together.

I had to wait forty years to read in Robert Irving's autobiography the reason for that near-debacle in New York, of which more – later.

Robert Irving *was a world-class bridge player, an international climber and holder of the Distinguished Flying Cross, awarded in 1943 for having flown a Beaufighter on a dangerous mission in appalling weather conditions up and down the Norwegian coast looking for the German battleship 'Scharnhorst'. He found it and passed on a message which led to its sinking by British Naval Forces.*

Hugo Rignold's *early career was as a violinist and vocalist in Jack Hylton's dance band. He became known as one of the three greatest jazz violinists in the world – the others being the American Joe Venuti and the Frenchman Stéphane Grappelli. He also served in the Royal Air Force and discovered his true vocation conducting what became the Israeli Philharmonic. After the war he never returned to jazz but became the Musical Director of the Liverpool and City of Birmingham Symphony Orchestras, which he raised to an international standard. He also raced his own Bugatti!*

CHAPTER 1

CROYDON, 1935

Death in the afternoon

Croydon in the 1930s

'Would you like a banana, dear?' said Auntie Nell. A sea of anxious faces swam into view through my tears. Would a banana help now that I'd been told that my mother would never be coming home again? The year before, when I was nine, Mum had said the same thing to me about Dad.

I remembered that morning when, as I played among the fuchsias in our front garden, Dad had come out of the front door carrying a Sainsbury's bag. I thought he was making his weekly visit to the Mayday Hospital just across the road, so I hardly looked up when he said, 'Ta-ta, son.'

I didn't know that this was the last time I would ever see him, or that he knew he was saying goodbye forever.

My earliest memory of Mum and Dad was a week's holiday

in Blackpool in 1930. We left Thornton Heath very early in the morning and travelled by John Bull coach from Victoria Bus Station. John Bull's were the first of the luxury coaches with a bar, sandwiches and a lavatory (I had never been in one that moved before), and after the longest journey I'd ever made, the tallest building I'd ever seen finally came into sight – Blackpool Tower.

Then we walked to our digs: a small terraced house within sight of the sea with an aspidistra in the window, where, after a warm northern welcome, our landlady, Mrs Sloane, gave us a fish and chip supper.

It was a wonderful week in a paradise of seven miles of golden sand, with a seafront where coloured trams packed with happy people shared the promenade with donkey rides, fun-fairs, the 'big dipper' scenic railway, paddling pools, candy-floss, cheerful music and sticky rock; all in the shadow of a Victorian copy of the Eiffel Tower. The Tower had many wonders: a zoo where for the first time I saw lions, elephants and tigers, and a circus where beautiful white horses were ridden bareback by sequined girl riders. Tight-rope walkers, jugglers and clowns were led into the ring by a man in a red coat and shiny boots, who was wearing a top hat and cracking a whip – all to an exciting march played by a band, led by a man waving a white stick.

The music was Fucik's 'Entry of the Gladiators', which I was to conduct many times on the BBC's 'Friday Night is Music Night'.

At the entrance to the Aquarium was a mechanical instrument called an orchestrion, which clattered out waltzes and polkas, and through the doors, huge tanks teemed with multi-coloured and dangerous-looking fish. Some of them were pretty frightening, and they would have terrified Jerry, our goldfish. On the top of our piano at home, we had coloured postcards of King George V and Queen Mary, but in the Tower's waxwork gallery, they looked so lifelike that I thought they might have been there in person.

On YouTube you can hear the same orchestrion that I heard in 1930.

In the amusement arcade, the upper half of a pop-eyed policeman with painted rosy cheeks, being seemingly trapped in a glass case, moved his head endlessly from left to right, shrieking with demonic laughter. He was meant to be funny, but at the age of five I found him terrifying, burst into tears and was speedily removed.

A much happier place was the Tower's ballroom when, at teatime, the organist, Reginald Dixon, played 'Oh, I do like to be beside the seaside' and hundreds of couples waltzed, fox-trotted and quickstepped in their 1930s version of the BBC's *Strictly Come Dancing*.

But the happiest time of all for those of us who only knew yellow gaslight at home was at dusk, when the Tower and the whole of the seafront blazed with brilliant white and coloured electric lights – the famous 'Illuminations'.

Blackpool, 1930

In our snaps of that holiday, Dad looks very tall and rather bald, dressed in a sports jacket, grey flannel trousers and tennis shoes and is smoking a pipe. Born in 1891, he'd done well at school, winning prizes for the three 'rs' – reading, 'riting, and 'rithmetic – and somehow, somewhere, he'd taught himself to play the piano. But with an elementary education – compulsory only to the age of fourteen – when he left school, he had no trade. For a while he helped his mother to deliver milk to the inhabitants of Edgeley, Stockport from her two-wheeled dog-cart, but Dad wanted to see the world and so, at the age of seventeen, he followed the family tradition and joined the Army.

The Wetherells were traditionally British Grenadiers. Dad's grandfather, Thomas, was born in 1819, just four years after the battle of Waterloo, and he had been a sergeant of the Grenadiers. When he retired, Thomas became the landlord of the Greyhound Inn at Adswood, Stockport where, on high days and holidays, free entertainment in the pub field included sheep-dog trials, coconut shies, bare-knuckle boxing, a Punch and Judy show and dancing to a fiddle and flute.

His son, Edward, was born in 1843 and followed his father into the Grenadiers, where, as one of the tallest men in the Regiment, he was selected for the Sovereign's Company, quartered at Buckingham Palace. They were Queen Victoria's personal bodyguard.

Thomas Wetherell

Edward and Sarah Wetherell

At the Trooping of the Colour in 1991 – a hundred years after my father was born, almost to the day – my march, 'The Young Grenadier', was played by the massed bands of the Brigade of Guards when Her Majesty appeared on the balcony of Buckingham Palace. If you believe in such things, perhaps there were a couple of ghostly Grenadiers present that day, who would have been pleased that another member of the family had finally marched at the Palace!

Edward married a Stockport girl, Sarah, and they produced a son – my father, John (known as Jack) – and a daughter, my Aunt Maud.

A British soldier was paid a shilling a day. Regimental married quarters in London being available only to a few, and rented accommodation being beyond their means, Sarah remained in the family home in Stockport. Not having ever seen much of his, my father opted to serve nearer his mother and joined the Cheshire Regiment. But it wasn't long before the Cheshires were posted to India. He served six years as a peacetime soldier in the 2nd Battalion and was promoted to lance corporal, but in 1914 the Great War began, and the Cheshires were soon on active service in France on the Somme, where my father was twice wounded and gassed three times.

In 1916, Jack was posted to Salonika (now, Thessaloniki) where conditions were appalling. The Regimental History records that the Struma Valley 'must be one of the most unhealthy places in the world. To sleep on the low swampy ground without elaborate precautions means, to the Western European, at best, a sharp attack of malaria of a malignant form. The 2nd Battalion at Lozista was probably in the worst place in the valley. They had no mosquito nets and no gloves, or other protection, and practically no quinine. In three weeks, at this plague spot, the Battalion lost 700 hundred men, 400 of whom never rejoined. Men attacked by this disease dropped unconscious as if they had been shot.' (*History of the Cheshire Regiment in the Great War*, Colonel Arthur Crookenden, Naval & Military Press, 2004)

A sergeant of the military police, my father was in charge of burial parties when the 2nd Battalion were sent to bury the long-dead at Gallipoli. It was discovered that he was an amoebic dysentery carrier, and he was discharged.

His discharge papers described him as 'a sergeant of good character', but, on the basis that he wasn't actually ill, and even after serving eleven years with the Regiment, they refused him a pension.

Jack Wetherell (right)

Beatrice Reeve

Mum – Beatrice Annie Reeve – was born in Walthamstow in 1898 and was the daughter of the first wife of a 'gentleman's gentleman', a Victorian valet known in the family as 'Bluebeard', for he'd had three wives and fathered eight children, including Mum, her only brother Arthur and her three half-sisters: Alice, Nellie and Bess.

I know nothing about Bluebeard, nor the fate of his wives, and I hope that his nickname was only a joke, and not the reason for the family's move from Walthamstow to Croydon!

Mum went to Ecclesbourne Road Girls' School, where, like Dad, she received an elementary education, but with the emphasis on needlework and cooking. She won a prize for art, and her headmaster recommended that she stay on at school and train to become a teacher. But there was no money for that, and so, like her three half-sisters, she went to work as a domestic servant.

With the outbreak of the Great War in 1914, women found new tasks, and for the next four years Mum filled artillery shells. The photographs of her in her teenage years are of a slim, pretty girl with a charming smile. She had many young men friends – rare when so many men had not survived 'the war to end all wars'. But it was all perfectly innocent, for in the working-class, a baby outside marriage branded the girl a 'loose woman'.

When the war ended in 1918, 'Beat' (as she was affectionately called) gave up making food for guns in a white overall and, similarly dressed, turned to making food for people. She went to work for Sainsbury's behind the butter counter. She became expert with the wooden paddles and could deftly cut half a pound and wrap it in greaseproof paper with geometric precision.

I don't know where the pretty Sainsbury's girl and the tall, handsome, ex-Army sergeant met – I was not old enough in their lifetimes to ask – but when Dad got a temporary job with the Board of Education, in 1923 they married and moved into a flat in Thornton Heath.

Mum and Dad: Beatrice and Jack

The newly-weds were able to buy a modest suite of furniture and, from the same shop, a piano. The makers of furniture often made their own pianos too, but, sad to say, these cheap instruments were not of great durability. The frame was usually made of wood which warped easily, and after a few years, they became untuneable and only useful as a place to stand the family photographs!

In 1925 they had their only child – me – and were happy until 1929, when the Wall Street Crash and the Depression cost Dad his job. Like thousands of others, he joined the dole queues of the unemployed – many of them were men who, like him, had served their country and were promised 'a land fit for heroes'.

As a young boy

The dole money couldn't cover the rent, so we were forced to move to a one-bedroom upstairs flat in a terraced house in Eridge Road, Thornton Heath.

**Beatrice and Jack before the
Great Crash of 1929**

Mum and Dad had the bedroom and I slept in the sitting room, facing the wall of the Mayday Hospital. There was no electricity, but the cold-water kitchen had a gas-stove. The WC was in the garden and so, as the ground floor was occupied by 'Grandma' – a courtesy title for our landlady – we had to knock on her kitchen door and ask permission to 'come through'.

Her name was Sarah and hers was a sad story. One day her husband went out to buy a paper at the local shop and didn't return. Sarah thought he'd abandoned her, but a few months later, the police brought him home, still in the clothes he'd been wearing when he went out for that paper. He had no money, no memory of what had happened to him and, tragically, no memory of this strange woman whom everyone assured him was his wife. He never did remember her, and not very long afterwards he died in what was, for him, a stranger's bed.

Grandma needed our rent, but she also needed our company. The front room in her part of the house had the usual aspidistra in the window, framed prints of *The Lily of Killarney* and

Landseer's *Stag at Bay* on the wall and, because we couldn't get it up the stairs to our flat, our piano. Luckily, Grandma enjoyed music, and Mum and Dad were always welcome to come down and play.

The few shillings of dole were supplemented when Mum earned a little money cleaning and washing-up for the better-off families in the adjacent streets, but our small flat became a prison to a man who'd soldiered all over the world. The tide turned slightly when Dad got a job as a night watchman at a factory in Mitcham. I remember how proudly he showed me the time clock, which he took round the factory to register his nightly inspections at key points. But someone else also knew his routine, for one night they broke in and robbed the place, and Dad lost his job.

One morning soon afterwards, Dad was having his hair cut when the robbery was being discussed by the customers. One man – not knowing who was listening – told everyone that the night watchman must have been in on it. Dad got out of his chair and, with the skill of an ex-military policeman, laid the man out. The Magistrate took into account Dad's record and the provocation, and he dismissed him with a caution.

Aunt Bess

Mum's half-sister, Bess, now became a great support to us: a basket of groceries, a bottle of beer for Dad and some money to buy me a Christmas present. Somehow or other, Dad found me a model locomotive which ran on methylated spirits, and on Christmas morning, it roared around its track, shot off the rails and set fire to the table. Mum was not best pleased, but Dad and I giggled – a memorable Christmas!

Then one day Dad started to cough blood. Everyone knew what that meant, for tuberculosis – TB – was as much a household word as TV is today. He moved out of the marital bedroom to a cot in the kitchen and I moved in with Mum. Now he always wore a gauze mask in the house to protect us both and, as he was always feeling cold, the fire in the sitting room was kept alight.

Dad's solace was music. No longer able to ride his bike, he sold it and bought a wind-up gramophone. Sometimes, in his last winter evenings, we'd hear the bell of the muffin man and, if there was money, Dad would take off his mask and then, just like any ordinary family, we'd scorch our hands as we toasted crumpets over the fire and listened to classical music. 'Dance Macabre' conducted by Stokowski was a great favourite, but I often fell asleep before the music ended. Then Mum would put me to bed, and Dad would put his mask on again and go back to the kitchen.

Before the TB became too bad, Dad and I would go by tram to Purley Way and then walk to Croydon Aerodrome where, from the penny enclosure, we had a grandstand view of the Imperial Airways Handley Page airliners arriving from all over the world and, in those great days of the British Empire, flying the Union Jack.

Croydon Aerodrome in the 1930s

We were there when Amy Johnson took off for her record-breaking solo flight to Australia. We were there when the famous American 'Birdman', Clem Sohn, wearing his rudimentary wings, jumped from a biplane and swooped and soared until, just as it seemed that he would crash into the ground, his parachute opened and he floated safely to earth. One day, it didn't!

Dad and I had great outings together until, suddenly, he began to go downhill very rapidly. Now he could only walk as far as the recreation ground at the end of the hospital wall. Often, without understanding, I'd urge him on. 'Come on, Dad! Why are you so slow?'

It was only later that I realised that his lungs were finally giving out, and that the frequent stops were so that he could get his breath and spit into his handkerchief.

I don't remember any doctors or medicine. The family just seemed to be left to get on with it, although, as a child at risk of TB, I received a small bottle of free milk each day at school, and every week a large jar of cod-liver oil and malt.

Finally, Dad became too ill to stay at home.

It is said that old soldiers never die, they only fade away, but in Mayday Hospital, Dad faded fast. One day he told Mum he fancied a pork pie. He took a couple of mouthfuls, laid down his fork and died.

My father's drawing of a Roman in my
autograph book for my ninth birthday.
I was Horatio to his Hamlet.

CHAPTER 2

AFTER DAD

The gramophone falls silent

Children don't mourn for long, and, for now at least, money was a little easier because Mum had been awarded a small widow's pension. Not a lot to pay the rent and feed and clothe a growing boy, so each Saturday we would walk the three miles to Surrey Street Market where the food was cheaper.

I loved our outings together – the shouts of the barrow-boys, 'Tuppence a pound, pears!'; the hurdy-gurdy which played Neapolitan songs, its handle turned by an Italian whose little red-coated monkey chattered from his shoulder at the passers-by; the tenor who stood in the kerb imitating Arthur Tracy (world-famous as 'The Street Singer') and belting out 'Martha, Rambling Rose of the Wildwood'; and a pianist who played popular classics from the back of a sloping cart on an out-of-tune instrument. Further down Surrey Street, a be-medalled, one-legged ex-serviceman turned the handle of a barrel-organ as it churned out the first-ever bicycle song:

Daisy, Daisy, give me your answer do!
I'm half crazy, all for the love of you,
It won't be a stylish marriage,
I can't afford a carriage,
But you'll look sweet upon the seat
Of a bicycle made for two.

Wandering through the market was Surrey Street's very own eccentric – 'Paper Jack' – who wore a suit of newspapers and was thought to be too poor to afford clothes. At least that's what everybody believed until, when he was killed in a road accident and prepared for a pauper's burial, the undertakers discovered, pinned inside the old copies of the *News of the World*, *Daily Mail*, *Mirror* and *Herald*, nearly a thousand pounds.

Not everything in Surrey Street was lovely. I hated the butchers' shops, where skinned rabbits (poor man's chicken) hung in obscene pink rows, only recognisable by their still-furry tails. On the fish stalls, glassy-eyed dead fish shared the marble slab with live mussels and cockles wriggling in vinegar. In the pet shops, puppies pleaded appealingly for the home we couldn't afford. But in all its rich variety, our Saturday visit to Surrey Street was the most exciting time of my week.

I'd now left Gonville Junior School, where I'd had some embarrassing times, particularly when I starred as a green rabbit in the school play. Mum had sewn me into my skin at home, but my long floppy ears wouldn't stay upright, and as she escorted me to school, the local kids gave me a hard time: 'Wot's the matter wiv yer ears then?' they jeered.

I was glad to say goodbye to all that, for my new school, Winterbourne, concentrated on manliness and sport. As Mum and I walked everywhere, my legs were strong enough to run for the school at the Crystal Palace where, once a year, all the South London schools held a combined sports day.

Crystal Palace

Before the races, we boys were taken on a tour of what was considered to be one of the modern wonders of the world. In 1851, it had been the centrepiece of Prince Albert's Great Exhibition, but a couple of years later it had been moved to Sydenham Hill. Two tall towers had been added, and Crystal Palace could be seen for miles around.

Now it was a great theme park of forty acres, with giant fountains and life-size models of dinosaurs. Inside the great Hall, under a million feet of glass, the Palace was ablaze with exotic plants and flowers from all over the world, over which towered a living plane tree, two hundred feet high. But there was much more to the Palace than horticulture. Each British Colony (and there was still a lot of Imperial red on the map in the 1930s) had its own exhibition. There were copies of great paintings and statues, and this visual cornucopia was matched by the sound of the largest organ in the world. What we boys didn't know was that, hidden away in the towers, John Logie Baird had opened one of the world's first television studios.

In the 19th century, the Crystal Palace Saturday afternoon concerts, conducted by Sir Augustus Manns, introduced classical music to millions and were the forerunner of Sir Henry Wood's Proms. Both conductors were the products of the Royal Academy of Music, where in 1952 I won the Manns conducting prize. Although nothing like as good or famous as either, I bet I was a better runner!

There was a lot to learn at the Palace, including how hot it could get inside – as John Ruskin described it – 'the largest cucumber frame in the world'. Even though the school had provided me with running shorts, a singlet with a large yellow 'W', white ankle socks and plimsolls, I was glad to get out into the fresh air.

Finally, we under-twelves were called to the starting line for the 'hundred-yard dash'. There being no starting blocks, I crouched like a marathon runner, right knee forward.

'Get ready, get set…' Muscles tense… mind alert… and on the crack of the pistol and to the cheers of my school chums, I ran like hell.

I won!

Winterbourne School Team, 1936
(front row, second from left)

With my prize

My prize was a flying model of an aircraft resembling the Spitfire, which had made its first flight that very year. This exciting day concluded with a grand firework display by Brocks, when hundreds of packets of sweets were rocketed into the air to float down by parachute into our grasping hands. I returned to Winterbourne the hero of the hour.

It had been a perfect day. Except that I missed my dad.

After my success at the Crystal Palace, I became the unchallenged leader of the Eridge Road gang (made up of boys like myself who played cricket against the hospital wall and collected horse manure to sell to gardeners keen to improve their rhubarb). Although Dad's gramophone was now silent, I still had a memory of the records that he'd played at bed-time, and I foisted on the gang a game called 'Orchestras'. I waved my arms about to the music that only

I could hear and they followed my strange gestures with kazoos, combs and paper and saucepan lids – anything bangable or blowable. It was a terrible noise, but it seemed they enjoyed Orchestras as much as I did.

Mum seemed to do very well after Dad died. There's always so much to do that grieving is sometimes delayed, but one night after I'd gone to bed, I heard her crying as, one by one, she read his letters and then put them on the fire.

She found some release from her depression for a few hours in the magical world of the cinema. There were twelve of these in and around Croydon, from 'flea pits' like the Scala at the end of Surrey Street to the Rolls Royce of cinemas – the Davis Theatre.

The Davis had a Compton organ, a restaurant and a small orchestra. This picture palace held close on four thousand, but it was often full, and then Mum and I would have to join a queue supervised by a Commissionaire, who looked splendid in a long military-style overcoat which bore his war medals. From time to time, he'd call from the head of the queue, 'Room for two in the stalls!' or, 'I've got a single in the gallery!' with always a reminder that there were: 'Armchairs in the Royal Circle!' Fat chance!

But it was well worth queuing, even in the rain, for the cheapest seats. The three-hour programme included two films, the Gaumont British or Pathé Gazette newsreels, trailers of forthcoming attractions, a stage act, and always an organ interlude of popular classics. The performances were continuous, and if we only got seats halfway through a film, we'd stay on until it came round again, and 'This is where we came in' became a phrase common in everyday life.

I first heard the music which I later conducted played on the Davis Theatre Compton... Ponchielli's *Dance of the Hours*... Lehar's *Merry Widow*... *Intermezzo* from *Cavalleria Rusticana*... Tchaikovsky's *Waltz of the Flowers* – the list of popular classics which everyone knew back then was endless.

With each change of tune, the beautiful crystal dome of the auditorium matched it in sparkling colours, until the lights began to dim, the organ cross-faded into the title music of the film and we joined Greta Garbo as Anna Karenina. (I thought Mum looked a bit like Garbo and I fancied myself as her son, Freddie Bartholomew.)

**Mum's sketch of her favourite Academy Award-winning film star,
Claudette Colbert**

In Edgar Wallace's *Sanders of the River*, the steel-jawed Leslie
Banks (it really was steel, for he had been wounded in the First
World War) was rowed up the Zambezi by the fine-looking
African Bosambo (Paul Robeson). As the paddles parted the
water, Robeson sang 'The Canoe Song': 'Ah yee yum bo, ah
weegan det. The rivers runs, the current swings, the water sings'
– I'd never heard such a wonderful voice.

Horror was there aplenty. In *Mad Love*, Peter Lorre, a
brilliant surgeon, lusted after the beautiful wife of a concert
pianist who'd lost his hands in a train crash and, for a price
payable only by the wife, Peter Lorre cuts off those of a
guillotined murderer and grafts them onto the pianist's wrists.
When Lorre demands his just reward and is grappling with the
lady, her husband breaks the door down and throws a knife at
him. With a surprised and resentful look (and the knife sticking
out of his back), Peter Lorre drops dead. I thought he got a raw
deal. But the film ends happily ever after, for the double-crossing
pianist never played the Tchaikovsky again.

To save the tram fare, on Sunday afternoons we'd walk to
Streatham Common to listen to Sir Oswald Mosley – always
guarded by his private army, the young fascists known as
'blackshirts'. He paid them three pounds a week – more than the

many unemployed ex-servicemen in the crowd who, like my father, had not found post-war Britain a land fit for heroes. As an ex-serviceman himself, Mosley struck a chord with many of these men, for he still limped from an injury sustained in a plane crash during his time in the Royal Flying Corps in the First World War.

Mosley told us that, under Hitler, Germany had been reborn and that there was now full employment. His slogan (based on that of Ancient Rome) of Empire, King and Fascism was very compelling – and not just to an eleven-year-old but to many in high places in the land. After the meeting, Mum and I would wander down to the Streatham Common Pond to sail my little boat before setting off on the three-mile walk home for tea and, if there was the money, the evening cinema.

One of the last outings I had with my mother was in January 1936, when we took a tram to London and joined a queue nearly two miles long to see the Lying in State of King George V. It was nearly three hours before we passed through the doors of the Great Hall of Westminster. There, in total silence, we shuffled past a raised bier on which – covered by the Royal Standard and surmounted by the Crown – lay the body of the King. At each corner stood a Life Guard in red tunic with gold buttons, polished spurred riding boots, shining silver helmet and head bowed as he clasped his sabre in the traditional mourning stance – a never-to-be-forgotten sight.

Mum had seemed to be getting better. Eight months after Dad's death, she saw me off to school on a Friday afternoon with a kiss and my lucky threepenny bit, saying, 'Spend it on something, son. It's not brought you much luck. Go to Auntie Bess after school. I'm going out tonight with Auntie Win.'

She didn't go out with Auntie Win. She closed the door, went upstairs, wrote her farewells (asking Aunt Bess to look after me and see that I got my dad's watch, wind-up gramophone and tools) and – so they told me – died of a broken heart.

I took the banana.

'Good boy,' said Auntie Nell.

CHAPTER 3

CANADA

The Chapel in the Moonlight

The problem now was what to do with me.

Croydon's Reedham Orphanage wouldn't accept me because I had living relatives. Mum had a brother, Arthur Reeve, a Chatham policeman who said his house was too small. He turned me down, but Dad's sister in Canada, Maud, and her husband Stanley, agreed to take me. The perfect solution, everyone thought: a new start in a young country. Bess would take me to Canada, and if I didn't like my new life, I could come back and live with her. So, with that promise, and having somewhere or other found twenty pounds, in October 1936 the great adventure began, and we sailed for Montreal on Cunard White Star's *S.S. Alaunia*.

Like all the big ships of that time, the *Alaunia* carried cargo, and although it wasn't like the floating hotels of today, Aunt Bess and I had the time of our lives. Tea in bed was followed by a six-course breakfast in the palatial dining room, mid-morning bouillon on deck and an eight-course lunch. Tea at 4pm meant cucumber sandwiches, and at 7pm, a gong was struck by a white-coated steward to call us to an eight-course dinner. There was no cinema or theatre, but nightly the third-class passengers – European migrants on their way to a new life in Canada – would gather on the deck to sing and dance to the sound of fiddles and guitars.

I spent my days playing shuffleboard on deck, in the small swimming pool or the gymnasium, where I sparred with an American boy several years my senior who showed me how to rub the laces of a boxing glove across an opponent's eyes, a foul difficult to detect. After seven exciting days, we sailed up the mighty St Lawrence River, littered with ice-floes, docked in

Montreal and began the six-hundred-mile train journey to my new life.

Windsor turned out to be a disappointingly small town on the Canadian side of the river Detroit, overshadowed by that city's skyscrapers. It seemed to have no real heart but to be just a place on the way to somewhere – which it was for most of its population, who crossed the river daily to work for the Ford Motor Company and earn the better wages paid by the Americans.

Aunt Maud, Uncle Stan and Cousin Roy lived at 1144 Moy Avenue, a wooden two-bedroom bungalow about half the size of Bessie's house, and so Aunt Bess had to sleep in the living room and I shared a bed with my twenty-two-year-old cousin.

The day after we arrived, I was taken out of English shorts and given my first pair of long trousers – a big moment in a boy's life. Now with fur-lined boots and hat and a heavy parka, I was ready for a Windsor winter. As it grew colder, I realised why we had an enormous furnace in the basement, and even sharing a bed with Cousin Roy didn't seem so bad. I was given a toboggan and, as Windsor was as flat as a pancake, I learnt to run on the ice, clutching the toboggan to my chest, and throw myself face down – 'belly-flopping'. It required a lot of nerve – almost as much as for the ice hockey which I learnt to play with the local boys.

The first days at any new school are pretty daunting for a new kid, but at the John Campbell School, I had the disadvantage of an English accent. I was mocked by my classmates – a mixture of the descendants of French settlers and migrants from Ireland, Wales, Scotland and Middle Europe. Windsor had a small town mentality and these groups banded together, some factories only giving jobs to migrant workers from their own background. Some advertised: 'No English Wanted.' One teacher asked me, in front of the class, if there was electricity where I came from. Were there flush lavatories and were there street-cars and buses? All this produced howls of laughter. What were Buckingham Palace and St. Paul's Cathedral like? How about the Tower of London?

I'd only been to London once, when I went with Mum to see King George V lying in state, and so I just replied miserably:

'Don't know.' I was bullied for quite a long time until, provoked once too often, I spoke up for myself and told the class that, where I lived in Croydon, we had an airfield where more aeroplanes took off and landed in an hour than street-cars came down Windsor's main street in a day, and that my home town, London, had ten million people.

I won that one: the letters from indignant parents about the lies their children had heard from the English boy led to an investigation by the school principal. The baiting stopped, and I began to enjoy what turned out to be a very good school.

Although it was a small house, we had a piano, and one day Cousin Roy came home to find me picking out the top line of 'The heavens are telling' from Haydn's *Creation*. He was a pianist in a dance band and a natural teacher, and he soon had me playing a popular song of the time, 'The Chapel in the Moonlight'.

Cousin Roy at the piano with his wife Anne on drums

I'd play it at every opportunity, which must have been rather tiresome, but as I was obviously musical, Aunt Maud and Uncle Stan were very patient.

They certainly found me unusual, for on my birthday, they gave me the choice of a new pair of ice-skates or some tap-dancing lessons. I chose to tap-dance and learnt to 'wing, break and slip step' my way through 'Turkey in the Straw' – a modest achievement, which I was to make the most of when, thirty years on, I came to direct musicals in London's West End.

'The Professor' by Aunt Maud

After a few months, I was becoming quite Canadian. I could skate backwards, play hockey, 'belly flop', dance 'Turkey in the Straw' and play and sing 'The Chapel in the Moonlight'. I began to feel at home, but on 30th November, 1936, the Crystal Palace where I'd run for Winterbourne caught fire and molten glass ran through the streets I knew so well. Eleven days later, Edward VIII abdicated after the shortest reign by a king in English history, and my thoughts were all of home and Aunt Bess.

So when the immigration man called for the umpteenth time, with always the same question – 'Do you want to stay in Canada?' – I said: 'No.'

I seemed in those years to be always saying 'goodbye' – firstly to Mum and Dad, then to Aunt Bess, and now to my Canadian family, kind Aunt Maud and Uncle Stan, of whom I'd grown very fond, and Cousin Roy, who'd started me on the musical journey of my life.

To judge from my autograph book, my classmates seemed sorry to see me go back to an England about which they now knew a little more than before I arrived.

One classmate wrote:

'Our teacher is a lovely man who goes to church on Sunday and prays to God to give him strength to kill us kids on Monday.'

But the teacher who'd given me a hard time now kindly wrote:

'May you sail on the ship called Good Fortune and arrive at the port of success.'

The ship I did sail home on was the S.S. Athenia, which, on 3rd September, 1939, the first day of the Second World War, was the first U-Boat victim. It was torpedoed with the loss of 128 lives. The Athenia was sunk during Sunday dinner and then the U-Boat Captain shelled the survivors. Later, the Nazis denied responsibility and blamed Churchill.

CHAPTER 4

ENGLAND AGAIN

Little Lady Make-Believe

I was back among my own kind, and it felt good.

In my last year at Winterbourne, I'd won a scholarship to Whitgift Grammar, but my trip to Canada had lost me my place. However, Aunt Bess worked her charm with the Board of Education and I became a pupil at John Ruskin Central School, where I could obtain the 'School Certificate' – the gateway to 'white-collar' employment.

John Ruskin School was then in Tamworth Road, West Croydon, and had previously been called the British Boys' School. One of its pupils had been Samuel Coleridge-Taylor.

Samuel Coleridge-Taylor

He was the mixed-race composer of *The Song of Hiawatha*, which I was to record for Decca in later years. Our paths seem to have crossed, but in a parallel universe. 'Coley', as he was known at school from the colour of his skin, had lived in Dagnall Park, Selhurst, nearly opposite where I lived with Aunt Bess, and he'd been married and I christened at the same church, Holy Trinity.

But music was not the school's strong suit, and it had been renamed for the famous artist and man of letters, John Ruskin. Fittingly, our Headmaster, J. W. McCloud, was a personal friend of Walter de la Mare and had been a teacher at Croydon's Davidson Road School, along with the author who set the cat among the pigeons with *Lady Chatterley's Lover*, D. H. Lawrence.

Picture a Scottish Mr Pickwick and you have the look of J. W. McCloud. With his small glasses perched at the end of his nose, he wore a waistcoat of more than ample proportions, across which stretched a watch-chain heavy enough to anchor a battleship. At assembly each morning after the opening hymn, he would command us to sit and then, jowls shaking like a Great Dane, his voice rising and falling in the manner of Frankie Howerd, he'd parade before us our schoolboy misdemeanours. We knew when he had reached the climax of his peroration, for he would pause and, with 'Let us pray', he would call on God in a sorrowful tone to forgive us our trespasses. It was an impressive performance, and we boys were proud of 'Mac'. He was to be seen every Saturday morning in Wilson's coffee shop with his companion, Mr Barber (inevitably known as Ali), our school music teacher – Croydon's own Dr Johnson and Boswell.

'Mac' had a very strong team of teachers, both academically and in the arm. Even little Ali Barber could hand it out with the cane. He filled the dual role of music and maths teacher, and may have been good at teaching algebra (and I suppose I shouldn't blame him for my memorable twelve percent in the exam), but at our first lesson in musical theory, Ali carefully drew five parallel chalk lines on the blackboard and below them another line, much shorter. We dutifully copied this into our exercise books. Then, with an air of revelation, on the small line Ali drew a reclining hollow egg. Pointing at it, he revealed the secret. 'That's middle C. *Learn it!*'

Art Master Mr Drummond was also of the old school.

Perspective was all, and we copied bowls of fruit and vases in pencil. But he soon retired and was replaced by a young man who didn't mind how well we drew as long as we used our imaginations. Prosaically named Smith, he possessed long, well-oiled hair, a Dali-like moustache and at school wore a paint-stained smock and suede shoes known as 'brothel creepers'. Best of all, he was seen about Croydon with *girls*, and we boys christened him 'Smoothy'. Now our art classes became exciting – a world of poster-paints, colour washes and charcoal, with not a pencil in sight. Smoothy talked of 'self-expression' and of 'choosing a subject from life'. I created quite a stir with my first figure-composition. It depicted, in glorious poster-paint, a prisoner strapped to the guillotine, head-basket gaping greedily and guarded by uniformed men in black wearing swastika arm-bands. Above the dreadful waiting blade was a sign bearing one word: 'JUDE'. I must have absorbed from the papers and wireless more of Hitler's doings than I thought. Smoothy was very pleased that Art and Life had been reconciled, and he hung my figure-composition on the wall for all to see.

At Ruskin, caning was always in the offing: 'six of the best' – three on each hand.

We boys would bravely accept *just* punishment, but our French master was a man who believed in keeping us in a constant state of anxiety. Typically, he'd set the class a translation to be completed in 'absolute silence'. He informed us at the beginning of every lesson, 'My doctor says I have very bad nerves, and everyone should be quiet and considerate.' He'd then sit back with his feet on the desk and set about picking his nose.

I shared a desk with a boy called Billings – a golden-haired, cheeky-looking thirteen-year-old, who one day looked up from his work and stiffened like a rabbit to the stoat as the teacher caught his eye.

'Billings,' murmured the teacher (as he took his finger out of his nose and slowly unwound himself from his desk to move towards ours).

'Billings, you are most unkind.' He came closer and his voice rose.

'Billings, you are not getting on with your work.' The class froze.

Now, much louder, and *very* close: 'You know how this upsets me, and the Doctor' (his voice became a roar) 'said it was *bad* for me.'

On the word 'bad', he hit Billings so hard on the side of his head that *I* was knocked out of *my* seat.

But not every teacher was like him.

Our geography master, Mr Matheson, was a gentle soul, and his blackboard maps of the world were works of art. A third of the world was still coloured pink, being the British Empire, in defence of which Matty had lost most of his hearing in the Great War. When he had his back to the class, all hell broke loose, but he would suddenly swing round and, catching some boy with his mouth moving, thunder, 'Take a hundred lines: "I must not talk in class." Give them to Christopher.' Christopher was the Head Boy. Since Matty never asked to see the lines, Christopher made a small fortune by charging a halfpenny a hundred, with a discount for every fifty.

I last saw Christopher in the 1950s stamping dates on books in Croydon Public Library. I was surprised that he'd accepted the tranquillity of a public library when he had shown such talent for the hurly-burly of the Stock Exchange.

John Ruskin was a disciplined school where English history was taught with pride, something that strengthened us boys in the years to come. Although Ali Barber roped me into the school choir, it met only occasionally. As I was fast becoming keen on music, Aunt Bess suggested I join the choir of St James's Church, Addiscombe.

St James's had been built in the early 19th century especially for the church

St James's Church, Addiscombe

parades of the cadets of the East India Company Training Seminary who, from the age of fourteen, learnt to become officers in the Company's private army. In 1857 the Company issued new rifles which required that its bullets, stored in pig's grease, be bitten before firing. The native troops refused, the Company wouldn't listen and the soldiers mutinied, threatening the whole British presence in India. Many Europeans were slaughtered and the British regular army had to take over control of Indian affairs. Queen Victoria became the Empress of 'the Jewel in the Crown' and the Seminary was closed.

As a young choirboy at St James's, I was fascinated by the war-like nature of the church. There were the memorial plaques to the officers killed in the mutiny and the many who perished of cholera. On the walls hung the shell-torn battle flags from the Great War and a bullet-scarred wooden cross brought back from the great battle of the Somme, where my father had fought.

Under its young Organist and Choirmaster, Cecil Arnold, St James's had a fine musical tradition, second only to Croydon Parish Church. Its forty-strong choir comprised twenty boys, three male altos, seven tenors and ten basses. Choir practices were twice a week – boys only on Tuesdays and full practice on Fridays. There were two services each Sunday, 11am and 6.30pm, with Holy Communion at midday on the first Sunday of the month. In summer, we frequently sang for weddings, but the occasional choral funeral seemed to be a winter activity when the old were carried off by the cold.

The choir I joined: all of the bigger boys went to war

Church was cosy. I have very happy memories of Sunday evening services in winter, when the distant lights from the church and the evening bells would hurry me up the dark path to the vestry door; of opening it to a blaze of light to reveal the animated faces of friends of all ages; and of donning my cassock, surplice and celluloid Eton collar (kept clean with a pencil rubber) and transferring the sweets reserved for the sermon to my cassock pocket. Then, with a minute to go, the Vicar, the Reverend Lee, led the choir into an invariably full church. The cold white electric lights were softened by the many candles, and as our treble voices soared in descant during the first hymn, I was transported to a place where no chill winter winds blew.

It was here in this very simple but beautiful church that I learnt to love the sound of the organ. It was a three-manual Noterman, and in the hands (and feet) of Cecil Arnold, it produced, to my ears, a sound of great grandeur. When at Easter we sang Stainer's *Crucifixion*, I experienced for the first time what it was like to be part of a thrilling musical performance. Christ's entrance into Jerusalem, 'Fling wide the gates, for the Saviour waits to tread his royal way,' was a splendid noise, and we gave it the full treatment. Being boys, we giggled when we sang that 'Christ was in a basement' (what was he was doing down there?) and our solo tenor who couldn't roll his r's sang of Christ being 'cwownless'. In the Lord's Prayer, we asked God to 'Lead us not into Cheam station'.

The Reverend Lee's prayers for peace on Sundays 9th and 16th October, 1938 had not gone unheard. Hitler had invaded Czechoslovakia, and Prime Minister Chamberlain had flown to meet Hitler in Munich. He had come back waving a piece of paper promising 'peace in our time', but even we choirboys could recognise a con.

Hitler met Mr Chamberlain and shouted, 'I want peace. I want a piece of Czechoslovakia, a piece of Poland and when I get Hungary, I want a piece of Turkey dipped in Greece.'

The threat of war seeming to have receded, I was keen to have piano lessons, but Aunt Bess told me I'd have to pay for them myself. It sounds very hard but, as she explained later, she'd paid for her son Jamie's lessons but he'd not practised, and they had been a waste of money. She told me that, if one wanted something, one had to work, save and wait, so I took on a paper round. I rose at six and cycled, wet or fine, winter and summer, to pick up my morning papers, finishing my round at just after eight, and then back home for a wash before a quick breakfast. (Printers' ink has an unpleasant smell and doesn't taste very nice). Then I cycled two miles to school, barely in time for the assembly hymn. It was hard work, but my reward was a half-hour piano lesson each week with Cecil Arnold.

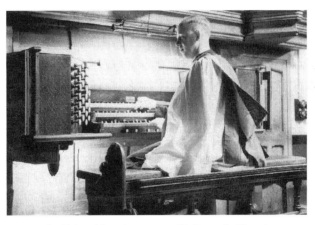

Cecil Arnold at the organ of St James's Church

Although I loved playing our old piano rescued from Eridge Road, I'd now met the king of instruments at close quarters, and after a few months Cecil thought I'd progressed well enough to start organ lessons. But organ practice cost two shillings an hour. My pay as a choirboy was paltry and my paper round paid only five shillings a week. I needed more money, and so the answer was an evening paper round. Now, instead of going home after school, I cycled to a yard in the Fairfield, opposite East Croydon Station, where they printed the stop-press editions of the *Evening News*, *Star* and *Standard*. The ink would still be wet, and after I'd finished the evening round at about 6.30pm, I'd have to spend a good five minutes washing it off my hands for my quick tea and keyboard practice, reduced to about half an hour on Tuesdays and Fridays, before jumping on my bike and cycling to choir.

I still wasn't able to afford enough organ practice, so I took on another paper round – this time on Sundays. This had to be finished in good time for church. Sunday papers were far too heavy to use my bike, so I walked everywhere. No one had warned me of what to expect when, on my first Sunday, I crossed a footbridge over the railway lines which led to a settlement of about twenty cottages built especially for employees of the Southern Railway who had been injured or become too ill to work. My first knock was answered by a man with no arms. I offered him his *News of the World* and he indicated a tin just inside the front door.

'The money's in there, son. Put the paper on the table.'

I didn't waste a minute wondering how he'd opened the door but went quickly to the next cottage. This time, a woman opened the door with a smile of greeting, but she had no nose, only blackened nostrils. Each door was opened by a poor soul with some kind of disfigurement. They were all kind and welcoming, but I dreaded Sunday mornings.

When I travel by train to London nowadays, I pass the place where once those poor people lived and wonder what happened to them, for many bombs were dropped around Selhurst Junction.

Life at home was hectic for all of us. Everyone seemed to be always on the go. Aunt Bess's husband (Uncle) Bill Spall remained a porter at Leadenhall Market, but his son Jamie had a white collar job as a meat marketing manager at Smithfield. He could now afford a car – a Wolseley – and drove to work. Bess was very proud of him and cooked him delicious meals served with the best cutlery and a starched white linen napkin.

On the other hand, his father caught the train to London at 10pm and did a hard day's night with a dawn breakfast at the market stall. He would arrive home at about two in the afternoon and throw half a pound of pork chops and a piece of steak into the frying pan, adding yesterday's cabbage and potatoes (the delicious 'bubble and squeak') and cook himself a fry-up. The debris in the pan was left to give the next meal a good head start, sometimes with dire results. I was very ill after one of his delicious concoctions.

Jamie and I got on very well and we had a common interest in music. He took some lessons from my teacher Cecil and was soon able to give a passable performance of Schubert's *Impromptu in E flat, Opus 90* – not an easy piece. His big chance came when the professional producer Ralph Reader chose the South Norwood Scout Troop to present a 'Gang Show' and put Jamie in charge of the music.

Talent being a bit thin on the ground in South Norwood, Jamie included me. I could offer 'Hear My Prayer', 'Oh, for a closer walk with God' and 'Jerusalem' but he rejected these as, sung in cassock and surplice, they would lack entertainment value. Gang Shows were jolly affairs! I offered to sing *and* play 'The Chapel in the Moonlight' or to tap dance 'Turkey in the Straw', but Jamie rejected these as not representing 'the true spirit of scouting'.

In our piano stool at home was a song called 'Little Lady Make-Believe' which was a great hit for Bing Crosby. It was a song by a widowed father to his little daughter whose mummy has died and who, to make her daddy happy, has dressed up in her mum's clothes. Girls do sometimes sing men's songs (Marlene Dietrich had a great hit with 'Lily Marlene'), but I was a boy dressed as a girl in her dead mother's clothes singing a man's song in a boyish treble.

Please do not refer to boys whose voices have not yet broken as sopranos. Male sopranos are castrati, and I certainly was not one of those!

At the first rehearsal, in costume (and carrying a doll), from my carmine lips emerged:

Dressed up in a gown that trails upon the floor,
In a picture hat your mother once wore,
Living in a world that you never saw…

I could hardly hear myself against the clamour of Jamie's enthusiastic orchestra, and even though in church I could easily be heard, here on the stage of the Stanley Halls, Norwood, most of my words just disappeared into the curtains; what little sound was left was drowned by the band – a lesson which was to stand me in good stead when later I came to conduct opera. I cannot believe that this song represented the true spirit of scouting, but Ralph Reader brought his magic to bear and dispensed with my doll. On the day of the performance, the curtain rose on twenty heavily-made-up Boy Scouts standing sideways on to the audience, left hand on the left hip and right hand on the downstage knee as they sang the signature tune of Scouts throughout the world, 'We're riding along on the crest of a wave, and the sun is in the sky.'

The television series about a wartime military concert party called 'It Ain't Half Hot, Mum' with the incomparable Windsor Davies as the sergeant in charge of his 'lovely boys' owed much in style to Ralph Reader and the Gang Show.

'Little Lady Make-Believe' went down quite well with the audience, but my fellow scouts were not kind, and I vowed never again to wear a dress.

Then came an accident which was to change my life. One Sunday at the end of Evensong, when 'Stuttering Stan' (a fellow choirboy whose stutter disappeared when he sang) and I were chatting away outside the vestry lavatory door, Cecil rushed past us to answer an urgent call of nature and slammed the heavy oak lavatory door on my finger. I felt no pain until Stan's jaw dropped.

'Your f.f.f.f.. ' he stammered.

'Your f.f.f.. ' he tried again.

Then I realised I couldn't move my hand.

'Sir, open the door, please. I've got my finger in the door!'

'His f.f.f…' Stan tried again.

'Go away, boy!' replied Cecil, sensing a boyish prank.

'But Sir,' I pleaded, 'I really have!'

With a good deal of understandable grumbling (for who likes to be interrupted at these times?), at long last there was the welcome sound of the cistern flushing and the great bolt was drawn.

I was free.

'Oh my God!' exclaimed Cecil. Still in cassock and surplice, my hand in my school cap to catch the blood, we walked the mile to the local doctor, who popped the top back on and plastered it tightly.

Now it hurt!

Cecil walked me home, but there was no one in, and this talented chartered accountant with a lovely family and nice house in Addiscombe waited with me until Aunt Bess came back from shopping.

A kind man.

The finger eventually healed, but was somewhat shorter than I was to need.

The tension between James and his father was increasing. The troubled soil was ready for the seed, and one morning at breakfast, it was sown. From behind his newspaper, Jamie made a remark of some kind and the overstretched Bess, the kindest of women, suddenly lost her temper and threw his breakfast at him. The paper broke the full force, but there was a shocked and deadly silence as he carefully folded it, looked coldly at his mother and left for work. The next day he booked his passage to Australia and ten days later said goodbye to his now heart-broken mother, to his father and to me.

The effect on me was that I began to blink uncontrollably.

The young curate at church ('Call me Syd') was very kind, as was Cecil, who gave me some extra music lessons and entered me in the piano class of the Croydon Music Festival where I won a medal for my performance of Norwegian composer Jensen's *Elfin Dance* – a musical description of jolly little Scandinavian elves running up and down the keyboard in happy mood.

Cecil decided that it was time I had some experience of playing before a paying audience, so I became the youngest member of his amateur concert party, 'The Strawhatters', and was programmed to play my *Elfin Dance* at their next concert.

To be sure where the little elves were going next, I'd had to memorise the music and look at the keyboard. However, on the morning of the concert I was still blinking, and Aunt Bess took me to Croydon General Hospital to have my eyes examined. The doctor flooded them with atropine to enlarge the pupils and when I left hospital, life was a blur and I had to be guided everywhere. My eyes were no better by the evening, but the show had to go on, so, wearing my small straw hat, Cecil guided me to the piano. Off I went, and although the elves danced merrily, there were so many wrong notes that it was obvious they had been on the Aquavit! On the last drunken chord, I stood, bowed, raised my hat and groped my way off the platform to the sympathetic applause of an audience who were convinced that I was blind.

My first public performance had been in a dress and my second as a blind straw-hatter, but there was a good side to my piano debut. My blinking ceased, never to return.

Jamie's departure for Australia had left a bedroom free. I was still sharing one with Bill, but I didn't get a room to myself, for Bessie decided to take in a lodger – one Claude, known as Basil. Bas was a 'spec' builder, dispensing with an architect and doing all the work himself. He was a cheerful bloke, a snappy dresser with a small moustache, who at weekends, dressed in plus-fours and smoking a cigar, would drive his Hillman Minx Saloon to the dogs at Catford, football at Selhurst Park or horse-racing at Epsom.

A few years before, he'd nearly died on the table during an operation for a duodenal ulcer – not uncommon in the 1930s – and had been warned to take it easy on the beer. But that wasn't Basil's way, and one day he came back from work early, ashen-faced. Bess got him to bed and called the doctor, whose verdict was that Basil was bleeding internally, was too ill to be moved and was probably going to die. But Basil wasn't going to die if Bess could help it. For three days and nights she nursed him until, on the fourth day, he showed a little improvement. 'A miracle!' said the doctor. The miracle was bread and milk laced with brandy, and two weeks later Basil was well enough to leave his bed.

Bess had saved Basil's life and he knew it.

A special bond was created between them, but I do not believe that it was physical. Bill and Basil got on very well and would occasionally join Bess and me on Basil's weekend joy-rides around the inns and pubs of Box Hill, Reigate, and Warlingham. Kids not being allowed in pubs, I had to stay in the car and eat Smith's crisps or arrowroot biscuits washed down with Tizer.

It was an unusual set-up: a husband who shared a room with a troubled orphan teenager, a wife who slept alone and a lodger whose life had been saved by his landlady.

But 17 Dagnall Park was at peace.

Basil suggested to Bess that I spend my summer holiday in the village of Great Bardfield in Essex with his sister, Dolly, her husband Harry and their adopted daughter, Freda, a rather pretty ten-year-old who'd arrived from an orphanage somewhere. Dolly and Harry became my honorary Auntie and Uncle and, being a fellow orphan, Freda became a make-believe cousin. Auntie Dolly was very fat and had only one breast, but she was immensely kind and cheerful. Uncle Harry was diminutive, and I should think that Dolly had to be a bit careful not to roll on him in bed.

I'd arrived in time for Sunday dinner and, after thanking the Lord for what we were about to receive, he saw fit to serve plums and custard. They were followed by a very large portion of Yorkshire pudding, swimming in gravy. Finally came roast beef, potatoes and cabbage. This meal in reverse was apparently quite usual in the Essex of the 1930s.

Great Bardfield had neither running water nor electricity, so Monday was an exciting time, for it was village wash-day. At 6am the 'copper' – a cement bowl in a small outhouse – was filled with water, brought in buckets from the village pump. Then Auntie Dolly lit the wooden fire under the copper, and at about 8am it was hot enough to add a Rickett's blue whitener and the sheets, shirts, pillow cases and even handkerchiefs (I often wondered where the catarrh went). Dolly skilfully directed her labour force, all the while stirring the copper with a large rolling pin. 'Bring more water, Ken!' she'd command, and off I would go to the village pump. Then, as the steam rose and the water cooled, 'Look after the fire, my little love,' and Freda went off to chop wood. The wash-house resembled a Hogarth print as, through the steam, mountainous Mistress Dolly, her red face pouring with sweat and cotton dress clinging to her one breast, held a bottle of lemonade in one hand and the rolling pin in the other.

Then came my favourite task – mangling – when the wet clothes were passed between wooden rollers turned by hand. 'Manglers' had to be careful, for mangling might mean mutilation, as in the warning known to all:

Never let your braces dangle,
Dingle, Dingle, Dangle.
Poor old sport, he got caught,
Pulled right through the mangle!

On Tuesday after I'd gone to bed, Freda invited me to her bedroom, for this was the exciting night when the 'Night Soil' men visited the bottom of the garden, not to frolic with the fairies, but to empty the privy. We watched from her window as, under the full moon, men in waders and gauntlets carried the brimming buckets to the cart in the lane. They were very quiet; the only sound was the clop of the horses' hooves as they moved on, taking the not entirely unpleasant country smell with them. My holiday was during the harvest, the time of the great rabbit hunt. I joined the local lads who, armed with sticks, followed the horse-drawn 'binder'. As each swathe of corn was cut, a rabbit or two would make a dash for safety, but none of the boys bothered to chase them, for they knew what was to come. As the field of uncut corn became narrower, the remaining rabbits huddled together, still out of sight. Then when the corn was down to a narrow strip, hundreds began to stream out, seeking safety. But it was a long and perilous journey, made between boys with sticks and excited dogs. Few survived. At long last, the final swathe was cut and, in a terrible climax of barking, yelling and the screams of the rabbits, the massacre ended.

17 Dagnall Park being a butcher's home, I was used to seeing bits of dead animals, but I never ate rabbit again.

Each Christmas, Bill made extra money by bringing home turkeys from the market, which he bought at knock-down prices. He gutted and plucked them in the scullery, and on Christmas Eve we would be awash in giblets, feathers and his friends.

On Christmas Day, we always had a party and played 'Consequences', 'Charades' and, for those who could still keep their eyes open, 'I Spy'. Then it was time for tea, Christmas cake and music.

I played and sang 'The Chapel in the Moonlight' and – wearing a paper hat – 'Little Lady Make-Believe', but once that ordeal was over, I opened the *Daily Express Songbook* (found in every piano stool) and played some of the popular songs of the day, some of which I was later to conduct on the BBC's *Friday Night is Music Night*: 'A Batchelor Gay Am I' from *The Maid of the Mountains*, 'Tea for Two' from *No, No Nanette*, and Bessie's favourite song, 'Smilin' Through':

> *And if ever I'm left in this world all alone*
> *I shall wait for my call patiently,*
> *For if Heaven be kind, I shall wake there to find*
> *Those two eyes of blue*
> *Still smilin' through*
> *At me.*

I hope she did.

Christmas Day 1938 fell on a Sunday, and it was to be the last peace-time Christmas for seven long years.

With Aunt Bess in our garden

CHAPTER 5

THE LAST DAYS OF PEACE

The last choirboys' outing

1939 had begun peacefully enough.

As a special reward for singing a solo at our annual prize-giving, Mac gave me the *Schoolboy Diary for 1939*, and henceforth I recorded the daily events of my none-too-exciting life. One of the first entries read: 'Mac took Choir to the Croydon Rep to see *1066 and All That*. Jolly good.'

The cast of this tongue-in-cheek version of English history starred Leslie Henson. Twenty-five years later, I was to cast his young son Nicky as Mordred to Laurence Harvey's King Arthur in the London production of 'Camelot'.

At school, our far-sighted Headmaster set about making us boys aware of the history of a town we might one day have to defend; of how, in the 16th and 17th centuries, Croydon had strong ecclesiastical connections and was the home of the Archbishops of Canterbury, Tenison and Whitgift; of how, in the 18th century, the town burnt all its trees to supply charcoal to London; of how, in the 19th century, it possessed, uniquely, an 'atmospheric railway', the carriages being sucked along the rails by a vacuum tube; and, of how in the 20th, the grass field of Croydon Aerodrome became famous throughout the world.

At St James's, Cecil Arnold kept us very busy with a new anthem each week. I was now one of the two 'top boys', taking most of the solos. Dvorak's 'Thou who art forever blessed', 'Oh, for a closer walk with God' and Mendelssohn's 'Oh, come let us worship' were wonderful to sing, except that I was now of an age when my voice (like other parts of my anatomy) was beginning to descend, and my days as a treble were numbered. I was top boy of Decani, and the top boy on the opposite side of the chancel (Cantori) was Ron Greenfield. We were good friends, and I became a regular visitor to his home in Addiscombe, where his father was an undertaker.

We took pains to appear tough and to show that an Eton collar and surplice didn't make us sissies. Boys joining the choir had to be interviewed by Ron and me among the empty coffins, with their sweet smell of fresh varnish. Possession of an adult bicycle meant the right to use the choirboys' bicycle shed. It was the scene of many interesting discussions – mostly about sex, of which we were woefully ignorant. Being now fourteen, and, as a top boy who had been confirmed by the Bishop of Croydon, who had had his finger amputated in the church lavatory door (the story had grown), had won prizes in music festivals playing Bach, was an orphan who'd been to Canada, had shot a bird with an air gun, had won a fight with 'Fatty' (a boy from another choir) and who had then gone straight on to church to sung Mendelssohn's 'Love one another', my opinion was sought, for I was obviously a worldly boy.

One of our smallest asked me if it was true that, if a man put his winkle (a rather charming description of the male member) into a girl's (nudge-nudge, wink-wink), it produced a baby. I felt I should provide an answer. I explained that all stories of the winkle being any good for making babies were nonsense. I explained that *intimate kissing* produced babies. Kissing made the mother's tummy grow into the shape of a baby which, when ready, could be tied off like a small balloon and snipped off with a pair of scissors. Quite a neat system, if not as much fun!

Apparently, I was very convincing, and a lot of young choirboys took to heart the perils of kissing girls.

In choir, Ron and I imposed *our* rules. No farting or dirty stories were permitted in the vestry and church. No eating sweets whilst singing or during prayers. Only small sweets were to be sucked during the sermon, and gob stoppers were forbidden. All communications were by passing – not throwing – a note or, in an emergency, signs across the chancel using the 'deaf and dumb' language learnt by all choirboys.

Breaking our rules could lead to expulsion from the choir, missing our quarterly pay nights when we all went for fish and chips or – even worse – missing our annual day at the seaside. Early in spring, the vicar would make the welcome announcement, 'The collection this morning is for the choirboys' annual outing.'

Came the great day and we boys, in the charge of Cecil, the curate Syd and a choirman or two, would gather at East Croydon station for the hour's journey to Brighton. The town in those days was clean, friendly, fun and comparatively quiet, even when full of holidaymakers – no drugs, no sex, no rock and roll: just sticky rock. The beach was pebbly and the sea was very cold and, as few were able to swim in the 1930s, people mostly paddled, the men rolling up their trousers to the knees and the women holding their dresses between their legs as high as they dared. Those few who could swim wore one-piece bathing suits, rubber shoes and hats, seemingly designed to reduce the female form to a few barely recognisable bulges. Sadly, the beauty of the female anatomy remained a mystery to us choirboys.

On Brighton beach (eighth from right)

The high spot of the day was a visit to the West Pier and there, in the 'Penny Arcade', a peep-show with the title *What the Butler Saw*. With one of our number keeping a look-out, we boys would cluster around its small screen, which we hoped would reveal the sex life of the upper classes, but the flickering black and white images of a fully-dressed couple in a chaste clinch was certainly not worth the penny. Brighton had a reputation as a family resort to maintain, and sex was certainly not on the menu!

Nevertheless, there was masses to see and do. To the sound of the merry-go-round, we wandered amongst the coconut shies, candy-floss, plates of whelks and winkles, pin-ball machines, fortune tellers and rifle ranges (soon to be put to good use in the war), but most fun of all were the dodgem cars, which we drove straight at each other to crash with bone-shaking force, our shouts exceeded only by the screams from the Big Dipper as it hurtled earthwards. The music and noise were wonderful, but at the end of the pier it was heard only distantly over the gentle lapping of the summer sea, as a holiday fisherman with baited line patiently waited, hoping to take a fish home for his tea.

As this grand day drew to a close and dusk fell, the promenade would glitter with thousands of coloured lights, and we knew that it was time for the train back to paper rounds, church and school. We said goodbye for another year and sadly made our way past the clock tower and up the hill to the railway station, as the glorious sounds of Brighton grew ever fainter. That choirboys' summer outing of 1939 was the last one.

My diary entry for Friday 1ˢᵗ September read: 'On the brink of a World War. Hitler seizes Danzig and bombs eight Polish Towns.'

CHAPTER 6

LIGHTS OUT

The blackbird on the cross

On Sunday 3rd September, 1939 a large blackbird perched on the cross that surmounted the tower of St James's. The only time I had seen it before was on the morning that the ninety-two-year-old Reverend Mason died in his seat by the high altar during prayers (we choirboys had thought him asleep – again).

The service began at eleven, and as we entered singing 'Onward Christian Soldiers', the country was already at war, but we had to wait until the sermon to know it, when, instead of 'In the name of the Father, the Son and the Holy Ghost,' a grim-faced Reverend Lee began with, 'I have just been informed that we are at war with Germany. Let us pray.'

The war was not unexpected. For weeks we had been filling sandbags, taping windows and digging air raid shelters. The government had arranged to evacuate children to the safety of the country, but I was fourteen – almost an adult – and I persuaded Aunt Bess to let me stay and take my chances in Selhurst. John Ruskin School became a first-aid post, and so I was moved to an elementary school in Selhurst, where a make-shift curriculum rationed us to five half-days of education each week. My music lessons stopped, and when Cecil's marriage sadly ended just before the war broke out, he enlisted in the Royal Air Force. The last tune he played on the organ at St James's was his improvisation on the popular song 'I'm nobody's baby, I'm blue somehow' – an unforgettable moment for the many who loved him.

Cecil's replacement was viewed with great suspicion, for he brought to St James's the music of the 16th century English composer John Merbecke. We preferred Stainer and Mendelssohn, but the new man's greatest sin was when he opened up the choir to girls! In 1940, boys like us were familiar with Richmal Compton's *William* and shared our hero's view that girls were not suitable for any serious activity – an opinion soon to lose credibility when they began operating searchlights and firing anti-aircraft guns.

With Cecil gone, I continued lessons with Hoppe Leslie Smith, the organist of Croydon Parish Church. The church rated a suffragan Bishop, the choir wore red cassocks and ruffs and there were no female choristers. The music was even better than at St James's, and I began to dream of a life in the environment of a great English cathedral, perhaps as a choirman.

Meanwhile, there was a war to be won, and music had to take second place.

'Mr Merbecke', as we called him, didn't last long at St James's, and, as though on cue, my voice broke and I began to speak like a man. There being no one else, at the age of fifteen, the Reverend Lee appointed me Organist and Choirmaster. Although rather nervous to begin with, I discovered that if one puts the music first, a conductor can be forgiven much – even by choirmen old enough to be one's grandfather.

The young men in the choir had left to fight, so as well as playing, I sometimes sang tenor, baritone and occasionally bass. Although this changing about was good for my musicianship, it was ruinous for my voice. Who knows, I might have become a world-class tenor but for the war.

That winter we entered the strange world of the 'blackout' with its unlit streets, blue lights in trains, cars with a white paint trim and shuttered headlights, and Air Raid Wardens exhorting us to 'Put that light out!'

But we *could* see the stars more clearly.

Church bells were silent, only to be rung as a signal that we were being invaded. Every theatre and cinema was closed, and the BBC began introducing newsreaders by name so that, in the event of an invasion, we would not be fooled by a false broadcast by the enemy.

I only went to school for three hours a day, so I became an errand boy for Yardley's General Stores at Thornton Heath, delivering groceries and beer on the company bicycle. Over the tiny front wheel was a basket which could hold two crates of a dozen light ales with a large basket of groceries. Fully laden, I had to be launched by one of the shop assistants, and the only way of stopping was a controlled crash into a tree or lamp post. I was paid fifteen shillings a week and tips, but Christmas 1939 was white, and on an icy hill, my little wheel lost grip and my precious load of whisky, eggs, sherry and two dozen bottles of Tolley Ale were lost in a Thornton Heath gutter. Yardley's decided that I was really not big enough for the job, and I was fired.

At the beginning of 1940, the forecast air raids had not materialised, and many parents brought their children back to Croydon. Now our classes were overflowing, and so education was reduced again to three half-days every second week. Aunt Bess decided that I may as well get a full-time job and sent me to work for Ben, the Commissionaire at Creed's, a factory on war work which was manufacturing secret equipment designed to transmit military information by teleprinter. Ben and I were housed in a glass cubicle as reception officer and 'gofer'. Ben wore a dark blue uniform and the medal ribbons from the First World War, when he'd lost his left arm. His prosthetic left hand was covered with a leather glove and he wore a matching one on his right, so that when he saluted, he looked a whole man again. The factory hands worked ten-hour days to the BBC's *Music While You Work*, played loudly enough to be heard above the continuous roar of the machines. At dinner-time (eaten in shifts between 12pm and 2pm), the BBC often broadcast variety shows, and occasionally classical performers tried to rise above the clatter of cutlery and conversation.

But later in 1940 came the miracle of Dunkirk, when, between 26th May and 4th June, a third of a million Allied troops – almost the entire British expeditionary force – were taken off the French beaches by ships and boats of all sizes and brought home to England.

Years later, for the Festival of Britain of 1951, the almost-blind composer Dr Thomas Wood, for whom I was acting as amanuensis, collaborated with Ivor Novello's librettist, Christopher Hassall, on a cantata called *The Rainbow*, which I will return to later in this book. It was the story of one of the little ships crewed by amateur sailors who went to Dunkirk. It was performed by six hundred male voices (mostly Welsh) and six bass bands, all conducted by Sir Adrian Boult. The composer wrote in an organ part for me, and so I played that mighty Albert Hall organ. Having myself seen the haggard returning members of the BEF, I found Hassall's words very moving:

A long the beach at Gravelines,
The skies adrift with murk,
For they've made a belching cauldron
Of the oil tanks at Dunkirk,

And there's a silent multitude
That seems to stretch for miles,
The stranded tens of thousands
Keep their long unwavering files.

The army was back, but now Britain stood alone – a feeling only truly understood by those of us who were there. Within a month, a million men aged between seventeen and sixty joined the Local Defence Volunteers. They had no uniforms but wore a simple armband. They had few firearms (we'd left rather too many in France), so their makeshift weapons included farm implements, old souvenir pistols, spears, bayonets, revolvers from the first war and the occasional shotgun – hardly a match for the expected German parachutists.

The summer of 1940 was hot, and while we waited for the invasion, the LDV (now renamed the Home Guard) was trained by professional soldiers. Uniforms and weapons were found: light automatics, heavy machine guns, grenades, carbines and bayonets. For, as Corporal Jones in 'Dad's Army' rightly said, 'They don't like it up 'em!'

Bill was issued with a First World War 303 Lee Enfield rifle and ten rounds of ammunition, which he kept in the shoe cupboard with Felix the cat. I acquired an American Colt revolver ('the gun that won the West'), a German Ortgies gas-operated pistol with some sinister notches on the butt, an American 'Little Boy' '38 and a single-shot Derringer, designed for ladies and known as a 'muff' pistol – but all with no ammunition!

Behind the scenes, we knew nothing of the Nazi blacklist of important men and women destined for immediate execution, nor that, all around us, underground shelters were being equipped with supplies and equipment so that Britain too would have an underground army.

CHAPTER 7

THE WAR MOVES ON

The Battle of Britain

In June 1940 Italy declared war on us, but by that time there was a devil-may-care spirit in the country. 'In for a penny, in for a pound', and as for the 'Wops' (a pejorative term for Italians), we'd take them in our stride. It was a very exciting time to be a teenager. My choirboy pal 'Gus' had joined the Royal Navy at fourteen and had already seen active service (and the inside of a Far Eastern brothel) by the time he was sixteen.

Serious music began to take second place to songs designed to strengthen morale. One song broadcast frequently by the BBC was 'We're going to hang out the washing on the Siegfried Line', but we never did get anywhere near Hitler's strong line of defence, with washing or anything else.

Hitler was preparing for the invasion of Britain by bombing our ports, our shipping in the English Channel and, to gain control of the air over his invasion fleet, the RAF airfields. In the late afternoon of 15th August, an RAF Hurricane squadron returning to Croydon Aerodrome was followed in by German fighter bombers. They came in out of the sun and attacked our aircraft as they landed. As well as destroying many planes, some of the bombs fell short and landed on the factories around the airfield. At the Bourjois Scent Factory, home of the popular 'Evening in Paris', sixty women workers were killed, and production ceased.

That raid on Croydon was the beginning of the Battle of Britain, often fought so high that the aircraft were almost invisible. Only their vapour trails, the distant sounds of engines and the clatter of machine-gun fire told of the life and death duels in the sun as the planes, in the words of Spitfire pilot John Magee, 'wheeled and soared and swung... through footless halls of air'. Minutes after the fight had moved away, the skies were clear again, and the only sound was the tinkle of machine-gun clips hitting the pavement or the sight of a lone parachute carrying a pilot down to a friendly earth or prison camp.

One day I watched a parachute descending my way. I jumped on my bicycle and followed it to where it finally landed, a few hundred yards from home in our local allotments. There, half covered by his parachute and lying in a ditch of muddy water, was a young pilot. He was quite still, but before I could get to him, the police and ambulance arrived, and I was told to clear the area. Later, I heard that he was Neville Chamberlain's grandson, a Pilot Officer, and that he had survived.

Pilot Officer Chamberlain is included in the official RAF list of those who took part in the Battle of Britain.

The head of the Luftwaffe, Hermann Goering, expected the RAF to collapse, but by September, it was clear that the Germans had failed to gain control of the English skies. 'The Few' had won the battle, and Hitler postponed the German invasion and turned to attacking the civilians.

In Croydon, we were again amongst the first to witness the change of tactics. I was standing outside the Creed factory at East Croydon one afternoon when I heard the roar of aircraft engines and looked up to see a Dornier 215 at rooftop level, so close that I could see the face of the pilot. There had been no air-raid warning, but it was on its way to bomb London.

So began the Blitz. Every dusk, as regular as clockwork, the air-raid sirens sounded, and down we went to the garden and our Anderson shelter. All was quiet until, in the distance, we heard a strange, low-pitched and intermittent grunt. Every internal combustion engine produces its own sound (the Spitfire's Merlin is unmistakeable), so if the two engines of a bomber are each tuned to a different pitch then, as in music, the different notes, sounded together, will produce a third note (a harmonic). The Germans deliberately set up the engines of the Junkers, Heinkels and Dorniers to be 'out of tune' so that this third note – the grunt – was a dread warning of the horror to come. The trick was intended to be frightening, and it succeeded.

As the bombers got nearer, the intermittent grunt of the engines changed to a steady throb, the searchlights criss-crossed the sky, seeking a target, and our anti-aircraft guns began. I learned to recognise the crack of the mobile 3.7s firing from the railway line near Selhurst station and the heavier, static 4.5s. Many of the guns and searchlights were manned by girls. Gunners rarely hit anything, for there was (to quote one) 'only a cat's chance in hell of ever hitting one of the bastards!' – but at least we were fighting back.

An air raid meant noise: collapsing houses, shattering glass, Air Raid Wardens' whistles, the shouting of the Rescue Squads and the bells of fire engines, all to the continuous background of guns, bombs and engines. It was a savage attack on one's ears. The experts who claimed to know such things said, 'You never hear the bomb that kills you.' How on earth could they be sure of that?

At the height of the Blitz, air raids went on all night, and the only chance of getting any sleep on the fourteen-inch planks that passed for beds was to keep the heavy shelter curtains closed. At least one felt safer, and, even though hot and stuffy, with water running down the steel walls, if one stopped one's ears with the little rubber plugs provided by the government, a few hours' sleep might be possible.

It was not a comic time, but it was a time for comics, and good old 'Auntie' BBC did her best to cheer us up by saying every Friday, *It's That Man Again* ('ITMA'). The programme was funny, but for me the best part was when, each week, the BBC Variety Orchestra played a new arrangement of a traditional British tune. Dr Gordon Jacob, whose ballet *Mam'zelle Angot* I later conducted at the Royal Opera House, surpassed himself with a knock-out version of 'Cherry Ripe'. All the arrangements were so good that I was still conducting them, forty years on, for *Friday Night is Music Night*.

The Blitz continued, and one morning, after a very noisy night, I was the first to arrive at the Creed offices. The War Reserve policeman, who nightly guarded the entrance, was leaning against the protecting sandbags. He didn't reply to my 'good morning'. He couldn't: the nose of an anti-aircraft shell had buried itself in his steel helmet and he was dead, killed by 'friendly fire'. It was a shock to meet death for the first time, but people were dying everywhere.

My way to work – but not that day:
Queen Victoria Street, London

With so many away from home, Sundays saw half-empty churches, but Saturday weddings boomed, when young servicemen made their girls brides, hoping for a few days' happiness before going to war and an unknown fate. I was much in demand for Mendelssohn's 'Wedding March' and Wagner's 'Bridal March' from *Lohengrin,* with the words known to every choirboy: 'Here comes the bride, fair, fat and wide. Can't get in the West Door so goes round the side!'

The Germans continued to try to bomb us into submission. There was not much we could do about the high explosives but, as long as we could get at the incendiary bombs, it was reasonably easy to cover them with sand and use our stirrup pumps to put out the fires. It was exciting, but not particularly dangerous. However, the Germans had a trick up their sleeve, and on the night of 24th December, 1940, they gave 17 Dagnall Park an unwelcome Christmas present: the *exploding* incendiary. We were sitting around the dining table as the doctor bandaged Basil (who'd caught a nasty cut from some anti-aircraft shrapnel) when there was the clatter of an incendiary hitting the roof. It shattered the lavatory, exploded, and came through the ceiling to finish in the fire-place, where it burnt away in a merry yuletide manner. The Germans unloaded tens of thousands of them on the East End and London docks, starting fires so bright that I could read a newspaper by their light in our garden ten miles away.

Clapham Junction was bombed many times. Indeed, with its fifteen tracks running in and out of London, it was hard to miss, but it remained open, and it was on the night-train home from Victoria that poor Aunt Bess, travelling alone, came to grief. Her train stopped at the signals just before the station, but thinking she had arrived at Selhurst, she opened the carriage door and stepped onto the track four feet below. The train drove on. Bess picked herself up and walked the hundred yards beside the live rail, up the slope and onto the station platform. The porter looked at this middle-aged lady, hat askew and stockings all torn, and asked to see her ticket!

Ben, my boss at Creeds, told me I ought to 'better myself', and so I applied for a job with Docwra's, a firm of chartered accountants based in the Temple, London. There was an acute shortage of teenage labour, and on the basis that he could get two or three years out of me before joining the Forces, Stephen Docwra (whose great-grandfather had founded the 'Penny Post') took me on as a junior audit clerk. I knew nothing about accountancy, but I could write clearly and add up, and my choir training had given me an elocutive voice, so I had moved up a class into the world of white-collar workers.

Each morning I caught the train to London Bridge and joined thousands of city workers (known as 'Billy Browns of London Town'), still in their pre-war uniform of black jacket, striped trousers and bowler hat, but now all carrying gas masks as well as briefcases. We crowded over the bridge, not more than a few yards from where, nearly three hundred years before, the Great Fire of London had begun in a baker's shop in Pudding

Lane. My way to work took me along Queen Victoria Street, past St Paul's Cathedral, down Ludgate Hill, up Fleet Street to Temple Bar and the Law Courts, and finally past the Royal Air Force Church, St Clement Danes, to the Temple. Each morning there were new fires and new bomb damage. The fire brigades were often still at work in the morning, their hoses strewn across the roads from the emergency water tanks, which were vital because the mains were often broken. Many taxis had become emergency fire vehicles, carrying four or five firemen and towing water-pumps. The City policemen, with their distinctive portcullis badges, stood guard by the signs 'Danger, Unexploded Bomb', and around each corner were those incredible men who risked their lives many times a day, the Bomb Disposal Squads.

Over fifty years later, an unexploded German bomb was discovered under runway 25 of Shoreham Airport and, as the Chief Flying Instructor of Southern Aero Club, I hosted the Bomb Disposal Squad of the Royal Engineers. Corporal 'Nobby' Clark defused it and, as he had the German manual giving details of the fuses, it was a comparatively simple task. 'What makes you volunteer for such a dicey job?' I asked him. Then I learnt that the squads are not volunteers but ordinary soldiers, carrying out one of the routine tasks of the Royal Engineers. I later heard that Corporal Clark had been killed in the Falklands attempting to defuse a bomb without the Argentinean manual.

Some cinemas had re-opened, including the Davis Theatre, which had suffered a direct hit during a daytime performance, the bomb shattering the beautiful crystal ceiling. It didn't explode, but it crushed several members of the audience. It was at the Davis that, in 1941, I saw the film, *Dangerous Moonlight*, the story of how, during the German bombing of Warsaw in 1939, a Polish concert pianist decided to give up music and become a fighter pilot.

I wasn't a pilot, but I played the piano a bit, and the film affectedly me deeply. How could I know that Richard Addinsell's music would become perhaps the most famous of all war film scores and that I – a mere junior audit clerk – would eventually conduct no less than four recordings of the *Warsaw Concerto*?

But that was still to come, and it was the reality of a 1941 film called *Target for Tonight*, a documentary made by the Crown Film Unit during an actual night raid on Germany by the Wellington Bomber 'F for Freddy', that convinced me that my future lay with the Royal Air Force, and so I joined the 66 (Croydon) Squadron of the Air Training Corps.

CHAPTER 8

THE ATCATS

My first dance band

Every weekend, we cadets of the 66 Squadron Air Training Corps paraded in smart blue uniforms to be taught the military facts of life – who rated a salute and a 'Sir' – and to obey the shrill commands of Cadet Non-Commissioned Officers, some as young as fourteen. My fellow choirboy, Ron Greenfield, was already a Cadet Sergeant, so he who had once been my equal was now my superior: very galling. However, on learning that I missed Sunday morning parades to play at church, the 66 Squadron Commanding Officer, Flight Lieutenant Davis (the owner of the theatre where Mum and I had spent so many hours), ordered me to form a Squadron dance band.

I knew nothing about dance bands (one can't do much waltzing and fox-trotting to *Hymns Ancient and Modern*), but he set me on a road that was eventually to lead to working with one of the best dance bands in the world, The Royal Air Force Squadronaires.

I set about trawling through the cadets for anyone who could play anything at all. It was lean pickings, but eventually I came up with Danny and his 120 bass Soprani piano accordion, Don, a clarinettist, and a violinist whose name I've forgotten. I turned to our 66 Squadron Bugle Band for Steve (who was learning the cornet) and a drummer, Bob, who said he'd like to join but had no drums of his own, just a pair of drumsticks With a little financial help from F/L Davis, I went shopping, and, in a junk shop, found a drum-kit for three pounds. It was very basic: a single-sided snare drum, a bass drum with a skin decorated with a painting of a rampant Zulu, three Chinese blocks (useful for horses hooves and novelty effects), an excellent Turkish Zilgen cymbal (worth three pounds alone) and an American Charleston hi-hat, played with the left foot whilst the drummer pumped a large bass drum pedal with his right.

At our first rehearsal, Drummer Bob sounded as though he was building a shed. When Danny squeezed his bellows, we couldn't hear ourselves for the noise. Steve was still experimenting with his valves and Don was trying not to squeak, an ever-present danger with clarinets. The anonymous violinist, a very small cadet with red hair and pebble-dash glasses (certainly not destined for aircrew) spent a long time tuning, but since he didn't know any of the popular songs of the day, disgustedly packed up his violin and was never seen again. We had no music but played by ear (busked) 'Tea for Two', 'Honeysuckle Rose', 'The Lambeth Walk' and two waltzes, 'Ramona' and 'Who's Taking You Home Tonight?'

Our 'arrangements' depended on who knew the tune well enough to play the bit that the others didn't know. The instruments neither blended nor balanced naturally, and the piano was out of tune. All in all, the RAF Squadronaires had nothing to fear.

We gradually improved, and I came up with quite a catchy name for us: 'The Atcats', 'cats' being a jazz word, which suggested that we boys were what is known these days as 'cool' (the girls were 'swing chicks'). The war-like Zulu on the bass drum was hidden behind a smart blue cover carrying the Squadron's crest and 'Atcats' in silver letters.

F/L Davis confirmed that the Atcats were now 66 Squadron's official dance band and would make their debut at the Croydon Parish Church Hall on the first Saturday in August 1942 from 7.30pm to 10.30pm (air raids permitting). Tickets were sixpence, with no admission after 9pm (a rule designed to keep out those who turned up when the pubs closed). The Atcats were each to receive one shilling – my first professional fee as a musician!

On that August Saturday, our debut was going well until I realised we were running out of music. Now that America was in the war, we'd added 'Chattanooga Choo-Choo', 'Deep in the Heart of Texas' and 'Where Yawning Canyons Greet the Sun' ('Idaho'), but a three-hour dance needs about ninety minutes of music. As one tune plays for only about three to four minutes, the Atcats needed about twenty-five tunes. We had twelve!

I solved the problem by announcing that we were going to repeat a number 'by popular request'. The other way to spin out our meagre repertoire was to 'feature' our players. The Atcats didn't know 'Jealousy', but Danny did. At my suggestion, he took off his tunic to reveal red braces, and the youth club ladies were captivated as he played 'Jealousy' as though not from a little house in Pawsons Road opposite the cemetery but somewhere south of Granada. I 'featured' in 'The Chapel in the Moonlight' (without vocal). Steve, with a sweet-sounding mute stuffed in the bell of his cornet, 'featured' in the waltz 'Ramona'. Clarinettist Don 'featured' in 'Mood Indigo' without a squeak, all of us accompanied by Bob, who swished his brushes and kicked his bass drum with a measure of discretion. I popped a chord or two in from time to time, and things were going better than I could have hoped until, after buns and lemonade at the interval, there was a commotion at the door and in came twenty or so Canadian soldiers.

They'd got to hear about our dance, and having had their 'ceegarettes and whisky' in the local pub, were ready for the wild, wild women. Alas, ours were virginal young ladies from the Church Youth Club. But the girls were polite to these real soldiers, and so the Canadians, who had a reputation for enjoying a fight, responded like gentlemen.

'Question and Answer' by Samuel Coleridge-Taylor

All too soon came the last waltz of the evening, a new one with music by a local lad, Samuel Coleridge-Taylor, and words added later that year by an American. The song was 'Question and Answer'.

It was to be the very last waltz for some of these Canadians, for many were to die a couple of weeks later in the disastrous Commando raid on Dieppe, which was a trial run for D-Day.

The Atcats were now

twelve-strong, and pretty good for a bunch of untrained amateurs – so good that F/L Davis commanded me to produce a variety show for the Royal Air Force station on Croydon Aerodrome.

Once again he gave me a push in the right direction, for I knew nothing of 'showbusiness', but if F/L Davis, who ran the finest picture theatre in South London, thought I could do it, I was not going to let him down. I found a couple of singers and a few ballet girls from the Grandison School in Norbury, but the show lacked a top of the bill. Then I spotted a picture in the Croydon Advertiser of a young girl from Norbury who was doing her bit by taking her top off for the troops at the Windmill Theatre. Her name was Anita, a gorgeous seventeen-year-old red-head with a lovely figure. Although her dancing fell somewhat short of Ginger Rogers, the pilots (and the pianist of the Atcats) loved her.

In September 1942, now seventeen, I volunteered for the Royal Air Force, and after passing the Aircrew Selection Board, I was graded as suitable for flying training and was passed onto the Medical Department. I managed to hold my breath supporting twenty-nine inches of mercury for the required two minutes, and after passing the coughing test, when the stability of one's wedding tackle was tested, I was herded into a room with twenty or so others to take the oath of allegiance to King George VI.

Volunteer Bandsman AC 2 1892517

I was now AC 2 1892517, an aircraftman 2nd class in the Royal Air Force (Richard Attenborough was AC 2 1808294) and was issued with a lapel badge bearing silver wings and the RAF motto 'Per Ardua ad Astra' to show everyone that I was waiting to begin aircrew training and not dodging the column.

The predicted one-year wait before beginning pilot training was too long for some of us, and many re-mustered as air gunners, who, after a six-week course, were promoted to sergeants and posted to Lancaster Squadrons, bombing Germany nightly. Their life expectancy was about six weeks.

I wanted to be a fighter pilot and was still prepared to wait. Then I received a letter from the RAF offering me a preliminary Aircrew Training Course, designed to bring people like me, who'd left school at fourteen, up to the required educational standard of aircrew. The courses lasted six months and were held at universities and technical colleges. I jumped at the chance, for I would not only benefit academically but would also get into uniform much sooner. I accepted, and settled down to wait for my call. Meanwhile, I was kept very busy with music in the evenings and at weekends, and the daily journey to Docwra's offices overlooking the Thames.

After the Blitz in 1940, when the docks were set ablaze, all London buildings were required to maintain a twenty-four-hour fire watch, and one night a week it was the turn of Docwra's staff. At the end of a day emptying waste-paper baskets, tidying filing cabinets, cleaning typewriters and adding up columns of figures, I'd set up my camp-bed with a pillow and a blanket and check that there was enough coal to keep the office fire alight and enough milk for the morning tea.

Fire Watchers were allowed to sleep unless there was an air raid, and then it was not down to the shelter but a long climb up to the roof of our Victorian building, where the chimneys and glass skylights waited to swallow the firebombs which could ignite the masses of paper in the offices below.

Being a 'junior', I was paired with a former Territorial Army captain who had been invalided out after having been wounded at Dunkirk. Before the raids began (the timing was usually predictable), Henry and I dined at the Aldwych Restaurant, using our Government Fire Watcher's allowance of three shillings a night, drinking wine and smoking. All this high life was new to me, but I found it very much to my taste. If things were quiet, Henry and I would stroll as far as Fleet Street, where the Black and White Milk Bar stayed open all night for the pressmen from the *Daily Express*, *Mail* and *Mirror*, and we'd buy a couple of cheddar cheese rolls for the very early breakfast which marked the dawn of a red-eyed day.

Henry was an unusual man in every sense. We slept in our underwear, and I noticed that when he stripped to his vest, the left side of his chest was concave, almost as though his ribs were the wrong way round. When I got to know him well, he told me that, at Dunkirk, he'd received what should have been a fatal wound to the heart, but survived because he was a dextrocardiac, his heart being on the right side of his chest.

I learned a lot from Henry. We discussed everything from Einstein's Theory of Relativity to the relative merits of Tissot, Longines and Rolex wrist watches. Not that I knew anything about them, but at least I now had an opinion, even if it was his.

Sometimes, 'by kind permission of the Commanding Officer of 66 Squadron ATC, the Atcats would play in London. Our repertoire now reflected America's entry into the war with songs of love, longing and optimism: 'You Are My Sunshine', 'As Time Goes By', 'Jingle, Jangle Jingle', 'Skylark' and a song about the flight back to an English airfield of a badly-damaged American Flying Fortress, 'Coming in on a Wing and a Prayer'. Its composer was a man whom I later got to know well when I conducted his musical, *The Most Happy Fella*: Frank Loesser.

After the dance ended, if the line had been bombed, I'd have to wait until the 4am milk-train to Selhurst, getting home and to bed at about 5am. Then, after a couple of hours sleep, it was back to the station and the train to London. If I missed that, I'd cycle the ten miles to the office with a change of clothes in my saddlebag.

In preparation for full-time service in the RAF, we ATC cadets were sent for a week's camp at Kenley Aerodrome amongst the Spitfires and Hurricanes that had fought in the Battle of Britain. It should have been enjoyable, but during a game of rugby, I caught the ball awkwardly and damaged my left hand. The little finger stood out a strange angle, which the

Physical Training Instructor judged to be a dislocation. The idiot grabbed the finger and gave it a few yanks, and it was only when my pain got through his thick skull that he sent me off by bus, alone, to Croydon General Hospital. There, the X-rays showed a split knuckle, but as I was in ATC uniform, the hospital sent me back to the RAF Medical Officer at Kenley. As bad luck would have it, he was nowhere to be found, and I finished up in the hands of the two RAF Medical Orderlies. They admitted that they'd never set a broken finger, but decided to have a go. It had now taken the shape of a question mark, so they put it between two pieces of wood and gradually straightened it out, bandaging it very tightly – all without any kind of painkiller. They then sent me back to my camp (and a sleepless night), telling me to return on the morrow so that the Medical Officer could have a look at it. He did, and when he saw my black finger, he could scarcely conceal his anger. He did his best, but I was never afterwards able to stretch an octave.

Fate moves in mysterious ways, for had I not broken my finger, perhaps I might never have become a conductor! I continued with the Atcats and played as best I could only using four fingers of my left hand.

I was still one up on the great jazz guitarist Django Reinhardt, who had only three!

Life was very exciting, but very busy, and it was with a sense of relief that the long-awaited letter arrived from 'my obedient servant', an Air Commodore, requesting me to report to the Aircrew Reception Centre at Lord's Cricket Ground at 0900 on 23rd September, 1943.

CHAPTER 9

THE ROYAL AIR FORCE

Dancing at Covent Garden

One Thursday morning, I bought a one-way ticket from Selhurst to Lord's, where I'd spent many happy hours watching cricket before the war. But it wasn't the Lord's I knew with its immaculate wickets and beautifully-manicured grass. Now, young men in civilian clothes trampled the hallowed turf, and the sound of ball on willow and the applause for a good stroke was replaced by the shouts of non-commissioned officers as they brought some semblance of order to hundreds of men away from their homes for the first time and amongst strangers.

When we were finally assembled in our respective flying categories, we were inoculated and vaccinated, had a haircut, were fitted with uniforms, steel helmets and gas masks, were issued with a tin mug, knife, fork and spoon, and were then marched to Abbey Lodge a block of luxury flats in St John's Wood, where we learned how to make a bed the RAF way.

After a night's sleep (broken by a young Irish international rugby player who cried most of it, having been told that the spot on his lung was tuberculosis and he was to be sent home), we paraded at 4.40am for breakfast. We were red-eyed zombies, necks chafed by new, coarse flannel shirts, in ill-fitting uniforms and uncomfortable new shoes, with shorn hair under forage-caps and faces bleeding from the cuts of a cold-water shave.

We were brought to attention and told we needn't swing our swollen left arms as we marched by the light of the moon to breakfast in the vast underground car park of luxurious Bentick Close, where once Jaguars and Bentleys abounded. Now this cold cavern was filled only with long lines of wooden tables and benches.

The sergeant who excused our arm-swinging was Max Faulkner, later to become the British Open Golf Champion and founder of our local West Chiltington Golf Club.

At the entrance, we broke ranks and shuffled down the slope to join the long blue lines of young men who were slowly making their way to the distant servers. As we got closer, one of our number exclaimed eagerly, 'Look! Those cooks are WAAFs!' Even at this moment, just before dawn, when the human spirit is at its lowest ebb, our spirits rose at the thought of sharing our service lives with women, and WAAFs were women, weren't they? As we neared the hot-plates, in the poor lighting, we began to make out their shapes. They wore white overalls and turbans and were undeniably feminine. There was a sudden acceleration of the queue, and I found myself face to face with one of these visions. She had a deathly pallor, disguised by coarse face powder, with bags under her bloodshot eyes, pencilled eyebrows and smudged lipstick. Leering at me, she thrust something burnt and bony across the hot plate, and, in a smoke-wrecked voice, she croaked, ''Ere's yer fuckin' kipper.'

A month of basic training included a lot of sports in Regent's Park (where a number of cadets were killed in a surprise German air raid) and a swimming test where, totally naked, we were ordered to jump in the deep end of Seymour Baths. Anyone who didn't surface was rescued by a physical training instructor with a long pole and graded a non-swimmer who would need enough training so that, in the event of their aircraft coming down in the sea, they could get as far as the dinghy. Gradually, we began to look and feel more at home in our uniforms, and, with our basic training over, we were looking forward to our posting to university. Finally, one hundred eager cadets, proudly wearing the white forage-cap flashes of aircrew under training, marched smartly out to the waiting RAF trucks in great high spirits, bound for an unknown destination. Oxford? Cambridge? Exeter? They were all possibilities.

We turned south, but the trucks bypassed all the main stations and headed down the Waterloo Road for the Elephant and Castle in an ancient part of London known as the Borough. Then they turned left into the Old Kent Road and drew up at the

Oliver Borthwick Memorial Home, a Victorian workhouse. It was now empty, for its inmates had been evacuated to somewhere nice in the country to make room for us.

With a clang, the iron gates closed behind this home for the destitute, now ours for the next six months.

In training at Elephant and Castle (sixth from right)

I was only a bus ride from Selhurst, but I was not permitted to go home, as this could affect my morale – or so said the two officers who commanded us: a flight lieutenant (a middle-aged portly man with no flying brevet) and a sergeant (who had probably been a physical training instructor at a borstal, or some such other house of correction).

We slept fifty men to each dormitory. There were only six light bulbs, and the two lavatories on each floor soon became almost unusable. The next day, in low spirits, we marched to the Borough Polytechnic, originally conceived to provide the working classes with a technical education.

It was a revelation. During our six months there, we cadets had our minds opened to politics, philosophy and the kind of education provided by universities. An elderly retired professor, a Jewish refugee from Hitler, was un-retired and given a hundred reasonably-bright young men to instruct in European Political History. Never did he convey bigotry or hate but, as a true academic, was always objective and led our minds to truth. We learnt from him about Garibaldi and the Italian 'Risorgimento', about Kemal Atatürk's modernisation of Turkey, and of how we should have gone to war at the time of Munich to defend Czechoslovakia, the most democratic country in Europe. His lectures were fascinating and always relevant. Our studies included surprisingly few subjects that were directly connected with flying but, apart from machine-drawing, these were the subjects which we would have taken at school, had we been able to stay on.

We were allowed out of the workhouse each evening to savour the delights of the Elephant and Castle. The local cinema managers provided us with free seats, and the fish and chips helped us to forget the workhouse food. We were ticking over nicely. But then the air raids began again, and the Elephant was right in the middle of them. Although much shorter than the first Blitz, they seemed planned to disrupt, rather than an attempt to destroy London completely.

About 2am, the sirens would set up their unholy wail, our alarm bell would ring and the sergeant, always fully dressed, would roar, 'Shelter! Now! MOVE!'

Amongst the grumbles and curses of waking cadets and the rasp of cigarette lighters, we would scramble into uniform and, complete with gas-mask and steel helmet, crowd into a small brick building in the workhouse yard, where one bomb would have seen off the lot of us.

Two hours or so later, on the 'all-clear', the procedure would be reversed, but then after an hour or so, the whole thing would be repeated. It was exhausting, and after a couple of weeks of this, we were all suffering badly from lack of sleep. I managed to get some by buying a tube ticket on the Circle Line and dozing for a couple of hours before the stations closed for the night to become air-raid shelters.

As well as threatening our coursework, the air raids affected our tempers. One morning, with a headache and red-rimmed eyes, I was waiting in line for my cold-water wash and shave when a young Scot from Paisley contested my position. The next thing I remembered was my fellow cadets pulling me off him, for I'd suddenly 'seen red' (it does happen) and was doing my best to break his skull on the wet concrete floor of that awful smelly washroom with the overflowing lavatories.

I seemed to have stirred up the ancient war between the Scots and English, for a cadet from Stirling (with an incomprehensible oath and race memories of English soldiers snatching the haggis from the mouths of Scottish bairns) took to tipping selected Englishmen out of bed at any time of night. I was a prime target, and decided that this must stop, so I plotted revenge. I volunteered as a permanent fire picket, a duty generally disliked, for it meant having to get up before everyone else. The advantage was a room to oneself. For seven mornings, I gave him my full attention, tipping him out of bed half an hour before 'reveille' and whispering that I liked sleeping alone and might decide to remain the fire picket for the whole six months. It broke his spirit, and he gave up his antics.

Fifty young men in one room provided a unique education in self-control.

After lights out, the cadet in the bed opposite, a jolly Cornishman, told us that when he and his girlfriend went down to the beach to swim, she always took her top off. The thought had a profound effect on the cadet in the bed next to me, who confided that he could not sleep unless he relieved himself at least once every night. Why I should be his confidant made me wonder if I was sending out the wrong signals.

Two beds down was the Junior Sussex Lawn Tennis Champion, a chap called Frawley, and, opposite him, a red-haired Scot from Aberdeen, who danced for our delight a Schottische as he sang:

Ahm the saftest o' the family,
Ahm a little Johnny rover,
All the fam'ly like ter lamb me,
And ma faithers got it in for me an' all!

All of us passed the exams except a policeman from Devon. We were sad for him, because he'd been something of a father figure. As his bed was under one of the six lights, he'd let us sit on it to write letters home. One night it collapsed, he spent the night on the floor and the next morning was put on a charge for destroying government property!

One morning, after yet another broken night's sleep, we sadly waved him goodbye, he to return to his old life as a village policeman, apparently having failed to make the grade, and we again to the Aircrew Reception Centre at Lord's.

I was now better educated, I had learnt how to live with friend and foe, and, thanks to the attentions of a very pretty ballroom dancing teacher at the Borough evening classes, I had learnt the intricacies and intimacies of the shuffle, whisk and progressive side-step well enough to win my first medal – a Bronze for ballroom dancing!

'Strictly Come Dancing' – wartime style – at the Royal Opera House, 1943

CHAPTER 10

LORD'S AGAIN

On Wenlock Edge

The fact that we arrived from the Elephant and Castle in uniform and had been in the RAF for seven months seemed not to have penetrated the minds of those at the Lord's Aircrew Reception Centre, for we were shown the same film about VD. The first time, a couple of the cadets had fainted at the grisly sight, but now we'd lived in one of the toughest parts of London, where razor gangs still flourished, and had learnt how to defend ourselves with the buckles of our webbing belts. This time, the damaged wedding tackle produced coarse jokes!

Within a few days, we were split into our flying categories, and I was posted to the delightful Shropshire village of Bridgnorth, home of fifty-seven pubs and the Initial Training Wing, where for three months I would study Meteorology, Theory of Flight, Aircraft Recognition, Astral and Terrestrial Navigation, the Morse Code and Guns.

This time, there were only forty men in our Nissen hut. I shared a double bunk with Marius Camps, one of five Dutchmen who'd escaped from occupied Holland. One day they were absent and returned the next morning, each wearing an orange medal ribbon. They'd been to London to see their Queen Wilhelmina, who had decorated them for bravery. For the first time, I met men who'd lived under the German occupation, and suddenly the war seemed very close.

Marius was in his early twenties and came from Limburg in southern Holland. Though his spoken English was pretty good, the technical words posed particular difficulties. After lights out, he'd study by flashlight and, taking literally my offer of help 'at any time', would lean down from his upper bunk, prod me awake and whisper, 'Ken, for what is an Anemometer?'

At break-times the Dutch were glad to be able to relax into their own language, and I took to listening in the hopes of learning a little. I did, but it was mostly a collection of swear words and the phrase, 'Alleen tien daagen en wej hebben een tit in de hand!' The Dutch word for breast is 'borst', but they used our word, so you'll appreciate that I was learning the sort of Dutch which was useless to me when I later conducted in Holland.

In common with the rest of wartime Britain, we cadets worked ten hours a day for seven days, and the eighth day we were free. Our first day off fell on a Wednesday, and Marius and I planned to take the bus from outside the camp through the beautiful county of Shropshire to Shrewsbury, twenty miles away.

Having passed the gate inspection by the RAF police, we were waiting at the bus stop at 8.30am on a lovely spring morning. Opposite, a man, too old and bent for war service, was scything the grass verge. We nodded to each other. 9am came and went, then 9.30am, then 10am. As a matter of security, there were no bus timetables on display (after all, we didn't want the German parachutists to know the time of the buses to Shrewsbury), and so I asked the old man if he knew the time of the next bus. Slowly, he removed the straw from his mouth and, without a flicker of humour, replied, 'Thursday.'

'That's very English,' said Marius, to which I retorted, 'The man's a fool. Does he think we've been here all this time just to watch him cut the bloody grass?!'

Knowing that the one train a day from Bridgnorth had already gone, we decided to walk the twenty miles to Shrewsbury, hoping for a lift. I was just walking, but Marius was, for the first time for four years, enjoying a walk in a country free of German occupation.

It became hot under the clear blue sky, and we took to carrying our jackets. After a few miles, we passed a field where former Italian prisoners of war, who were now our allies (they'd changed sides), hailed us with 'Ciao!' I 'Ciao'ed back, but Marius, a devout Roman Catholic, turned to me and said, 'You know, Ken, the Italians were Hitler's allies, and if I had a gun now I'd probably shoot them all. But you can't understand that, can you!'

I couldn't, and we walked on in silence until his black mood passed and he explained more about his life under the occupation. With his fiancée and her brother, he'd been a member of a team that escorted Jews, French prisoners of war and Allied airmen on the escape route into Belgium. The fliers were the most difficult to get through, for they had to learn to ride a bicycle the Dutch way – knees akimbo – and when to say 'Ja' convincingly to Marius's bogus question at the German check-points.

One night, things went wrong and Marius was arrested. He talked himself out of trouble, but life under the German occupation took a turn for the worse when the government decreed that all the Dutch must now take an oath of allegiance which made no mention of Queen Wilhelmina. Marius refused, and it was time to leave Holland. He walked across the Pyrenees, in company with a Jewish escapee and a dog, but was captured. Marius escaped from fourteen prisons, including the notorious Miranda concentration camp, which was overrun by giant cockroaches. The prisoners took turns at killing them with rolled-up newspapers so that the others could sleep. He escaped yet again, and finally reached England in an unheated RAF Dakota. There, he learnt that his future brother-in-law had been shot and that his own fiancée was missing.

All this Marius told me as we walked between the red rocks of Shropshire, a county that had inspired so much poetry and music, on a road where we hoped no German jackboots would ever tread. When we reached the lovely village of Much Wenlock, I introduced him to the only food on offer – rock cakes and cider – and, thus fortified, we merrily sang our way to Shrewsbury, arriving just in time to catch the train back to camp.

As we stood waiting on the platform, an American troop train slowly passed through on its way to the south and the impending invasion of Normandy on D-Day. The soldiers were all black, and they were in high spirits, showering us with free cigarettes and Hershey's chocolate bars. Black soldiers did not fight alongside white Americans but instead fulfilled the vital role as drivers and armed escorts of the 'Red Ball Express' – huge trucks that took supplies right up to the front line. Many were decorated, including a sergeant who was awarded the America's highest decoration, the 'Medal of Honor'.

Marius and I never again strayed far from Bridgnorth on our days off. We went each evening to the camp cinema, where the programmes included documentaries from the Crown Film Unit. One of these, *Coastal Command*, had music by Ralph Vaughan Williams, which, years later, I was to record with the Philharmonia Orchestra. Worthy though these documentaries were, any other kind of film was doomed. When a distraught father is led into the morgue to view the body of his daughter, a wag would shout, 'Kit inspection! Stand by your beds!' All love scenes, no matter how sincere, were received with catcalls, whistling and shouts of 'Get in there, knob! It's your birthday!' The cinema was always good for a coarse laugh.

Fortunately, the camp had music: a band under the direction of a Flight Sergeant known to us as 'Bandy', who was very sympathetic to my curiously-shaped little finger and let me play the camp's Hammond organ. My music was certainly on hold, and for me the high spot at Bridgnorth was a visit by the Atcats's role model, the RAF Squadronaires. Fate was certainly smiling unseen.

Failure to pass the exams would mean a 'return to unit' (RTU), so we worked very hard, but on the parade ground, our Dutch friends gave us plenty of laughs. Although their English was now excellent, they appeared to have special difficulties with the commands of our Drill Sergeant – known more for his strength of voice than its elocution.

'Hon the command, Squad will hadvance in threes: right turn, on the word "turn", you will hall swivel on the right 'eel through ninety degrees, and to the timin' of, one (pause) two, bring the left foot smartly up to the right, forming han angle of thirty degrees… Squad atten-(wait for it!)-SHUN!'

Dutifully, we would bring the left foot smartly to the right and bang it down hard (heaven knows how much long-term damage we did to our joints). The sergeant then began, 'The squad will hadvance in threes.'

At this point, a Dutchman would interrupt with, 'Pliss, Sergeant, vot iss der trees?'

Quickly came, 'Three a-breast, son.'

Another Dutchman enquired, 'Pliss, vot is a brest?'

We listened eagerly for the sergeant to explain 'a breast', but after raising an eyebrow at the Dutchman, he began the whole sequence again. He was a good soul, and he knew we were taking the p**s.

We began our final exams on 6[th,] June, 1944: D-Day. But if the Normandy invasion had failed, Europe would have remained under German occupation, perhaps for many years, and there was still the war in the Far East. Aircrew would still be needed. And so, at last, after two years in the ATC and a year of the RAF, I was finally going to get my hands on an aeroplane.

In 2008, at the Shoreham Air Show, I asked the Dutch pilot of a Mitchell Bomber how I might find out what happened to Marius after he left Bridgnorth. By the most extraordinary coincidence, he'd spoken, just two days before, to Marius' daughter, Monica, who lived in California. I contacted her and she told me that her father became a Mosquito navigator (<u>now</u> he knew about an Anemometer!) and had been decorated many times.

CHAPTER 11

ELMDON

Come fly the Tiger with me!

Like the vast majority of the British population in 1944, I'd never flown, and, keen though I was, I wondered how I would react. I had heard that even Nelson was sometimes sea-sick, and I knew that some 66 Squadron ATC cadets who'd been lucky enough to fly had made a mess in the aeroplane – not popular with the pilot or those that followed. There was also the possibility of vertigo, disorientation and plain gut fear, so it was with some trepidation that, wearing a Sidcot flying suit, fur-lined flying boots, leather gauntlets, flying helmet, oxygen mask, goggles and a parachute, I clambered into the rear cockpit of a Tiger Moth – the 'Tiggy'.

A Tiger Moth

'So, you're my sprog?' said my instructor, a Sergeant Pilot on rest from wartime operations.

'Yes, Sir.' (All instructors were called 'Sir').

'Fasten your Sutton tightly, son.' (The 'Sutton' is a five-point harness, designed to keep its wearer attached to the aeroplane, even when upside down). He then went through the important starting-drill which, if mismanaged, can take off the arm, or even the head, of the man swinging the propeller.

'Throttle set, switches on, CONTACT…' and the Gypsy Major engine roared into life. Then he called 'Chocks away!' (there are no brakes on a Tiger Moth) and we bumped across the grass field (which is now Birmingham's International Airport) to the take-off point. He turned into the wind, opened the throttle and, as we gathered speed, eased the stick forward, and the Tiggy took to the air.

How can one describe one's very first flight? The Spitfire poet, Pilot Officer McGee, wrote that he 'slipped the surly bonds of earth', but my feelings were just of great excitement as, instead of climbing into the blue, we spent the next few minutes 'hedgehopping'. I'd never driven a car or ridden a motorcycle. The fastest I'd ever been was on a push-bike at twelve miles an hour downhill, yet here I was, a few feet above the ground, flying at over seventy!

The noise of the wind through the flying wires and the Gypsy Major engine made communication very difficult in the open cockpit, so short 'key words' were the order of the day. As we approached a five-bar gate, my instructor eased the stick back and, as we just scraped over, from my flying helmet came his nasal voice, 'Elevator equals – pitch. Got it?' We climbed somewhat higher and, as he pushed the stick over to the left, feeding in some left rudder, came, 'Aileron equals – Roll. Rudder equals – Yaw. Got it?'

Then we climbed again and, on the way up to what seemed to me a dizzy height, he asked me, 'Is your harness tight?' 'Yes, Sir,' I replied. Then he ordered me to lock the slots. Locking the slots should have warned me of what was to come, but this was my first flight! From that moment, the world went slowly mad as our turn to the left became steeper and steeper, and I realised that the green fields of Warwickshire were appearing over my head. In a panic, I desperately gripped the sides of the cockpit. When we were finally completely upside down, my harness lurched, and I fell a full three inches *upwards* into the sky.

Now, with quite a few thousand flying hours under my belt and a flying instructor rating, I know that was a very good 'slow roll', but I think I should have been warned.

'You have control', said my mentor, and, under his guidance, I flew back to the aerodrome. He demonstrated the landing and, as I walked back to the Dispersal Hut, trailing the parachute which I thought I was going to have to use, I was pleased that I hadn't been sick and determined that, the next time I flew, my harness would be really tight.

Apart from almost decapitating an airman cycling along the perimeter track on take-off, and a steep spiral dive the first time I made a turn to the right, eventually, after ten hours' instruction, a rather snooty flight lieutenant climbed out of the Tiger and said, 'Get on with it, LAC.' Being alone in the sky for the first time concentrates the mind wonderfully, and I got the Tiggy down in one piece.

Since then, I have sent many student pilots on their first solo flights and, without exception, they have found it to be the greatest experience of their lives. Thirty years after my first solo, I again flew a Tiger Moth at Shoreham, and I had the experience of re-living that day in Elmdon. The years dropped away, the air was like champagne and the colours of the sky, the sea and the green fields of Sussex were as though freshly painted. I was nineteen again.

I'd passed, and was sent on leave. From Birmingham to my home in Croydon is less than a hundred and fifty miles, but far enough to take me back into the front line of Hitler's renewed attacks on London – this time, not by Dorniers, Heinkels and Junkers but by unmanned aircraft: the V-1s (Flying Bombs). They came across the Channel in small, scattered formations at only two or three hundred feet. These nasty weapons were unpredictable, for they were each programmed to behave differently when the engine stopped. Some would dive and hit the ground very quickly, others would glide as much as two miles, the only warning being the whistle of the wind over the wings. If you could hear that, you were much too close.

I was therefore quite glad to leave the rigours of Croydon to take the train north to the peace of the Aircrew Dispersal Centre at Heaton Park, Manchester.

CHAPTER 12

HEATON PARK

Death from the stratosphere

In Manchester, it is either raining, has just rained, or is about to rain, and it was certainly teeming 'cats and dogs' when I arrived in August 1944 at Heaton Park Transit Centre, from where I was to be sent for further pilot training, under the Empire Air Training scheme, to either the USA or the Commonwealth.

It looked as though I'd have to wait three months in Manchester for an overseas posting, and so I was delighted to receive a letter from Aunt Maud telling me that I had cousins living in Salford, including Alice Mary Broughton, known as Molly. Her mother, Lily, helped her husband, Christopher, to run the Unicorn Inn at 10 Broughton Road, Lower Broughton, Salford.

The Unicorn was Salford's answer to Coronation Street's Rovers Return, but Chris had no spirit licence and had to sell a lot of beer and sherry to make a living. Nevertheless, the family seemed to be comfortably off, and I was immediately invited to a meal of 'cow-heel pie' (one cow heel and stewing steak, with the odd oyster or two!)

Cousin Molly

Molly turned out to be a very pretty girl with auburn hair, large brown eyes, a shapely figure and a twenty-year-old boyfriend in tow, one Edward. 'Eddie' was slim, wore leather gloves and a white riding mac, had glossy black hair, an assured manner and had recently graduated as a

Batchelor of Science in Engineering. I was impressed by them both.

After a couple of weeks getting to know my new cousins, I went home again to Selhurst for seven days' leave. This time, Hitler had a really nasty trick up his sleeve, 'Death from the Stratosphere'. I think I was one of the very first to survive the experience. When walking home, the peace of a lovely starry evening was shattered by a gigantic explosion, a chilling blast of wind and, seconds later, a sound like the Flying Scot passing at arm's length as the noise of the bomb's passage through the air arrived from outer space after the explosion. It was truly frightening.

This was one of the first of the V-2 rockets, the German 'terror weapon' which, weighing over a ton, arrived from seventy miles above the earth at over three thousand miles an hour. The V-2 could have easily reduced London to a ruin. The V-2s were kept secret by the government until, in November, Churchill admitted that as many as eight rockets a day had been falling on London since September and that thousands had been killed. I was glad to get back to the comparative peace of Manchester, where they knew nothing of what was happening in the south.

Now having relatives near the camp, I found that I could get a sleeping-out pass with a food ration and travel allowance, so I moved into the Unicorn and, for the first time, had a bedroom of my own. Molly was a classical music fan with a wind-up gramophone, and it was she who took me to my first symphony concert – the Hallé Orchestra, conducted by Sir John Barbirolli. This was a time of 'firsts': my first flight and now my first symphony concert, two loves which were constantly to interweave in my life.

Sleeping in a room of my own in a pub was a novel experience, and I had to report back to Heaton Park for the 8am morning parade. Many cadets without sleeping-out passes stayed out all night, climbing over the miles of stone walls that surrounded the park and sneaking into their huts just before dawn. The RAF police knew what was going on, and, late one night, daubed the walls with a combination of tar and creosote. It was a carefully-planned operation, and instead of the morning parade being held by a sergeant, things took a nasty turn when it was held by an Officer (whom I shall call Flying Officer Kite), accompanied by the Station Warrant Officer. The inspection went reasonably well until F/O Kite reached the rear ranks. These were the lair of the night owls who would arrive on parade at the last minute, and the slaughter of the sluggards began.

'You, LAC. Why are you wearing Wellington boots? It's not raining!'

Came the reply, 'It was when I left the hut, Sir.'

Without bothering to reply to such an obvious falsehood (for this was one of the few days when it wasn't raining), Flying Officer Kite turned to the Warrant Officer. 'Take that man's name and number, Mr Warren,' and he moved on to the next apparition.

'Why are you wearing a striped pyjama jacket and a black tie, LAC?'

Came the ingenious reply, 'I forgot to take off my shirt for bed last night, Sir, and changed into my pyjama top this morning by mistake.'

This was so complicated that W/O Warren, with a twinkle in his eye, merely said, 'Name and number, son.'

Flying Officer Kite moved on. 'Why are you wearing your rain-cape, LAC? What have you got on under it?'

The cadet raised the green rubber tent to reveal a uniform ruined by a black line of tar and creosote.

Things were tightened up, and although there was still no set daily programme after morning parade, it was extremely unwise to loll around the hut playing cards or reading. For there might be a sudden raid by prowling sergeants, eager to round up cadets for posting to Lincolnshire to load the Lancasters, which were nightly taking the war deep into Germany.

Loading bombs was a much-feared and back-breakingly boring occupation on freezing airfields, miles from anywhere that resembled civilisation.

Although we would no doubt be assisting the war, when I heard that the Officers' Mess needed washers-up, I, not being proud (and determined to stay near Molly, to whom I'd taken a great fancy), volunteered for this mucky job. There were compensations: the left-overs from the officers' meals, such as eggs, liver, steak, puddings and cheese. A veritable cornucopia of a quality, rarely seen in the Airmen's Mess.

When I recounted my luck to fellows also trying to avoid the Lincolnshire posting, I had so many offers of help that, with the aid of the friendly Cookery Sergeant, and equipped with my badge of office (a red lanyard), every morning I marched my own private Air Force – proudly named 'Headquarters Flight' – to the Officers' Mess. I'd start with about twenty, but on the way, most of them would disappear into the bushes and climb the walls to freedom and a day out in Manchester.

But when our bombing raids on Germany were stepped up, more bomb-loaders were required in Lincolnshire, and the activities of the sniffer-out sergeants increased. I needed another reason to stay in Manchester, and when I heard that RAF Fencing Classes were poorly attended, I sensed a possible solution.

My first lesson was a revelation. I knew I'd found a sport I might do well in.

There were few postings from Heaton Park for pilot training, but I was having fun with Molly's many friends, who were a merry crew. Led by Eddie, still with her on his arm (I had no luck there), we included Jo, a buxom blonde with a hearty laugh (an early Bridget Jones), serious Gladys and a tall, dark beautiful girl called Joan, whose fiancé had been posted to Southern Rhodesia for flying training nine months before, but (now a Sergeant Pilot) had returned to marry her. It was a beautiful baby!

The Salford Hippodrome was open again, with a variety show that included a Chinese magician (probably from Salford) and his lady assistant, whose fat legs were encased in spangled tights which, like the lady herself, had somewhat lost their lustre.

To draw attention to his next trick, she would strike a cracked gong, and the inevitable laughs (for a gong that is cracked lacks charisma) imperilled the phoney Mandarin's attempt to balance a sword on his chin.

Another of our gang's visits was to the Sale Hippodrome, where Frank H. Fortescue and his famous players were performing twice nightly.

Frank could be found in the Circle Bar between performances in full costume and make-up, and I saw for the first time what the sticks of Leichner grease paint looked like at close quarters – the fleshy tint of No. 5, the rosy No. 9 and Lake Liner.

When later I appeared in the West End as a professional actor, I used the same make-up as Frank H. Fortescue. Fortunately, my fellow actors took me in hand.

Although parties, plays, concerts, films and fencing were fun, I began to realise that I'd better start thinking about what I should do after the war. Remembering the advice of that wonderful Jewish professor at the Borough Polytechnic, I sought self-improvement and made a reading list: Shaw, Stendhal, Dostoevsky, Tolstoy, the Koran and other worthy books. I read Benham's *Economics* and passed a Manchester University College course in Elementary Psychology.

And so the last months of the war saw the end of the long-hoped-for flying training and brought another experience which was to affect my future.

On my way to the train to London, I developed a severe earache. Ancoats Hospital was close to Oxford Road station, and there a nursing sister syringed my ear (with cold water). I collapsed, and I made the long train journey to London with a punctured eardrum. Doctor Freitag told that I'd probably always be deaf in that ear, and with hopes of perhaps making a living in music, this was a bitter blow.

To be deaf in one ear, unable to stretch an octave with my left hand and to have also lost the tip of a finger did not seem to be a good start.

On 8th May, 1945, Germany surrendered and, in the summer, we aircrew trainees were made redundant and sent to the unpopular RAF 'knacker's yard' at Eastchurch on the Isle of Sheppey.

In 1911, Sir John McLean allowed his farm to be used for training Royal Navy airmen. Pilots who learnt to fly there included Tommy Sopwith and Lord Brabazon. One of the instructors was Ben Travers, who wrote many West End farces starring Tom Walls, Ralph Lynn and Robertson Hare. Those were the days before dual controls were fitted, and the first time that students (called 'passengers') actually handled the aircraft was on their first solo. I have seen Ben's flying log book from this period, with an entry typical of many: '10.30am. Passenger crashed on first solo. Killed.'

Eastchurch was the only RAF station in England that issued mosquito nets, which we slept under, for the last death from home-grown malaria on the island was as late as 1952.

The dining hall – a converted aircraft hangar – was the home of hundreds of colonically-challenged birds, which bombed us and our food unmercifully. However, the food was so bad that some of their deposits made little difference, and we became accustomed to removing them from our shepherd's pie and cabbage. The cook's sweet specialities were soggy jam sponge and rock-hard jam tarts.

The day of my very depressing interview, when I was re-mustered to Clerk General Duties, I was toying with my food. Having pushed away some inedible main course (with bird dressing) I was gazing aghast at my spoon (which had been bent by the jam tart at ninety degrees), when the cultured voice of high rank came from behind me. 'Food all right, lad?' I turned and there, complete with four rings and a cap laced with scrambled egg, stood a 'Groupie' – a Group Captain – and behind him a line of Officers of diminishing rank, ending with the Station Warrant Officer, with notebook, pencil poised and a nasty look in his eye.

The birds were diving like Stukas, my tin dinner plate was half-full of cabbage water and I'd just bent my bloody spoon on the jam tart. What kind of a damn fool question was that? I thought of the camaraderie at Bridgnorth, my first solo at Elmdon, my high hopes at Heaton Park and my present gloomy prospects, and I surrendered. 'Excellent, Sir. Thank you, Sir.'

And so at the birthplace of British aviation, where Tommy Sopwith and the holder of Flying Licence Number One, Lord Brabazon, began their flying careers, mine ended.

Or so I thought…

CHAPTER 13

THE AIR MINISTRY

Pilot officer passe

On our last night on the Isle of Sheppey, a few of my fellow 'redundants' and I decided that we'd go into nearby Sheerness for the evening. We were in low spirits, but finding this little fishing port rather depressing, we decided to return to camp. There was no transport and so we faced a walk of six miles.

Conversation turned to the future. 'What are you going to do when you leave the RAF?' I asked one. His answer was to take a deep breath and launch into the opening phrase of 'E lucevan le stelle'. The glorious sound of that Welsh tenor, the music of Puccini and that lovely English summer night under 'the stars brightly shining' lifted us all in a way that only music can achieve.

The tenor was Lewis Henry, and the next time we met was when I was auditioning singers for my first musical, Peter Greenwell's 'The Crooked Mile'. Lewis sang very well, and I asked him if he remembered a night on the Isle of Sheppey under the stars. He had no idea who the voice was from the darkened auditorium, but when I walked into the light and said, 'Mr Henry, I'd be glad if you would join the cast,' it was a memorable moment for us both. Henceforth, Lewis was always the first tenor I asked to join my casts, and we worked together many times during the ensuing years.

I was re-mustered from Eastchurch to the Air Ministry

Maintenance and Repair Unit (AMMRU) of Technical Training Command in Woburn Place, London. It was an easy posting, for I was billeted with Aunt Bess at Selhurst and allowed to wear civilian clothes off-duty.

Until AMMRU was formed, aircraft servicing was not planned. All too frequently, time was wasted, until an Engineering Officer, Squadron Leader McKelvey, introduced a 'Time and Motion Study'. My task was to meet and greet the senior technicians – mostly, grizzly old Warrant Officers who'd won the war using their methods – make them a cup of tea and try to persuade them that new was better.

I now worked office hours and was able to make good use of what delights wartime London had to offer. My fencing skills improved rapidly, for I could now get regular lessons from London's leading fencing master, Leon Paul.

Paul had been the European Professional Foil Champion and, even in his sixties, there was no one who could lay a point on him. He would turn all five foot three inches of himself square on and challenge me with ''it me, 'it me!' No matter how hard I tried, he parried me easily, and my lesson only ended when, fit as I was, I was too tired for even one more lunge.

The wrist work required to fence has a great deal in common with the physical control of the conductor's baton. Paul's insistence on a light-handed control of the foil served me very well and prevented the repetitive strain injury that might easily have occurred during the thousands of movements required for just one concert. Even now, more than sixty years later, I have no problems.

Under Paul's tutelage, my fencing improved well enough for me – now equipped with an international licence – to be included in his inner circle of twelve fencers, known as Salle Paul, which included Cooke, the English Foil Champion, and Leon's son, Raymond, an Olympic gold medallist.

My new prestige led the RAF Master-at-Arms to make me a

member of the Combined Services Fencing Team. Service swordsmen fought with foils, sabres, épées and bayonets. Bayonet fighting involves a lot of padding – both of the contestant and of the heavy rifle and spring-loaded blade. The general idea is that, if you couldn't get your bayonet 'up 'em' in the approved Corporal Jones manner, with a smart cross, you should thump them under the chin with the rifle stock. Contestants were quite often knocked off their feet; it was very rough.

We seemed to be unbeatable, but we met our match – the Royal Naval Cadets of Dartmouth Training College. Their traditional and rock-steady technique, coupled with youthful reaction time, proved too much for our rather flashy style (Nelson would have recognised their sabre work), and, as some of them were barely fourteen, we were humiliated.

Life at the Air Ministry was proving unbearably boring, but there was always the hope that I might be required in the almost-forgotten war against Japan. However, on 6th August, 'Enola Gay' changed the world for ever, and the war was over.

For me, it had been a year of waiting: waiting to enlist, waiting to get into uniform, waiting to go overseas. Now came the hardest part: waiting two years to get back to Civvy Street and an unknown future. I had no chance of becoming a professional musician, for I had no money to pay for the training, but when I heard that there was to be an afternoon concert by a new orchestra at the Davis Theatre, I caught the tram to where Mum and I had spent so much time together.

At 2.30pm on Sunday 15th September, 1946, Sir Thomas Beecham lifted his baton to conduct the very first concert by the Royal Philharmonic Orchestra. The orchestra's first rehearsal had collapsed after 'Tommy' mounted the rostrum, said 'Good morning, gentlemen,' (no women in his band), stroked his beard and, with a twinkle in his eye, announced, 'We'll play the *Faust* first.' He raised his short sharp baton and, with his typical stabbing movement on the downbeat, thrust it deep into his hand. The first concert had been postponed until that afternoon at Croydon. He started with the *Faust* ballet music and, safely past the opening bars, his performance had all the panache and humour that a great conductor can bring to light music. He often used *Faust* as an encore – something he called 'a lollipop'. On the tram home, as when I was a child, the music stayed in my mind, and I dreamt my impossible dream of becoming a conductor.

Rodney Glenn, the chief clerk at Docwra's, where I had worked before joining the Royal Air Force, had become a great friend. He was a keen amateur pianist, and after our performance of Fauré's *Dolly Suite* for four hands on one piano, he persuaded me that accountancy and I were not made for each other and that perhaps I should 'try something in music or the theatre'. I joined the City Literary Institute in Drury Lane, a London County Council Evening Institute which specialised in teaching the arts to amateurs who would like to be professionals but could not afford full-time training. The description fitted me perfectly.

George Bernard Shaw wrote that whenever an Englishman opened his mouth, some other Englishman despised him. Still sounding 'Croynge' (as Tony Hancock described the mixture of Penge and Croydon), I joined the Speech and Drama Class of Vera Castell, who taught elocution at the Royal Academy of Dramatic Art.

After managing to say, 'He reads regularly in a government library, rich in Coptic manuscripts, excepting during the month of February', including every syllable (try it sometime), Vera cast me in the leading role of the composer Lewis in *The Constant Nymph*. Lewis had to play the piano in full view of the audience.

Unfortunately, my acting wasn't up to it. Vera took the part from me, and I was banished to the orchestra pit to play the piano while my replacement pretended to play it on stage. To soften the blow, Vera gave me the title of Production Music Director – a role I was to play many times in the future.

In the cast was a very pretty little number, a dark-haired member of the Women's Royal Naval Reserve. The Wrens were all volunteers and were permitted to wear black silk stockings, whilst the Women's Army Corps and RAF girls – the WAAFs – wore grey lisle. The joke of young servicemen – 'Up with the lark and to bed with a Wren' – was mere wishful thinking, for Wrens were 'nice girls' who could resign if they didn't like service life, which was not an option for the other women's services. Our Wren, Patricia Keysell, was a nice girl who had a naval boyfriend, Kenneth Linden-Travers. His sister appeared nightly on the West

End stage as the star of the spicy hit *No Orchids for Miss Blandish*. However, Ken was somewhere east of Singapore, and Pat and I became good friends.

I finally got my chance to act when I played Shakespeare in Bernard Shaw's *Dark Lady of the Sonnets*. Queen Elizabeth was played by a large lady, a sort of Elizabethan Lady Bracknell in a beautiful jewelled gown. I, somewhat smaller, had a black cloak and a feather in my velvet cap. I thought I looked pretty cool. But I received a couple of acting lessons.

Firstly, that no matter how well you perform, if your tights don't fit and your crutch is somewhere around your knees, you may as well save your breath to cool your porridge.

Secondly, do not kiss tall ladies with a large bosom whilst wearing a false moustache. On my closing line, 'Good-night, Madame,' I leant forward on tiptoe, my tights in close pursuit, and deposited a kiss (and my moustache) on her hapless Majesty. We didn't win, but we got the best laughs.

At the City Lit, I met Clément Picciotto and Lord Swaythling, two amateur producers who had formed an entertainment organisation called the 'Cabin Club'. It was run by its members, all keen to sell themselves to theatrical agents, but unable to get any kind of 'shop window'. The only answer was to hire a theatre and invite the agents, the BBC and the public to take a look. Clem appointed me (unpaid) Musical Director and we set to work to put a show together.

I was now seeing a lot of Pat, who lived in Petts Wood, and one night we visited a Conservative dance at the Daylight Inn. The cabaret was a young RAF aircraftman presenting a solo stand-up comic routine. He was very funny and, unlike most wartime comics – witty. I introduced myself, told him about the aims of the cabaret club and asked him if he was hoping to be a professional entertainer and if he would like to join us. 'Yes, Sir!' he replied, and so Bob Monkhouse became our first resident comedian.

The London scene was coming to life again very rapidly, and it was an exciting time to be young. The West End theatres gave members of the Armed Forces free tickets, and every night Pat and I were either at a play or at the Royal Albert Hall, where, on a typical evening, like that of Monday 3rd February, 1947, the programme included the RAF Squadronaires, Felix Mendelssohn and his Hawaiian Serenaders, the International Ballet and the Bertram Mills Circus – all in the same concert.

AMMRU was expanding and as I knew quite a bit about the new system (even contributing something to the script for the training film), my boss suggested that I make the RAF my career, and he recommended me for the much sought-after peacetime permanent Commission. One of my duties was to take AMMRU schedules and plans for copying to the only place in London permitted to handle top-secret material, the Prime Minister's Map Room in the basement of a heavily-guarded building in Whitehall. One day, in the small lift ready to descend, I unexpectedly had to shuffle to the back to make room for Admiral Lord Cunningham, Field Marshal Alexander, Air Chief Marshall Tedder and lastly… Winston Churchill.

As Churchill made to enter, the liftman said nervously, 'Very sorry, Prime Minister, but the lift only takes five.' There was a hesitation as all eyes turned to me, a lowly aircraftman, jammed against the back wall and unable to move. Then, in that unmistakable voice, and with a smile, Churchill spoke to me. 'All right, lad. I'll walk down.'

I must be one of the very few people who ever made Churchill change his mind.

I duly attended the Officer Selection Board, and because I had flown solo, had broken my finger playing rugby (they liked that), had made a record of the piano music of Debussy and (thanks to Vera Castell) could string my words together in BBC English, I passed.

I was to remain in the same Air Ministry department, but as a Pilot Officer. I now had an assured future, but I began to have my doubts about being a 'wingless wonder'. To be in the RAF and not fly. Would it work for me? Then, my impossible dream became a possibility when someone told me of the government's Further Education and Training Scheme for teachers, a fast-track, three-year training course for ex-service personnel, with all fees paid and a maintenance grant that would qualify me as a full-time teacher of music.

I applied to the Royal Academy of Music, and in a very short time I auditioned for Sir Stanley Marchant. I'd not played the organ for months and there were many wrong notes, but I was in uniform, and I felt that Sir Stanley, being an ex-soldier himself, was going to give me a chance unless I was quite hopeless. He'd been the organist at St Paul's Cathedral until he developed arthritis, and he quickly spotted my broken left hand. When I told him I wanted to be a cathedral organist, he told me there and then that I could start in September.

I left the RAM in a daze. For my generation, money was the golden key which opened the door to any professional future, and those twenty minutes with Sir Stanley changed my life.

Pat and I celebrated by seeing the newest show in town, *Oklahoma!* and, now with rosy prospects and on a high, I asked her to marry me.

My diary reads: 'She refused, of course.'

Pat told me that she had to wait for Able-Seaman Linden Travers to return from the Far East. She was a nice girl who wasn't going to be unfaithful to a man serving his country.

We spent the day in Stratford-upon-Avon and saw that famous Peter Brook production of *Romeo and Juliet*, a dramatic way to end our seemingly 'star-crossed' relationship.

With Pat Keysell

At my suggestion, Pat applied for a teacher training grant and went on to study at the Royal Academy of Dramatic Art.

As well as acting professionally, Pat became brilliant at signing and presented 'Vision On' for BBC TV. Her great achievement was to found The British Theatre for the Deaf.

I don't think she married Kenneth Linden Travers.

I was now due to begin my new career as a peace-time Officer. In a difficult interview with S/L McKelvey, I told him that I had changed my mind and that I was now to become a professional musician. He took it well.

Twenty years later, as Air Commodore running the Royal Air Force Benevolent Fund, and not knowing that I'd been on his staff, he invited me to conduct the London Symphony Orchestra in the Fund's Annual Concert at the Royal Festival Hall. I was the first former member of the RAF to do so.

Finally, after five years in blue, I was demobilised. It's an odd experience to enter one end of a Nissen hut in RAF uniform and to exit at the other in a blue-striped, double breasted suit, white shirt, maroon tie, brown suede shoes and a canary-yellow pullover (all the rage in 1947), and, together with a couple of hundred men all dressed in a blue-striped, double-breasted suit etc., to launch oneself into a world where most of the jobs had already been taken by men in blue-striped, double-breasted suits etc. But I didn't need a job. I was to receive £230 a year for the next three years whilst studying to become a Graduate of the Royal Schools of Music, London – the equivalent of a degree from King's College, London University. Me!

With only my RAF gratuity of £30 and a few weeks to go before starting at the RAM, I needed money, so I joined the Film Artists Union and did a spell as an extra at J. Arthur Rank's Gate Studios, Elstree. Rank, who had made his fortune selling flour, was a committed Christian and used a large part of it to fund religious stories, distributed free throughout the world. I appeared variously as a Jew, a Muslim, an early American pioneer and, occasionally, a Christian. Not exactly great parts, but £3 a day was not bad money, and in July, for reasons which had a lot to do with being near Pat, I left kind Aunt Bess again and took a bedroom in Petts Wood as the only paying guest of a local family. The husband was a plumber, who hardly ever spoke, but his teenage son occasionally grunted. We were all under the thumb of the excessively house-proud mother, who preferred us to wash and shave daily in the kitchen sink, but allowed one visit to the upstairs bathroom each week – an immaculate showpiece, where virgin tablets of Cuticura and Wright's Coal-Tar soap nestled in ceramic dishes, equipped with matching fluffy towels and face-cloths, and a loofah that had never taken a soapy voyage around anyone. The tooth glasses were of crystal and the brushes of pure white bristle. I was happier at the sink.

One morning, my puzzled landlady asked me what professional musicians did during the day. A good question, which I was about to find out for myself when, a few days later, I walked up the steps of the Royal Academy of Music and into my future.

CHAPTER 14

THE ROYAL ACADEMY OF MUSIC

Sir Henry Wood, Bob Monkhouse and Benny Hill

Sir Henry Wood

The Academy was founded in 1822 and was London's first school for professional musicians. In those days, the premises were in Hanover Square, and the students of both sexes lived under the moral supervision of a clergyman and the musical guidance of a former infant prodigy, Dr William Crotch. Accommodation then was so limited that students were forced to practise their various instruments (and even take their lessons) together in one large room, where a contemporary observed, 'The din was such that it could not be described as music.'

They battled on for nearly a hundred years until they moved to the present magnificent building where, on three floors, the students and their professors have glass-panelled soundproof studios to themselves. It is reputed that the glass panels were so that the Lady Almoner in charge of morals could keep her eagle eye on what was going on.

On my first morning, I was given a cheque for £230 and the news that my professor was to be C. H. Trevor, organist of Lincoln's Inn. With money in my pocket, and the knowledge that I was to study with a teacher who was arguably the finest at the Academy, I set about finding my way around my new home with its theatre, concert hall and student dining room.

It was a wonderful experience, but my first day ended with an anti-climax when, not having the slightest idea of the difference between the harmonic and melodic minor scales, I failed an elementary test in theory and was relegated to a musical kindergarten with my fellow musical illiterates – mostly singers, unkindly described as having resonance where their brains ought to be.

The next day I met C. H. Trevor in the Duke's Hall. He was a gentle, balding man in a quiet check suit, a white shirt with a blue spotted bow-tie and shiny slim fitting brown shoes. The shoes were highly visible from his habit of wearing his trousers two inches above the ankle – presumably to let his students get a good look at what he was doing with his nimble feet. In my years at the Academy, I never saw him dressed any other way.

I played to him rather badly, but he smiled and said, 'Kenneth, there are only three things you have to do. Play the right notes in the right order at the right speed. You can always do one and two straight off; all you have to do is to play at the right speed.'

It was a simple way of telling me not to rush my fences – understandable when we ex-servicemen were already five years behind the teenage RAM students who had been too young for the war.

The Duke's Hall organ was only available occasionally, and although there were two studios at the RAM with small practice organs, they were always very busy. However, some help was at hand when I entered an amateur talent contest at the

Commodore Cinema, Orpington with a performance of a popular Samba 'Tico-Tico' on the little two-manual Compton.

My competitors included a comedian who – unlike Frankie Howerd – raised not a titter, a magician whose tricks went disastrously astray and a soprano who teetered her way through Ivor Novello's 'Waltz of my Heart', more hauntingly than gaily.

One of the disadvantages for the cinema organist is having to perform with one's back to an audience, which then feels free to talk. As I was deftly tripping through the pedal part of 'Tico-Tico' (the organ and I bathed in blush pink), I heard a voice from the front row of the stalls, 'Cor, look at 'is socks! They've got big 'oles in 'em!'

'Tico-Tico' wobbled a bit, but perhaps the holes in my socks won me the audience's sympathy and their vote, for I came first.

More importantly, I met the regular organist of the Commodore who, when she heard of my problem, arranged for me to use the Compton each morning, where I would practise to the accompaniment of vacuum cleaners.

The social centre of Petts Wood was the Daylight Inn, a good pub with its own little theatre, which was the home of an amateur drama company, 'The Proscenium Players'. Their producer was my girlfriend Pat's dad, Peter Keysell.

Bob Monkhouse and I were persuaded to join them for their next production, *The Day is Gone*, a recent West End success by Warren Chetham-Strode.

In late October the curtain rose, and Bob revealed yet another of his many talents in a performance as a middle-aged army major with a posh voice. I played a detective in a grubby raincoat with an 'off' voice and the *Kentish Times* gave a special word for Mr Robert Monkhouse and Mr Kenneth Alwyn 'who gave two of the most convincing performances ever seen by amateurs' (sic)!

Bob's family business was Monk and Glass – famous makers of custard powder – and they had a very nice house in Beckenham where I sometimes stayed overnight. Mrs Monkhouse, although polite to me, seemed to be very cold towards Bob.

I was not experienced in the ways of mothers and sons, but something seemed very wrong. Perhaps, being a serious artist herself, she disapproved of his illustrations of nubile young ladies in panties and bras for the saucy magazine *Razzle*.

When he married Elizabeth, a young WAAF from Northern Ireland, her family came all the way from Belfast. But there was only one member of his: his mother, who, disapproving of the marriage, dressed entirely in black.

I was now living a double life: as an organ student destined for the cathedral close, and as the scriptwriter, pianist and composer of the Cabin Club's show, 'Spotlight'. Bob and I got together a cast of twenty-five performers, including some glamorous girl dancers, an unknown comedian called Benny Hill, a mime artist called Phil Burn, and a good-looking young singer, Garry Miller. We lured agents and the BBC TV director, Michael Mills, to the 20th Century Theatre, Westbourne Grove for our 'West End season' of two nights.

The show went well. Bob got a TV contract, Benny a series of BBC and theatre engagements and Phil Burn a seaside summer show. Two of my six songs (orchestrated by Stanford Robinson and conducted by his brother, Eric) were sung by Gary on the BBC TV programme *New to You* – much to the surprise of my landlady.

Bob Monkhouse (centre) in 'Cabin Club'

We all decided that the Cabin Club should be kept going and were given a room upstairs in the Hermitage Restaurant, Dover Street, which quickly became the Mecca for a lot of new talent.

One night, when the rest of his family was out, Bob invited Peter Sellers (in a flying jacket), Benny Hill and me to his home. A crate of beer set the ball and the stories rolling.

I soon realised that I was the only one laughing.

Bob explained that all comedy was based on three basic styles, and that they were comparing their completely different ways of putting them across: Benny was the naughty simpleton, Bob the slick American and Peter the mimic.

The cast of 'Cabin Club' at the 20th Century Theatre, London, 1947
(Bob Monkhouse: front row, third from left; Benny Hill: front row,
second from right; I am in the back row, fourth from left)

Fascinating though all of this was, I was still practising for six hours a day. My piano professor devised an alternative fingering for my left hand which meant not using my little finger at all. Her special attention included invitations to tea and cucumber sandwiches at the small bungalow in Denham where she lived with her cat.

Life at my digs without a piano was proving impractical, and I was getting tired of washing in the kitchen sink, so I went to see the ever-loving Aunt Bess and asked to come home again. She turned her best room downstairs into a bedsit, and I bought a semi-grand Broadwood piano for thirty pounds, under which I slept. I often knocked my head getting up in the mornings, but at least I hadn't far to go to practise.

In the last week of term, after examinations were over, distinguished lecturers and performers were invited to show us what life was like in the world outside the RAM. The Hungarian composer and pianist Ernst von Dohnányi, wearing a black cloak with a red silk lining, swept on to the stage, draped himself over the magnificent Steinway Grand and launched into Beethoven's *Waldstein Sonata*. His electrifying performance had its fair share of wrong notes, but was vastly preferable to our note-perfect but pallid student performances.

We students were not neglected spiritually. Dean Inge of Westminster Abbey talked to us about 'Imagination and God' and an Irish lady, Edris Stannus, otherwise known as Ninette de Valois, spoke of her days with Diaghilev and Stravinsky. I had no idea as I listened to this fascinating woman with the French name and the Irish accent that I was to spend seven years with her Company as conductor.

Bob had now joined Pat Keysell and me at the City Literary Institute, where our drama class included a young RAF pilot officer, Leonard, who was preparing to audition for the Royal Academy of Dramatic Art. He'd heard on the grapevine that the Embassy Theatre Company was casting a play which owed a great deal to Graham Green's *Brighton Rock*, but included music. Its title was *Symphony in Violence*. The director, Marjorie Hawtrey, was looking for an actor to play Louis, a sinister bodyguard to the villainous 'Big Jim.' That would have been relatively easy casting, but Louis had to be able to play Liszt's *Liebestraum* ('Dream of Love').

Once again, the theatre called and I auditioned. From the darkness of the stalls of the Embassy Theatre, Swiss Cottage a voice enquired what I had been doing lately. Flying with the RAF didn't seem to be the right answer, so I said I'd played the lead in J. B. Priestley's *They Came to a City*. At one point in the play, Priestley gives my character Jo a very long socialist speech, which I'd had a hell of a job remembering, so I thought this should cover it. It seemed to be enough, for from the auditorium, a voice enquired, 'Can you play *Liebestraum*?' I made my way to the out-of-tune mini-piano and began Liszt's dreamy prelude.

'That's fine,' said the voice. 'Any questions?'

'What about the acting?' I enquired. There was a good deal of muttering, followed by, 'Will you walk across to stage right, look over your left shoulder and say "Yes, Jim"?' Clearly this was not going to be a big part, but I accepted their offer of fifteen pounds a week on tour and ten in London. Suddenly I was a rich, professional actor. However, there was an Academy rule prohibiting students from working professionally, and to have my name on bills outside the Embassy Theatre, Swiss Cottage, which was just a stone's throw from the Royal Academy, could be courting disaster. So, in the manner of Oscar Wilde's Ernest, I was Wetherell at Marylebone and Alwyn at Swiss Cottage and for the rest of my professional life.

Big Jim was Eric Pohlmann, the star of many British films; the young murderer was played by Peter Murray, later a Radio 2 disc jockey; the policeman was Richard Pearson, a fine period actor; and a well-known character actor, James Page, played the respectable crook who found young criminals too violent. The scene of the crime – a flower shop – was run by Joan Matheson from the BBC Drama Rep.

I was in a very strong company, but I only had three lines: 'Yes, Jim', 'No, Jim,' and 'It's Cook!' However, I was on stage for most of the play doing nothing but listening - a true test of an actor. My big moment came in the last act when Big Jim – just about to beat the hell out of his moll – is brought up short by my performance of 'Dream of Love'. Music hath charms, even when played in the wrong key on an out-of-tune piano.

We opened in Eastbourne, where Richard and I were in theatrical digs run by a dear old soul who liked to go to bed early, leaving a cold meal for us after the show. On Friday when 'the ghost walked' (actor-speak for being paid), Richard and I decided that we couldn't face another cold meal and bought fish and chips. That night the old dear had left us a couple of cold soused herrings and, not wanting to hurt her feelings, we tiptoed upstairs out into the street and sought the nearest drain. As I was stuffing a cold fish down the grill, shiny black boots came into view, and I heard the voice of an Eastbourne policeman.

'Good evening, sir. May I hask what you are a-doin' of?' (They talked like Agatha Christie policemen back then).

I replied, 'Er, I'm just putting these herrings down the drain, Officer.'

He smiled. 'Sending 'em back to the sea, are we then, sir?', and with a relaxed salute, he continued on his beat.

At our next stop, Bournemouth, the weather was very hot and we played the matinée to just two people – an elderly man (who kept his cap on) and his wife. He was deaf and had trouble hearing what Pete Murray was saying, and he asked his wife 'What did he say?' so many times that Pete took to delivering his lines straight at him. The rest of the cast followed, and a good time was had by all. The tour went reasonably well until our first night at the Embassy, Swiss Cottage. The provincial audiences had tolerated the melodrama, but the sophisticated Londoners were not so easily pleased.

The rot began with Jimmy Page. He had a speech in which he condemned the two young criminals as 'products of the five-thousand-pound bomb factory'. With the careful enunciation of someone who had taken a little extra Scotch to steady his nerves, he announced that they were 'products of the five-thousand-pound *bun* factory'. The audience stirred a little, but the effect on the cast as we thought of a bun weighing five thousand pounds was to produce that irresistible need to laugh (known to all actors as 'corpsing').

The play limped on but, in the last act, having saved Mary Mackenzie from being beaten to death by my tinny performance of *Liebestraum*, the dramatic pause that followed was shattered by the telephone (a call from Jim's arch enemy, Detective Inspector Cook). I rose from the piano, slowly crossed the room (this was my big moment, for I had control of centre stage), picked up the receiver, listened carefully and, holding my hand over the mouthpiece, turned to Jim.

After another long and significant pause, I spoke my final line: 'It's Cook.'

To my total astonishment, the audience howled with laughter. I looked down to see if my flies were undone. I might have got away with 'Detective Inspector Cook', but 'cook' with a small 'c' raised the image of the kitchen, and turned what should have been high drama into farce. It was too much for this hitherto patient London audience.

The next day I got a rocket from the director Marjorie Hawtrey for not playing my two words seriously enough.

The drama critic of the *Evening Standard*, Beverly Baxter (whose post-war play whitewashing poor, young, misled Nazis had been booed off) gave us a terrible notice. I got a special mention as a 'piano playing oaf', and he awarded the play the

As Louis (far left) in 'Symphony in Violence', 1948

headline: '*Symphony in Violence* is even worse than my play.'

We carried on for a week, now playing to full houses and getting laughs never intended by the author. As so often happened in London in 1948, there were power cuts when the stage was suddenly plunged into darkness. When this happened, Liberace-like, my piano illuminated by candles, I led the audience in the sort of 'sing-along' that had been heard in the air-raid shelters during the Blitz. The audience loved it, and when the lights came back and we picked up the play from exactly where we had left it, we got our best applause of the evening. I loved working in the theatre, even if it was the worst play in the West End.

Back at the RAM after my short life as a professional actor, I was too busy again with music for much social life, but if a piano student, Arthur (who had captained a Liberator of Coastal Command and had a DFC to show for it) and I had three shillings to spare, we'd have a meal together at the popular Lyons Corner House near Piccadilly Circus.

Meat was still rationed but, apart from the fishy taste of the first mouthful, whale goulash was plentiful and nourishing. Alternatively, 'Chung King Special', a combination of chicken livers, scrambled eggs and noodles, was delicious; washed down by a draught lager, and followed by 'Wonder Ice-Cake' and coffee, it was excellent value for money

Arthur became a close friend, but it seemed we were the subjects of gossip among the female music students – a homely lot, except the blonde and petite singer, Elizabeth. It was she who later told me that the girls had Arthur and me down as 'queers'. I was twenty-three but had never to my knowledge met one, which was understandable because homosexuality was then a criminal offence and was kept under wraps. It was a complete shock to learn that a decorated pilot (with whom I had shared a bedroom on a holiday in Harlech) was gay.

When he told me that another of my RAF friends, Len, was also gay, I was amazed, (although perhaps I should have suspected something when Len knitted me a pullover). But my education was finally complete when Elizabeth told me that a beautiful blonde drama student I fancied was a lesbian.

I was working hard at the Academy and began teaching privately in the evenings, and so I was able to buy an Ariel 350cc 'Red Hunter' motorbike on hire purchase and to afford Chinese food, whale goulash and gypsy music – no longer with Arthur, who remained a friend for many years, but with Elizabeth, who also enjoyed a Chung King Special.

Elizabeth on my motorbike

Elizabeth decided that I should do something about my voice, which had reached the peak of treble perfection in the Boy Scouts and fifteen years later could imitate a sweet melodious tenor and a rich, resounding baritone, but which had neither the high notes of the one nor the low notes of the other. So for four pounds a term, I became the student of Professor Robert Alva – vocal coach to the Royal Opera at Covent Garden. He decided that I was a light baritone, but, to add the bright top notes of a tenor, we experimented with Mr White's method of 'Sinus Tone Production' – mooing like a cow and bleating like a sheep. I found I could bleat better than I could moo, and gradually I began to sound a bit more like a tenor, but not enough. At the end of one frustrating lesson, Alva told me of an operation that might give me something more up top.

'But at what cost?' I thought, for I was familiar with how, as late as the 19th century, a choirboy might keep his unbroken voice by losing his wedding tackle. However, having been assured that the surgery would have no effect on my sex life, I presented myself one morning to the Royal Academy's throat specialist at a clinic in Harley Street. There in a long room were six black leather barbers' chairs, each one occupied by a fellow patient, with only their open mouths and staring eyes visible above white smocks. Each was attended by a white-gowned, masked surgeon wearing rubber gloves and a headband bearing a shiny reflecting disc.

The surgeon's muffled voice came through his mask.

'Having trouble with your high notes, eh? Let's see if this will help. Relax and keep very still.' He then approached me with a soldering iron and there followed a smell of burning. The operation improved my high notes for a while, but sadly I was soon back to my boringly elocutive and entirely uninteresting baritone. Although I was awarded a silver medal, clearly my voice was never going to thrill, and for what other reason would one want to be a professional singer?

Professor Alva was a great technician, and I learnt the mysteries of the Ventricles of Morgani and function of the Intercostal Muscles, so when a singer declared at rehearsal that they were saving their voice, I could, with confidence, ask: 'What for?'

Although I was training to be a teacher I still had my conducting dream and, never having even picked up a stringed instrument, the Academy lent me a viola. My next four pounds were spent on lessons with the principal viola of the London Symphony Orchestra, James Lockyer. Jimmy knew that I was not going to be a professional violist (my little finger again), but his experience of what an orchestra looked for in a conductor was to prove invaluable.

Final Exams were now only a year away and I decided to work through the summer holidays at a summer school course at Queenswood, run by the RAM's Professor of Conducting and Henry Wood's successor: Ernest Read. There, I hoped to get a crack at one of the student orchestras. Although the food was good and the accommodation very sociable, the instrumental coaching was of the finest. Dennis Brain looked after the horns, his brothers Leonard and Aubrey the oboes and cor anglais, Jack Brymer the clarinets and Gareth Morris the flutes. The players got a very good deal, but the conducting class was over-subscribed, and it became obvious that very few of us would get the chance to get in front of the orchestra. Then a professional violinist from the Yorkshire Symphony Orchestra with conducting ambitions took it upon himself to get together a number of musicians to come and play for us on their one day off – Sunday.

After the morning service, this kindly volunteer orchestra duly assembled, and the Yorkshire violinist organised matters. All the orchestral music was with Ernie Read, and this brave fellow sent off a minion to collect it. Then he did a very strange thing! To keep the orchestra occupied whilst waiting, he conducted them in scales – a truly macabre sound. Suddenly the door flew open and Ernie – who had not known of this rehearsal – exploded onto the scene. The scales faded away, he ordered the chap off the rostrum and distributed the music to the now-reassured orchestra. Then with a snarled 'Not you!' to our poor violinist friend, pointed at us conductors and said, '*Jupiter Symphony*. Anyone know it?'

It was a moment that was to change my life, for I had been studying that very symphony for my graduation. I caught his eye, and very shortly I was enjoying conducting an orchestra in what some call Mozart's finest symphony. Never having conducted anything other than a small church choir before, the experience was indescribable. After the last chord I heard the shuffling of feet, which I was later to learn could mean failure, but with it was sound of the string players tapping their stands.

They approved of me.

'Why aren't you in my conducting class?' demanded Ernie, and within a few weeks he had arranged a year's extension of my grant. From then on, I allowed myself my impossible dream.

We are all subject to 'pot-luck'. We may be nearly killed by a pigeon which had suffered a heart attack a hundred feet above Oxford Street, or pinned through the shoe by a screwdriver dropped by a careless stagehand from the flies of the Royal Theatre, Manila (both were totally unexpected near-death personal experiences), but my luck that afternoon was being in the right place at the right time.

From my new status as a conducting student, I was appointed coach to the opera class, where I prepared Bizet's *Carmen* and Benjamin Britten's *Albert Herring*. It was a great experience to work on Ben's music for *Herring* and, feeling proud of my singers, during the comfort break at the public performance, I said to the chap in the next urinal:

'Well, what do you think of this modern stuff then?'

'I rather like it really,' he said as he did up his flies.

'But then, I suppose I'm biased,' replied the man who'd written the libretto: Eric Crozier.

As a student conductor at the Royal Academy of Music, 1951

Still studying voice myself, it was useful to play for lessons given by the contralto, Astra Desmond – to whom Vaughan Williams had dedicated his *Magnificat*. Astra was a very imposing lady, who, in her wonderfully fruity voice, once asked a timid young student contralto what kind of music the girl wished to make her career. Was it to be in opera, lieder recitals or oratorio?

The poor girl had no answer, but Astra had. 'Lift your skirt above your knees, dear!' she demanded. Examining the girl's sturdy legs and child-bearing hips, she delivered judgment. 'Oratorio, I think.' The girl went on to become one of our leading oratorio singers who, for the sake of kindness, I will not name!

At the end of term, I was required to play before the leading Professor of Piano, Harold Craxton. He approved of what he heard (I heard him say, 'I liked that'), and I became a Graduate of the Royal Schools of Music and could be let loose to teach music full-time. I had fulfilled my original commitment, but now the fun started as a member of Ernest Read's conducting course.

CHAPTER 15

RAM: THE FINAL YEAR

I beat Brahms at the Royal Festival Hall

Now I had a year to explore the world of the conductor, and, as I needed to be nearer the centre of London's musical life, I went looking for somewhere to live near the Albert Hall. Fortune continued to smile when my composer friend, Roger North, told me that the flat below him at 53 Caithness Road, Brook Green – a mere two miles away from the Hall – was let to a stage manager working in rep at the Clacton Repertory theatre, who had fallen so far behind with his rent that his landlord was about to chuck him out. The stage manager was sharing with the man who, according to critic Kenneth Tynan, 'changed the course of British theatre' with his play *Look Back in Anger* – John Osborne.

At the end of 1950, Elizabeth and I had cat-sat for the horn-player Dennis Brain whilst he was on a tour of the US with Sir Thomas Beecham. Playing house had been great, and when I suggested we might share Osborne's flat, Liz moved in with me. But, for the sake of propriety, she slept on a put-u-up in the sitting room and I took the bedroom, where the decor was gaudy if not outright vulgar. One wall was dominated by a badly-painted portrait of a nude young man sitting on a crescent moon. He didn't do a lot for either of us. Not surprising really, for it was the man who shared the flat with Osborne.

 Osborne wrote years later that he was only thirty percent homosexual. Nevertheless, with the remaining seventy percent, Osborne married five times.

Late one Saturday night, Liz and I were disturbed by a knock at our flat door. I opened it a couple of inches.

'Is there any chance of me kipping down on the floor?' said the voice. 'It's my flat, and I've nowhere else to go.'

I replied, like Alice's Mad Hatter, 'No room, no room!' and sent John Osborne into the wilds of Hammersmith Broadway.

In Osborne's flat, I experienced for the first time the delight of living with a young pretty woman. In the evenings we cooked together, listened to BBC concerts and, when night fell, played recordings of great music. Frederick Delius was a particular favourite, and I recommend listening in the dark to his opera *A Village Romeo and Juliet* with someone you love. Upstairs, Roger would play his clarinet (he gets a mention in *Look Back in Anger*) and compose until at around 3.30pm, when he'd put down his pen, don a long white coat and earn a little extra money supervising the school crossing at St Paul's School for Girls – the very crossing that the School's Music Directors, Gustav Holst and Ralph Vaughan Williams had used.

A letter to the *London Times* bewailing the dearth of young English composers asked: 'Where are they today?' It was answered by Roger's father, Admiral Sir Dudley North: 'I can tell you where one young and brilliant composer is,' he wrote. 'He's escorting schoolgirls across the road in Hammersmith!'

I was still with Professor Trevor, and one day, after a successful lesson, he asked me if I'd like an organ job at a London church. Without asking him what he had in mind, I told him I had a job already.

However, the organ job I'd taken on was not at any London church but was as Louis Mordish's deputy at the Gaumont Cinema in the King's Road, Chelsea. Each Saturday morning I became 'Uncle Ken' to hundreds of excited children, who, at 9am, screaming their heads off, exploded into the Gaumont. I pressed the 'up' button and ascended from the safety of the pit into the wild atmosphere of totally unsupervised children, and played jolly tunes until 9.25am, when the theatre manager came on stage with the lights still up and greeted this mob with: 'Good morning, boys and girls!'

The answering shout was 'Good morning, Uncle Jack!', and a great cheer went up, for they knew that there was only one hurdle to leap before the lights went down and the film show began. That hurdle was the 'Gaumont British Song'.

'Now,' said Uncle Jack, 'Uncle Ken is going to play our song, so stand up.'

After my spirited introduction, under his eagle eye they sang:

We come along on Saturday morning,
Greeting everybody with a smile.
We come along on Saturday morning,
Making our lives worthwhile.
As members of the GB Club, we all intend to be
Good citizens when we grow up,
And champions of the free!

The last hurdle crossed, Uncle Jack lowered the lights, and I pushed the 'down' button and descended back into the pit. That routine that worked quite well, but one morning Uncle Jack cowered in the wings and made signs suggesting that he'd lost his voice. I was left to bring order out of chaos, so I flooded my instrument in my gaudiest lights and ascended into the lion's arena playing 'Land of Hope and Glory' on the full organ. Swinging one leg over the stool, I half-turned towards the kids and shouted, 'Uncle Jack is not here this morning. Now we're going to sing the Gaumont Song, so stand up.'

I'd got as far as 'greeting everybody with a smile' when a shower of popcorn, thrown by my invisible enemies behind, descended and jammed between the keys. I knew I was beaten and, to the victorious cheers of the vandals, I descended again. Uncle Jack hurriedly lowered the lights, the curtains parted, and the cheerful music of Woody Woodpecker brought comparative peace to the morning.

I had kept rather quiet about my role as Uncle Ken, so I was a little apprehensive when, in my final year, I was called into Principal Sir Reginald Thatcher's office. However, all was well, and he appointed me the RAM's only student professor of organ. I was to receive £9 a term for each of my ten students – very useful money.

Then came the call which was life-changing.

'Kenneth,' said Sir Reginald, 'as a former master of music at Charterhouse, I have been approached by them to suggest students to interview for the post of Junior Music Master. You would play for chapel, take the choir and teach music. Would you like me to recommend you? I think you'd have a good chance.'

To teach music at one of England's leading public schools was something most would give their eye teeth for, but something troubled me, and I asked for time to think about it. Suddenly, here I was at another crossroads. Charterhouse could be my whole career, but I'd become used to an exciting life – acting in a West End play with ladies who went bare-bosomed on Eastbourne beach; being 'Uncle Ken' at the Gaumont; directing Comedy Carnivals with Bob Monkhouse, Michael Bentine and Benny Hill; writing music for BBC Television; and each Christmas playing in Norman Nankervis's Orchestra at the Hotel Bristol in Newquay.

Was I the sort of man who might, after a long academic career, become the 'Mr Chips' of Charterhouse? True, I was playing the organ well enough to justify my professorship, but was I really like my fellow student, Lionel Dakers? Lionel went straight from the Academy to become the Assistant Organist of the Chapels Royal, Windsor, hobnobbing with the Royal Princesses, and then moving on to Exeter Cathedral and becoming Head of the Royal Schools of Church Music. I realised that I was something of a gypsy, and I turned down Sir Reginald.

In the conducting class I continued, under Ernest Read's instruction, to shout at the student orchestra, but thankfully I had my RAM Madrigal group and the opera class, where I was coaching *Carmen*. I was able to do things my way in Croydon, with the choir from the Parish Church Youth Club and an orchestra of thirty hand-picked RAM students, led by Arthur Davison. I called it the 'Croindene Music Society' – the name from the early Saxon settlement. The choir were a lovely, lively bunch, all of whom could read music. Our staple fare was the madrigals, ballets and motets of Byrd, Wilbye and Gibbons, which they sang from memory. Under the auspices of the Parish Church, we gave a concert at the Croydon Civic Hall. The soloist was Norman Tattersall, later a professor at the Academy. C. H. Trevor came down from London, and it all went very well and pleased everyone, except the Bishop of Croydon. He summoned me to tell me that, as we were singing mostly secular music, the church hall would no longer be available for Croindene rehearsals. Furthermore, in his opinion, I was leading these young communicants away from the Church.

The Bishop had not reckoned with how much the choir enjoyed the 'buzz' they got from the audience (the local critic called us 'a choir to be reckoned with'!), and so, without exception, we all moved from the church hall to the upstairs room of the Sandrock Pub in Addington. Was that really what the Bishop wanted?

Now as Sub-Professor of Organ, opera coach and conductor of the Madrigal Group, I had my own niche at the Academy, to which was added Chairman of the Students' Social Committee. One of my tasks was to organise the Christmas Social held in the Duke's Hall. Formal dress was *de rigueur* and the dance music was provided by a professional band, but the cabaret was up to the Committee, which fortunately included Gordon Langford. As music was the only thing we were any good at, we put our heads together and decided to get a few laughs by poking fun at the gypsy band which accompanied our whale goulash and Chung King Special in the Brasserie of Lyons Corner House, Coventry Street. Mostly middle-aged and overweight gentlemen, costumed in tight black trousers and white frilly shirts, their ample waists encompassed by red cummerbunds, they played very well, but they were a warning that, if we didn't work hard, their fate – competing with the clatter of knives and forks – might be ours.

On the night of the dance, there was an hour or so of quicksteps, foxtrots and waltzes. Then the band repaired to the Music Library under the stage for beer, and it was our turn. I opened the cabaret with a performance for full organ of 'Jingle Bells', flavoured with a touch of Bach, and then donned a beard (God knows why) and headed for the piano. Gordon assembled his trombone, the cellist played some out-of-tune notes and a clarinettist (who'd lost a leg at El Alamein) practised a little of the Mozart concerto until the leader of the ensemble, Arthur Davison, in a red cummerbund, led us all in an extravagant version of the tango 'Jealousy'. Being intentionally funny is very difficult, but Gordon had cleverly arranged all the wrong notes in the right order!

It was all rather undergraduate, but we'd been denied our teenage years and needed to laugh.

Fortunately, none of our gypsy orchestra chose a career in comedy. Arthur Davison became the leader of the London Philharmonic Orchestra and led for me on a couple of recording sessions. Denis Vigay joined Kenneth Sillito, William Bennett and George Malcolm in the Academy of St Martin-in-the-Fields Chamber Ensemble. Gordon Langford became one of our finest arrangers and his compositions are heard at the BBC Proms, even as I write in 2014.

If the Royal Academy of Music was the powerhouse of my activities, it was my time in the Royal Air Force that had given me the opportunity to follow my star, and I was to be forever grateful. My friend and fellow airman Bob Monkhouse and I decided to arrange a 'Comedy Carnival' in aid of the Royal Air Forces Association, which helped ex-members of the service and their families. The performers were ex-servicemen trying to get started in the world of entertainment. Benny Hill and Spike Milligan had been in the Army, but Peter Sellers, Michael Howard, Dennis Goodwin, Bob and I were formerly RAF, as was one of our number who had already got started and was heading the bill at the London Palladium: Michael Bentine. However, he agreed to help the cause and to play for one glorious night at the Drill Hall, Tooting. Bob suggested that, as well as being Musical Director, I should take the afternoon rehearsal of this mighty handful of talent. There was not much I could do, except warn them that there were to be no blue jokes and not to go on for more than five minutes.

My only creative idea was that, on the final notes of our two-piano overture, the curtain rose and Bob Monkhouse, in full flying gear, was discovered suspended in a parachute harness above the stage.

It got a round of applause from the full house, but unfortunately the volunteer stage management, having got him six feet above the stage, couldn't get him down. He looked at me helplessly, and from my seat at the piano, and with a bit of inside knowledge, I shouted 'Bang the quick release button!' He did, hit the stage and got the first laugh of the show.

By the third hour of comedy, the audience was beginning to wilt, and some to steal away. But then Michael Bentine, in full stage make-up, rode his motorbike at breakneck speed from the

Palladium to Tooting, burst through the door, climbed onto the stage by way of the tops of the pianos and revived the audience with a series of off-beat impressions that certainly must have impressed Peter Sellers and Spike Milligan, who'd stayed on to see him. When Michael sat on the sharp end of a shooting stick, it must have lit a small fire in them. This was 1950, and in 1951 Milligan, Bentine, Sellers and Harry Secombe made their first broadcasts as the 'Goons'.

'Comedy Carnival' poster

In my last year, we student conductors finally had the second orchestra all to ourselves for the end of term concert. I conducted *Russlan and Ludmilla* and accompanied a little blonde Icelandic prodigy, Thorunn Tryggvason, in Beethoven's *First Piano Concerto*. She was only ten, but she played brilliantly and was charmingly self-assured. She later married Vladimir Ashkenazy.

In 1951, to mark the centenary of Prince Albert's Great Exhibition, the country put on the great 'Festival of Britain'. London was *en fête* and there were over eight million visitors. The heart of the Festival was on the South Bank of the Thames with a 'Dome of Discovery'. On the river bank towered the 'Skylon', a three-hundred-foot high, needle-like (apparently unsupported) steel shaft – a wonderful example of British engineering. The new Royal Festival Hall was complete except for the acoustic tests, which required a choir, an orchestra and a man with a revolver.

The Royal Academy of Music provided the orchestra (in

which I played percussion) and a two-hundred-strong choir, all conducted by Clarence Raybould. The Hall was already packed, and the choir and the student orchestra came onto the platform in the confident way of hardened professionals. Personally, I was rather nervous, for I was to play the cymbals in the first item on the programme, Brahms's *Academic Festival Overture*.

Brahms's brilliantly-orchestrated collection of German student songs was an ideal choice for us. Hugh Maguire, who was later to lead the London Symphony Orchestra on my Decca recording of *1812*, took his place on the first desk of violins and Clarence Raybould climbed onto the rostrum.

With an encouraging wink, he began the steady, *sotto voce*, march-like introduction. Everything was in perfect accord. The bassoon was quietly jovial, the horns dignified, the lower strings rustling and marking the rhythm, the bass drum making a gentle 'boom' and my gleaming twenty-four-inch Turkish Zilgens providing the 'tish'.

Brahms builds the music wonderfully in anticipation of that final great tune, the 'Gaudeamus Igitur' ('Let Us Rejoice'). At last my great moment arrived, and accompanied by the full orchestra, I joined in the rejoicing: 'Crash, ta-ta, Crash ta-ta, Crash ta-ta, Crash, Crash, Crash.'

There are thirty-six *fortissimo* clashes in the finale, and thirty-five were perfect. For the thirty-sixth, in order to give it all I'd got, I bent at the waist and my right cymbal began its journey from near my ankle, the left one from high overhead. Precisely on bar thirty-six, they met. A magnificent moment – except that something was wrong.

My left arm felt strangely light, and I caught sight of Raybould gazing with horror above my head. I looked down, and from my left wrist there dangled the knotted leather thong which passes through the hole at the centre of the cymbal, securing it safely to the player. Only there was no longer a knot and, worse still, no cymbal.

Somewhere, high above me, was a rogue, spinning, circular saw which threatened all below. Time stood still as I imagined the newspaper headlines: 'Brahms Overture ends in tragedy. Conductor decapitated by cymbal. Percussion expert warns all cymbalists to check their knots.'

The split second ended as the great gleaming disc, still spinning, descended past the brass, the woodwind, the horns, and a horrified harp, finally coming to rest, in the manner of a Tom and Jerry cartoon, before the great God of the Baton. He smiled and mouthed, 'You bloody fool!'

There came a roar of laughter, followed by huge applause for the orchestra, and a special bow for me. Then the man with the revolver appeared to test the Hall's echo. At Raybould's prompting, he fired, not into the ceiling but at me. I collapsed, apparently mortally wounded.

Such was my trivial contribution to the first concert at the finest concert hall in London. I certainly got the first laugh.

CHAPTER 16

RAM: THE CODA

Farewell to all that!

One morning Sir Reginald called me into his office to ask if I'd be prepared to help Dr Thomas Wood, the President of the Royal Philharmonic Society, with his Festival of Britain commission, *The Rainbow*.

I knew of Dr Wood as the author of *Cobbers*, a chatty account of touring small Australian towns examining for the Royal Schools of Music and of how, on one trip, to the accompaniment of the clip-clop of the pony's hooves, the driver sang him a song called 'Waltzing Matilda'.

Wood realised how good it was and had it published. It's probably true that, without Wood, Australia would have been short of what has become known as its second national anthem. By now he was practically blind and could only write large notes on special paper. My help would be to transfer these to normal manuscript and liaise with the lyricist, Christopher Hassall (who was well-known for his musicals with Ivor Novello), with Frank Wright (who would arrange my transcription of Tommy's music for the six-hundred-strong male voice choir, six brass bands and two soloists) and with Sir Adrian Boult, who would conduct.

It was a team worth knowing.

The Rainbow was the real name and story of one of the little boats crewed by amateur sailors that had brought back thousands of Allied soldiers from Dunkirk in 1940. Tommy Wood was an ideal choice, for he'd spent much of his youth at sea with his father, a Master Mariner, before going on to Oxford.

There was much to do, and I spent weekends with him and his wife, St Osyth, at their Tudor house in Bures, Suffolk, where after-dinner conversation included his account of hosting a dinner where his only guests were Richard Strauss and Vaughan

Williams. But these two great composers exchanged not a word. Tommy had to keep the ball rolling until after coffee when, with a surreptitious glance at VW, Strauss leant close to Tommy and whispered, 'Who is this man? Is he a composer?'

Finally, everyone came together for rehearsal at the Royal Albert Hall. *The Rainbow* was divided into six 'watches', each with its own brass band and a hundred male voices (mostly Welsh) occupying its own part of the platform. Sir Adrian opened the complicated score, lifted his long baton and, with a flick of the wrist, he began.

Amateur musicians are not used to 'flick of the wrist' conductors, and to be truthful, this was not a work for Boult. Sir Malcolm Sargent's 'bandmaster' style would have been easier for everyone. Before very long, Sir Adrian appeared never quite to be sure where the next 'watch' was coming from. He soon abandoned the full score and reverted to the easier-to-read vocal score. Tommy had written me an organ part, but on my first entry (a pedal E flat), when I looked into the driving mirror (my only view of the conductor), I saw Sir Adrian in as much distress as that urbane gentleman ever showed. The great Albert Hall organ was at a slightly different pitch from the brass bands. I stopped playing when a nearby Welsh euphonium player advised me to 'Get that box of whistles tuned, boyo!' Quite impossible, and my part was cut. Eventually, it all came together, but Tommy was not there. Sadly, a few weeks before the performance, he suffered a fatal heart attack – something he had forecast as being likely for someone who could not exercise.

There was only one performance.

St Osyth asked me to complete his unfinished commissioned work for the 'Three Choirs Festival' on the subject of the painter John Crome. It was called *Norwich Fair*, with words by Christopher Hassall. Hassall agreed to work with me, but I found continuing Tommy's sketches in his style impossible, and so *Norwich Fair* remains uncompleted on my shelves.

But then came a performance with my Croindene Orchestra which was to have unforeseen results. As part of the Festival of Britain, I programmed a romp for two pianos and orchestra by Madeleine Dring, playfully called *Nights in the Gardens of Battersea*.

It was her contribution to the Festival, where the Battersea Gardens were the scene of great festivities. Madeleine only lived a twopenny tram ride from the Civic Hall and came to the concert. I obviously made a good impression, for she insisted that BBC TV engage me to conduct her dance drama, *The Fair Queen of Wu*. The Queen was played by the beautiful Japanese girl, Sonya Hana. Looking back, I don't think I realised how lucky I was to be involved in one of BBC Television's first arts programmes.

Conducting the Croindene Singers and Orchestra
(leader: Arthur Davison) at The Civic Hall, Croydon, 1951

Although it was in black and white, the director Philip Bate defied the accountants by insisting on the finest costumes and decor, all in magnificent colour for, as he said, the performers must 'feel right'. In the studio, the great company of singers and dancers in full Chinese costume in the Palace of the great Queen of Wu was breathtaking, but it had lost a great deal by the time it reached the small screen. Nevertheless, the BBC learnt from this, and when it began transmitting in colour, the arts programmes revolutionised the concept of television as a serious artistic medium.

Madeleine was married to the principal oboe of the London

Symphony Orchestra, Roger Lord, and he recruited its best players to perform his wife's music.

My motorbike broke down on my way to my first professional orchestral rehearsal and I arrived late and oil-stained for these distinguished musicians. However, I knew the music (the key to players' respect), and it all went well.

Philip Bate, came to the Royal Academy to talk about it, and was surprised to see me in the front row. He'd had no idea that his Musical Director was still a student.

The choreographer of *Wu* was the graceful Felicity Grey. Her success led the BBC to give her a TV series called *Ballet for Beginners*, and she asked me to be her Musical Director. After a few weeks I'd learnt enough about the *entrechat, tour en l'air, plié, grand battement* and *pirouette* to stand me in very good stead later with the Royal Ballet.

At the final RAM prize-giving, I was awarded the Manns Prize for conducting, but prizes don't pay bills, and I joined my fellow graduates who daily scanned the postcards on the 'Appointments Vacant' notice board.

One morning there were two new postcards. One was for the post of Musical Director of the Royal Wellington Choral Union, New Zealand and the other was for Music Assistant to the Schools department of Radio Malaya in Singapore.

I applied for both.

No one at my Colonial Office Board had ever been to Singapore, but when I mentioned my great interest in conducting, these gentlemen assured me that there was a radio orchestra to which I would have access and that I would be very useful conducting the Singapore Music Society Choir. I got the impression that I would be welcomed by the culture-hungry citizens of the Colony, and so with an excellent salary and allowances on offer, I signed a three-year contract – the last Colonial Officer to be appointed to the Federation of Malaya and Singapore.

No one had thought to mention the civil war.

So, in my quest for conducting, it was goodbye again to Liz, Aunt Bess and my Croindene friends, and away on a midnight flight to Singapore. As I stood at the bar of the BOAC terminal at Victoria with a glass of brandy in hand, waiting for the bus to

Heathrow, I looked across the road to another bus station from where Mum, Dad and I had set off for our Blackpool holiday all those years ago, and I wondered if I was doing the right thing.

CHAPTER 17

SINGAPORE

The bodies in the garden

The BOAC bus deposited passengers bound for the Far East at Heathrow's Terminal One, which was in those days a large, draughty shed filled with wooden tables. But once aboard the aircraft, matters improved, for in the 1950s, airline travel was luxurious. It needed to be, for the Argonaut cruised at a little over two hundred miles an hour, and we were not due to arrive in Singapore until three days later.

The four Rolls Royce engines came to full power as we accelerated down the runway, and the take-off was so smooth that only the magnificent spectacle of London by night under the wings told me that we were airborne. I was flying for the first time since my solo in a Tiger Moth. But what a difference: no view over the nose, no reassuring parachute (with four engines, what could possibly go wrong?), no comforting sense of control but just total reliance on an unseen stranger, somewhere up forward.

The BOAC Argonaut

Under the influence of a first-class steak dinner and some excellent wine, I introduced myself to the man in the next seat as a new Colonial Officer, bound for Singapore. He revealed that he was an 'up-country' police inspector at Kuala Lumpur.

'Must be lovely, up-country,' I said encouragingly.

'It would be', he responded, 'but for the bandits.'

'Bandits?' I said. 'What bandits? They didn't tell me anything about bandits at the Colonial Office.'

'Those twits wouldn't!' he replied. 'They didn't want to put you off, and, anyway, you'll be OK in Singapore. The bandits use it as a rest centre, and we have an agreement with them. As long as they keep the war out of Singapore, we don't lift them.'

For the rest of the flight to our first stop for refuelling in Rome, the police inspector told me how, during the Japanese occupation, the backbone of the resistance had been the Chinese Communists, known as the 'The People's Anti-Japanese Army'. He said that they'd fought for a Communist Malaya and, with victory in the Far East, anyone (including the British) who stood in their way was the enemy. According to him, they attacked the British rubber-planters, whose homes became veritable fortresses, and the Malay villages were surrounded by fences and ditches in which razor-sharp bamboo spikes lay ready to impale intruders. He advised that the roads were subject to ambush, and that it was only the British Army – many of whom had fought with the PAJA and were skilled jungle-fighters themselves – that kept the lid on. It was no longer 'lovely' up-country.

No wonder my Colonial Office Board had kept quiet. I was going to war again, but this time it was civil war.

We re-fuelled in Rome and had been flying for about three hours when an elderly and distinctly nervous English lady on her way to visit her son, a captain in the British Army, left her seat and, looking through my window at the Italian coast illuminated in the bright moonlight, said, 'It's very lovely, isn't it?'

With all of my twelve hours of flying experience, I reassured her.

'Oh yes, and flying nowadays is very safe. You've more chance of being killed by a car than an aeroplane!'

At that instant, the moon disappeared.

Cloud, I thought.

But it wasn't cloud, it was oil. The port inner engine was on fire.

In the film 'Titanic', whilst the ship was sinking, four gentlemen in the first-class saloon, scorning lifejackets, continued their game of bridge. They must have joined the Titanic's orchestra and have gone down with the ship, playing until their hands were too wet to hold their instruments or their cards. Certainly, when we caught fire, the four people playing bridge across the aisle from me only paused long enough for one to say, 'We seem to be on fire – three, no trumps!'

The lady gave me one of those looks and returned to her seat as the captain, without a word to his passengers, began a gentle one-hundred-and-eighty-degree turn back towards Rome, at the same time jettisoning fuel.

'What could go wrong?' I had asked myself. Now I knew.

With three good engines, we landed safely back in Rome, and, after fitting a new engine (flown out from London), we took off and made an overnight stop at Karachi the next day, landing in Singapore four days after leaving Heathrow. My junior rank not rating the Raffles Hotel, I was driven to the Cosmos – a large, wooden boarding house, run by a Geordie landlady by the name of 'Hannah' ('Henna' might have been more appropriate, for that was the colour of her hair). Hannah favoured flowered dresses, wore long strings of beads and frequently mopped her ample bosom with a delicate lace handkerchief. She led me upstairs to my bedroom.

'The bathroom's at the end of the veranda, dear,' she whispered, again mopping her bosom. 'Why don't you have a shower? Breakfast's at 7am: eggs and bacon.'

In the ceiling of my tiny room, a large, lazy fan sluggishly stirred the soupy Singapore night air. The bed had just enough room for me and a 'Dutch wife'- a long, hard bolster, designed for cool embrace. The lamp flickered as small night fliers flitted in and out of the light, and tiny lizards darted about the walls and walked upside down on the ceiling, defying the laws of gravity in their quest for love. I closed my mosquito net and, with thoughts of Elizabeth, embraced my Dutch wife and restlessly passed my first tropical night.

Apart from finding a snake in the shower-room on my first morning, I was comfortable at the Cosmos, but it was rather like living a chapter from a Somerset Maugham novel, and I was glad to move into my Mess – a white Colonial mansion which, during the Japanese occupation, had been the Operational Headquarters of the German submarine unit, the famous Monsun Gruppe. It was said that it had been the scene of fierce reprisals, when the Malays beheaded the Japanese and Germans and buried their bodies in shallow graves in the garden. Only the old gardener now remembered where.

I shared the Mess with five other Colonial Officers. Our meals were prepared by a resident Chinese cook and four attractive Malay girls, who cleaned the rooms and washed the enormous amount of laundry that six young men produced when living only fifty miles from the Equator and changing twice a day.

Six Colonial Officers, six cars and six servants. It sounds as though we were pampered and lazy, but the reverse was true, for we worked from 9am until 5.30pm in a climate known to floor even the native Singaporeans.

I believe that we would have benefited from a siesta, but we British had just the usual hour for lunch and, as Noel

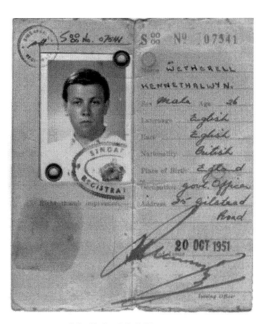

My Colonial Officer pass

Coward sang, 'went out in the midday sun.'

Radio Malaya was housed downtown in Singapore's only skyscraper, and a fellow officer who'd been appointed my mentor showed me to the studio where, in 1942, the British had broadcast their last farewells after their surrender to the Japanese – the very same studio from which, three years later, the Japanese broadcast their admission of defeat. It was still in use, and he told me that that, at night, there was sometimes heard from this dark, empty studio the high-pitched voice of the long-dead Japanese announcer's last words before he committed hara-kiri: 'Long Live the Emperor'.

The Cathay Building: headquarters of Radio Malaya

Radio Malaya broadcast in four languages: English, Mandarin, Malay and Hindi. The Chinese and Indian sections also included programmes in dialects. Each main language had a Head of Section, answerable to the overall Director of Radio Malaya, who was a Senior Colonial Officer by the name of Jackson and in close touch with government policy.

English programmes were controlled by a pre-war member of the BBC who'd fought in Malaysia and spoke the language fluently: Anthony Beamish. To the Malays, he was a 'Tuan Besar' – a real gentleman – and his assistant, David Kennard, was later to pioneer and produce wildlife programmes and was a colleague of David Attenborough at the BBC in Bristol.

I shared my 'mess' with a journalist, Derek Cooper, who organised our meals with the Chinese cook – experience he put to good use when he returned to the UK, joined the BBC, and hosted his long-running *The Food Programme* on Radio 4.

The Chief Administration Officer was Bert Reed. For many

years he had been an arranger for Geraldo's Dance Band, but he had nothing to do with the Radio Malaya Orchestra, which was the preserve of a former prisoner of the Japanese, the Dutchman Cor Ryff. From the violin, Cor led an orchestra of six in programmes of light music.

So much for the promised conducting opportunities.

I decided to bide my time and make plans for a bigger and better orchestra. I suspect my brief appearance as a professional West End actor and my work with Bob Monkhouse had appeared on my CV, because my first task was to write, cast and produce a series of twelve programmes, *Adventures in Music*, which would be broadcast to all the schools in Malaya and Singapore.

My first script was about the Czech composer, Dvorak, and I set about auditioning actors. Surprisingly, there were some very good ones amongst the British living in Singapore who worked at the Victoria Theatre (where, in 1930, Noel Coward had saved the day when he stepped in for an indisposed actor in R. C. Sherriff's *Journey's End*). I auditioned Eileen Attenborough who, as one might expect, was very professional; as narrator, I cast a school music teacher, Pam Stacey, who had a very good radio voice, and I cast Sergeant Willis Hall, later famous for his play about the lives of young conscript soldiers in Malaya, *The Long and the Short and the Tall*, starring Peter O'Toole. It was a very talented cast, and I had great fun writing and directing but more importantly, I learnt a great deal about radio.

Working for a multi-language radio station like Radio Malaya meant that we all had to write, take part and produce programmes for each other. Sometimes, I was called to the Indian studio to play the piano for a schools programme, and on one occasion I directed a Chinese flute player, who played non-stop for nearly an hour. My main work was with the English section, where I read the news and the rubber prices – which varied widely as the civil war took its toll. The war attracted the press from all over the world, including a reporter from the *Daily Mirror*, who described accompanying our troops on a night raid over the border into Malaya. Very exciting he was, but then I couldn't stop him talking about a Singapore dinner given by a Chinese host, where he had eaten monkey brains from a trepanned skull. The implications were very clear. Was this what our young conscripts were nightly risking their lives for?

My mentor, John, was great company, but I quickly realised that the long, scented tropical nights, and the presence of many beautiful Oriental women were beginning to get to him.

Mixed marriages were now acceptable. A Welsh Colonial Officer married an Indian girl, and another, a beautiful Thai princess; all this was a far cry from the days when Colonial Officers found their own solutions to loneliness. A popular after-dinner joke ran like this:

> *First Colonial Officer to Second: 'Have you heard about poor old Carruthers? He's gone troppo. Living with a baboon!'*
> *Second Colonial Officer: 'Male or female?'*
> *First Colonial Officer (shocked): 'Female of course! There's nothing queer about Carruthers!'*

I, too, was feeling the lack of feminine company, but although in Singapore there were many wives of soldiers serving up-country, they were considered off-limits. Attractive European women were very rare indeed, and I was very lucky to find myself favoured by the unattached Audrey.

Audrey showed me her Singapore and took me to dinner in one of the many open-air restaurants in Bugis Street, where the food was excellent and the entertainments colourful. The unofficial cabaret included noisy fights between boy-girls and girl-boys over territorial rights to their kind of customers. One of the most beautiful was a Chinese girl, whose elegance was not matched by her voice, for she could only utter guttural noises. It was said that, during the occupation, she had been very popular with the Japanese high military and, although unable to read and write, they decided that she might pass on Japanese officers' 'pillow talk' to the Chinese resistance, so they removed her tongue. Henceforth she was known as 'Dumbo'. It was also said that the ornamental spikes of Singapore's department store Robinsons often bore a severed head at that time.

I decided to see how well my first 'Adventure in Music' was being received in the up-country schools and, not fancying a two-hundred-and-fifty-mile drive through bandit country, I flew in a

Dakota to the capital, Kuala Lumpur.

It was not the great modern city of today. Hotel accommodation was short, and I had been booked into a Chinese hotel where the bedrooms, each equipped with a spittoon, were simply partitioned corridors. I was kept awake all night by non-stop Chinese chatter and the clacking of the Mah Jong counters, for I'd had the misfortune to be in a Chinese hotel during their New Year, the only time they'd ever take a holiday.

I tottered downstairs the next morning, but breakfast brought no comfort, for no one spoke English. The only words I had in common with the unsmiling waiter were 'Nasi Goreng', and it was with that delicious combination of chicken livers, fried eggs, banana, sundry spices and fried rice that I started a day to remember. This first morning, I was to listen to my Dvorak programme in a large Chinese school.

When my car arrived, it was driven by a worried-looking Malay, and I joined a nervous Chinese Education Officer. The third member of our party was an extremely worried Malay soldier, sporting a Lee Enfield 303 rifle. Not much good in a car, I thought – I'd rather have the short-barrelled Sten machine gun which I was handy with.

'Where are we going?' I asked the Education Officer. He looked around furtively.

'I mustn't say. It must be a surprise. If they knew beforehand, they'd arrange an ambush!'

Suddenly, the comic horror of the situation hit me. We were risking our lives to discover if a class of young Chinese students were benefiting from a programme about the Czech composer Dvorak. What could they possibly find of interest in the life of a 19th century European born in the province of Bohemia?

Then I answered my own question. Like Dvorak, they were citizens of an empire – his, the Austro-Hungarian, theirs, the British – whose people sought their own political and cultural identity.

My musings were interrupted by our arrival at the school, where my armed guard caused no comment.

'Oh, and by the way,' said the Education Officer, 'the Headmaster can't be here to greet you. The Communists came into the school last week and shot him for showing too much Western bias.'

I can't remember too much about the broadcast. As always, the radio was turned up full blast (the Chinese love their music loud), and I received polite applause from the students. I was rescued from another night of Mah Jong by the Malayan Head of Broadcasting, Lloyd Williams. That night, I stayed with him and his beautiful wife, and we dined in an open air restaurant beneath the stars and the grenade-nets. I was glad to get to the coffee.

The next morning I flew back to Singapore. Take-off was delayed as we waited for former Prime Minister Ramsey McDonald's son, Malcolm, who, with his great experience and love of Asia, had been sent by the British Government as a 'trouble-shooter' to reconcile Malaya's different racial factions in preparation for independence.

As our Dakota winged its way southwards, I looked down at the thousands of acres of bandit-infested jungle below and was glad that Malayan Airways had a 'nil accident' record, for a forced landing would have been unsurvivable.

Back in the safety of Singapore, one night I was having a drink with the Director of Broadcasting, Jacko, when he received an urgent phone call from the Senior British Army Officer with the news that the Governor of Malaya, Sir Richard Gurney, and his wife had been ambushed by the bandits and killed. Gurney's assassination could well have been the signal for a general uprising and the spread of the war to Singapore, and so, as Director of Broadcasting, Jacko had the responsibility of controlling the release of this dangerous news.

He slammed down the receiver and turned to me.

'Come on Ken, tonight we're going to break the law.'

We did, in a break-neck drive through the streets of Singapore to Radio Malaya, there to meet the heads of the Indian, Malay and Chinese Sections and to issue a short, low-key statement.

Jacko issued his orders: 'Keep it short, keep it calm. I want a simple statement that Governor Gurney has been murdered by terrorists. However, this will not alter our intention to overcome the forces of evil, and the British Army is in complete control of the situation.' Jacko was a great admirer of Churchill.

Incredible though it seems now, neither Jacko nor I, nor any of our English-speaking staff, were fluent in any language other than English. The Malayan announcement seemed about the right length, as did the Indian, but the head of the Chinese Section went on and on, to our increasing agitation and dismay. We had no idea what he was actually saying. Was it: 'Comrades, the moment has come to rise and sweep the smelly barbarians from our land?'

Jacko's worried question 'What's he saying?' was answered by his assistant, who explained that his boss had passed on Jacko's message in four languages – Mandarin, Cantonese, Hokkien and Haka – and there was nothing to worry about.

I had a weekly late-night programme called *Kenneth Alwyn at the Piano*, which was quite popular and led to an invitation to Christmas dinner at the home of the editor of *The Straits Times*. There, fifty miles from the Equator, Audrey and I ate turkey and all the trimmings in the company of his guests, who included a young lawyer Lee Kuan Yew (later to become Prime Minister of Singapore), Willis Hall and a defrocked Roman Catholic priest, married to a beautiful Chinese lady with a wooden leg. I kid you not!

No longer working for God, the former priest was looking for a job, and I arranged for him to audition as a Radio Malaya announcer. Unfortunately, having spent most of his youth in a seminary, he was not very worldly-wise, and his mispronunciations of such names as Debussy and Falla made him quite unsuitable.

I had no conducting opportunities, but I'd sometimes be asked to deputise for an Indian friend, Paul Abisheganaden, whose chamber orchestra was preparing Gerald Finzi's *Dies Natalis*, but apart from that, and a studio broadcast by a Chinese girls' choir of my arrangements of Purcell's *Nymphs and Shepherds*, the folk song 'No, John' and Handel's *Harryruja Chorus* (the Chinese tongue does not slip easily around the English 'l'), accompanied by the Cor Ryff Orchestra (all six players!), my baton stayed in its case.

It was time to find a rostrum somewhere.

In an awkward interview, my boss Jacko accused me of being ambitious (seemingly undesirable in a Colonial Officer) and dismissed my suggestion that perhaps I'd been misled about the conducting opportunities at Radio Malaya. I gave the statutory three months' notice, which astonished my colleagues, for with Malayan independence in the offing, Colonial Officers would be retired early with pensions and a handsome gratuity. Even when I was offered the post of Head of Schools Music in Singapore and the Federation, a government appointment, I turned it down.

Recording 'Nymphs and Shepherds' for Radio Malaya

I came under quite a bit of pressure to stay. A letter signed by Sergeant Willis Hall in *The Straits Times* was headlined 'Kenneth Alwyn must not be allowed to leave Singapore', but I was still looking for that rostrum, and time was a-wasting.

I decided not to work out my notice but do a midnight flit, and I wrote to Elizabeth, telling her that I was coming home to England.

Then, totally out of the blue, a cable arrived from New Zealand offering me the posts of Conductor of the Royal Choral Union and organist and choirmaster of St Paul's Cathedral, Wellington and – most importantly – access to the New Zealand Radio broadcasting orchestra.

I sent a cable to Elizabeth: 'Not coming home after all. Going to New Zealand.'

I quietly cleared my Radio Malaya desk on Friday evening, and that night Audrey secretly drove me to Changi Airport for my escape to Australia.

I never heard from Audrey again: a lovely girl, who would not be alone for long.

I'd been lucky.

CHAPTER 18

AUSTRALIA AND NEW ZEALAND

Tiny balls!

Fifteen hours after leaving exotic Singapore, I arrived in Melbourne – perhaps the most 'English' of the Australian cities – and met my cousin Jamie again from Dagnall Park, now a highly successful Australian business man with a flat amongst the possums of sophisticated Toorak.

It was a breath of home. We laughed about teenage experiences – the Ralph Reader 'Gang Show' and 'Little Lady Make-Believe' – but, sadly, Jamie had given up music. After a couple of very pleasant days, I flew to Sydney to meet the Australian composer, Alfred Hill, with whom I was to share my first concert in New Zealand. I was to conduct Bach's *Peasant Cantata* and he, his own *Hinemoa*, which was a kind of Maori *Hiawatha*.

It was a sunny evening when I took the ferry to Mossman where Hill lived in a Victorian house overlooking the Bay. He and his wife greeted me warmly and, as we drank tea sitting in his comfortable armchairs, complete with antimacassars, he told me of his early life.

Although Australian, at the age of four, his family had moved to New Zealand. One of his earliest memories was of a very old Maori woman, who remembered Captain Cook sailing into Wellington Harbour and purchasing the land, later to be called Palmerston, for a few axes and trinkets.

In 1888, at the age of 18, young Fred had been sent across the world to Leipzig to study composition, conducting, and the violin, which he played so well that, even though a student, he was invited to join the Gewandhaus Orchestra. In this great orchestra, he had the experience of playing under Brahms, Tchaikovsky and Grieg. He told me how Tchaikovsky would suddenly clap a hand to the top of his head as though he feared it would come off; how Brahms seemed rather bad-tempered (probably the result of the innumerable cups of strong coffee and cigars); and how the orchestra loved the gentle Grieg. Hill returned to New Zealand in 1893 where, single-handedly, he trained the country's first symphony orchestra, but he was tempted back to Sydney and became Head of Music of the Australian Broadcasting Corporation.

Our concert together was the first time he would be returning to the country which owed him its first Symphony Orchestra. The choir were looking forward to meeting us both, or so it was said.

The next evening, the setting sun framed the Sydney Harbour Bridge in warm pink and the lights of the houses on the hills sparkled on the water as I settled into my seat on 'C' deck of the Sunderland Flying Boat. Having assured his passengers that our take-off path across the water had been cleared of the jetsam which could sink us, the captain opened the throttles of the four Bristol Pegasus engines. Then, and unexpectedly, the lights of Sydney disappeared, the nose pitched down, and sea covered the porthole as the Sunderland took on the characteristics of a submarine seeking the safety of the deep. Thankfully, as we gathered speed, the water receded, the lights re-appeared, and we climbed into a star-studded velvet sky on the two-thousand-mile journey to my new home, and yet another attempt to put my baton to work.

As dawn broke at the end of our thirteen-hour flight over the Tasman Sea, I saw, low on the horizon, the land of the long white cloud: Aotearoa, as the Maoris called New Zealand.

If the take-off from Sydney had been spectacular, the landing at Wellington was certainly the most beautiful. The natural harbour is surrounded by green hills dotted with small white houses, and in the distance are the snow-capped Tararua Mountains. But it was raining as we taxied to our mooring, and what should have been an exciting day turned out to be depressing beyond measure. I was cold in my tropical, light-weight suit. I was also tired, unshaven and in need of a warm welcome. Instead, I was greeted by the chairman of the choir, who told me he'd taken time off work to take me to my digs and that they were 'respectable, clean and cheap'.

He drove me to the door of a wooden house, which was certainly clean, and there was no doubt about its respectability. The stringy lady, whose sole lodger I was, led me upstairs to a small bedroom, one wall of which featured a romanticised picture of Christ and the caption 'God is Love'. On the opposite wall, facing the Saviour, a sign read 'No Smoking' and, in the bathroom, which boasted a virginal bar of soap and a perfectly folded towel, another notice rammed the point home: 'Positively No Smoking'. When my landlady told me that she didn't serve meals, I turned my collar up and set off in the rain to find some lunch. My spirits were somewhat recovered by a dozen fried oysters, garnished with pumpkin, and lashings of bread with creamy New Zealand butter. The bill was one shilling and sixpence (about seven pence in new money), and I left a tip, which was returned with my first friendly smile and 'There's no tipping in New Zealand.'

If Day One was not a success, Day Two was even worse, when I met the Royal Wellington Choral Union – or rather, what was left of it after its former conductor had resigned and taken about forty of the best singers to form his new Schola Cantorum.

The remnants of my choir were three tenors, four 'pushed up' baritones (politely called 'second' tenors), nine basses, about thirty contraltos, forty second sopranos and twenty top sopranos – most of them the wrong side of fifty. The truth was out. I'd fallen in with a management – albeit this time amateur – which had brought me halfway across the world to a failing choir and a cathedral post which was only 'in the offing'. All I would have to live on would be the choir stipend: £165 a year, paid quarterly in arrears. This was a little over three pounds a week in a country where the basic minimum wage was nine pounds four shillings a week.

After rehearsal, and back in my cold room, without even the comfort of a cigarette, I realised I'd made a terrible mistake.

The next morning – Day Three – I walked to the offices of the New Zealand Shipping Line on Lampton Quay and put down a five-pound deposit on the cheapest berth on the first ship back to England after the concert. Meanwhile, I had to survive.

But just when everything seemed dark, fortune lit up Day Three with a telephone call from a fellow student at the Royal Academy of Music, Maurice Rossiter. He'd seen my photograph in the Wellington paper and asked me if I would like to meet.

Would I not!

Maurice had been the only pupil of Dennis Noble, the baritone who'd given the first performance of Sir William Walton's *Belshazzar's Feast*. But his voice, reared in the pure air of New Zealand, had fallen foul of the London smog, and Maurice had developed severe chronic sinusitis – thus ending his high hopes of a career sponsored by his famous teacher. I told him how things stood, and without further ado he invited me to live with his family. I moved that afternoon to his house in Haititi overlooking the harbour, where I could watch the flying-boats take off and land.

The Rossiters were a fine example of the New Zealanders of 1952 – loyal to the Crown, and a caring society which, though somewhat insular, was comfortable with itself. My small capital would have soon run out had I not tried my luck with New Zealand Radio and, modestly mentioning my West End appearance, auditioned for the drama director, Bruce Beebe. He offered me the part of 'Death' in Jean Anouilh's *Point of Departure* – a version of *Orpheus and Euridice*, which had premiered in London the year before. I got away with it, even if my accent was *awfully* French. However, we were a long way from Paris, and as I was a new voice to radio, I survived to act again and earn enough to pay the Rossiters a modest amount.

In an attempt to get the choir ready for *Hinemoa*, I held extra rehearsals, but only the enthusiastic members turned up.

Life had some compensations, for being an RAF 'Blue', I was welcomed into the Victoria University Fencing Club, and it was here that I met Mary, the great-granddaughter of the Prime Minister of New Zealand, who had commissioned Wellington's fine wooden town hall.

In her high-collared white fencing jacket, with its padding adding extra curves to her upper breastwork (a fine target), and her white pantaloons ending just below the knee (revealing very pretty calves and dainty white ankle socks), she was an enticing sight. She was also a very good fencer, and we hit it off, both on and off the piste.

As the new conductor of the Royal Wellington, I was invited to the family home. Mary had lived unchaperoned in London and so was familiar with the wicked ways of the big city, and we became good friends, spending a lot of time together in what was nicknamed 'the land of the long white weekend' where everything shut down at Saturday lunch-time – well, almost everything.

Finally, Alfred Hill arrived and, as the Choral Union had no contact with the New Zealand Broadcasting Symphony Orchestra, we had to make do with the local radio station band – a small and depressed group.

Hill soon made it clear that New Zealand's musical standards had declined since his day. Nevertheless, after the concert, which was a rather uninspiring affair (I could hardly make much of a mark with twenty minutes of Bach), the ever-polite New Zealanders gave their honoured guest a party, and in his honour, Maurice Rossiter sang Hill's best known song 'Waita Poi', which describes beautiful Maori maidens as they swing tiny balls – their Pois – on the end of coloured strings.

It's all very delicate – even coy – but with Maurice's fine baritone now fully restored, he gave it all he'd got.

The applause was enthusiastic, and we eagerly awaited the composer's words of thanks. In the expectant silence, Alfred Hill looked at Maurice, turned to the audience and snarled, 'Nothing like it!'

He signalled me to play it again and thereupon sang it himself. Though a beautiful Maori maiden he was not, his movements were delicate. But the sight of this octogenarian fluttering his eye-lashes, enticingly offering us his arthritic hips and singing about his tiny balls was too much for me.

I've learnt that, if at first, one says something positive with a smile, then the artists will take more kindly to a suggested improvement. Valery Gergiev, rehearsing the London Symphony Orchestra for Stravinsky's 'Firebird', stopped them with the words: 'It's good, but ordinary good.'

The sailing date of my ship home, the *Rangitiki*, was now imminent, and Elizabeth had managed to sell my motorcycle for the balance of the fare – seventy-five pounds – so I told the choir that urgent personal matters required my immediate return to England, but that I would return for their next concert.

The Rangitiki: saved by the captain of HMS Jervis Bay

Stupidity may be defined as making the same mistake more than once. First there had been Singapore, and now New Zealand. I wasn't about to make the third. Had I been offered a couple of dates with the New Zealand Symphony Orchestra, I might have tried to rebuild the choir, but nothing was planned, not even the next concert. I'd gone halfway across the world to conduct Bach's *Peasant Cantata* and to play 'Death' on the radio. It was time to go home.

I left New Zealand as I'd arrived – in the rain. As I leant over the ship's rail watching the *Rangitiki* prepare to sail, on Lampton Quay a Maori choir sang 'Now is the hour that we must say goodbye'. But we didn't say goodbye, and after they'd sung their song of farewell three times, the choir went home.

As Mary's small figure became lost in the drizzle, I turned my face eastwards towards the Pacific and the five-week journey to Southampton and, hopefully, Elizabeth.

During the war, the ship had been a troop carrier bringing Americans and Canadians to Europe, and in 1940, as the largest in a convoy of thirty-seven ships, it was being given special attention by the German Pocket Battleship, the *Admiral Scheer*, until the armed merchant cruiser *HMS Jervis Bay* took on the eleven guns of the *Scheer* and gained enough time for the *Rangitiki* to escape. The *Jervis Bay* was sunk, and the captain was awarded the Victoria Cross.

After the war, the *Rangitiki* was refitted with large

refrigerated holds to carry New Zealand lamb and butter to Britain, returning with British migrants who wanted to start a new life, and so, being 'destination driven', it was not equipped with all the refinements of the modern cruise ship. There were no frills. Entertainment was limited to a small cinema, deck quoits, a solitary ping-pong table with a net to prevent the ball going over the side (only one ball was issued per day), a small library and a couple of bars selling very cheap drinks.

I'd had the experience in the Royal Air Force of sharing a room with fifty airmen, but this hardly equipped me for sharing a six-berth cabin on 'E' deck below the water-line with five total strangers. The first was a Scot who had been a game warden in the North Island, a man not dedicated to the preservation of animal life but to its destruction. His reward for two lonely years of culling was a handsome bank balance and the ownership of two hundred acres of country, teeming with wild horses.

The second was a doctor. He and his wife were returning to England because he'd not been able to set up a practice. I asked myself why he had ever gone there at all. His wife, a pretty little dark girl with mischievous eyes, was also sharing a five-berth cabin with strangers, and I never saw them together, not even at mealtimes.

The third was a Cockney of Blitz vintage, who had been a post-war assisted immigrant (he'd paid only ten pounds for the trip). Though of the right age, he could not have been in the Forces, for he had no roof to his mouth. This, together with his accent, made him almost incomprehensible, but, being a sociable sort of chap and priding myself on having a discerning ear, I asked him why he was returning to the 'old country'.

He replied 'Ahillim!' several times, the words delivered through his nose. Then I realised that his answer to my question was: 'I'll kill him'. The 'him' turned out to be his daughter's husband, a violent man who got drunk and beat up his wife, so Dad was returning to England to murder his son-in-law. He spent most days in his bunk, only getting up to roam the decks at night.

The fourth member of our tight little group was a newly-married sailor, whose bride was sharing a cabin with middle-aged ladies, and so the couple were unable to enjoy their conjugal rights. He drank heavily to sublimate his natural urges and usually returned to the cabin in the early hours, reeking and reeling.

The fifth was a young New Zealand barrister who'd hit the headlines when he quoted *habeus corpus* to secure the release of his client and the dismissal of the case. He was going to England to 'dine in' at one of the Inns of Court so that he could continue his very promising legal career in England. His name was Bruce Weir, and we were to become great friends.

The cabin was so small that there was no room for our clothes, which had to remain unpacked on our bunks until we went to bed. We then transferred our cases to the floor, leading to a lot of cursing from anyone using the 'heads' for, of course the lavatories and sea-water showers were certainly not ensuite. The solitary porthole, which gave us a fine view of the underwater Pacific, was secured by two massive screws. Cabin air came through a single tube from the laundry next door.

After a couple of weeks, dolphins, sharks and a foot-long flying fish on the boat deck told us we were now well into the Pacific and sailing towards Pitcairn Island, home of the descendants of the Bounty Mutineers and their Tahitian women. There, we were to disembark the priest – a quiet man who played cracking table tennis – but the weather was so bad that the islanders couldn't launch their longboat, and he had to sail on to Panama, there to change ships and go back for a second attempt.

Life without any kind of privacy became increasingly intolerable, until I discovered, hidden away on deck, a piano. I managed a little time to myself, but it was not long before I had an audience including the doctor's wife, Betty. It was all quite innocent but, as is the way on a long sea voyage without much to do, people began to talk.

Passengers looked for privacy in the oddest places. One couple found it in a lifeboat down amongst the emergency rations and water butts. Unfortunately, the officer of the day spotted the loose cover and, discovering them in flagrante delicto, took them to the captain. He issued an order that the lifeboats were for emergency use only. The crew did rather better than the passengers, for the ship's second funnel – a dummy containing the radio room – was roofed with a deck, which they used for nude sun-bathing and *their* emergencies.

As the ship moved further into the Pacific, it became too hot on deck for deck-quoits and table tennis, and so life centred around the bar. Drink was cheap, and one night the frustrated bridegroom started a fight. Order was restored by a detachment of the crew, led by an officer armed with a revolver. The young man was taken before the captain, who sentenced him to spend the rest of the voyage in the Brig, but he was allowed conjugal visits.

The *Rangitiki* was now approaching the Panama Canal and Curacao, where we'd have a desperately-needed few hours ashore. Betty told me that her husband was not interested in seeing Curacao, and she asked me if I'd escort her.

I think the couple may have had what is called these days an 'open marriage', but I think it more likely that it had come apart in New Zealand. The doctor took to walking the decks at night, and I began to feel very uneasy when, in response to my cheery greeting, he merely gave me a funny look. I kept well away from the ship's rail. The sharks were only a few feet below.

In the colder waters of the Atlantic, passions cooled and, apart from being questioned by the purser about a missing suitcase found next to my bed (had I been framed by the doctor?), the rest of the voyage passed uneventfully.

After five weeks at sea, it was with a profound sense of relief that, on a beautiful English day, I saw the gulls wheeling over the green hills of the Isle of Wight.

At last, I was home.

CHAPTER 19

THE SADLER'S WELLS
THEATRE BALLET, 1952

At last, the fun begins!

Home is where the heart is, but it's also where one can afford, and, with only twelve pounds to my name, I hoped that I could have my old room, and that, perhaps, Elizabeth and I could start again.

I discovered I could do neither. She'd moved to nearby Brook Green to share the flat of cellist, Eileen Croxford, but more to the point, she had a new man in her life – my composer friend from upstairs, Roger North. He'd often given Elizabeth a lift to the Royal Academy of Music on the pillion of his Norton motorcycle, and cornering at fifty whilst clinging to the waist of a good-looking army captain, who was both a composer and the son of a famous admiral, had obviously set her heart a-flutter. He was in, I was out. However, she told me that there was a spare room in her new flat which I could rent, providing I understood that she was no longer mine. Now, not only did I have no job and no money, but I had no girl either. Cellos have a propensity for gloom, and playing Saint-Saëns's *The Dying Swan* from the room next to where Roger and Elizabeth spent their nights was, perhaps, not the most sensible thing to do, but it was Hobson's choice.

After a couple of very uncomfortable weeks, I was down to three pounds and no prospects, but then chance again took a hand when I phoned a dancer from my *Ballet for Beginners* TV days, Yvonne Cartier. She was now a member of the Sadler's Wells Theatre Ballet and told me that my call was well-timed because the Company was looking for a rehearsal pianist and assistant conductor. Ten minutes later, I rang the Musical Director, John Lanchbery.

'Are you Royal Academy or Royal College?' he asked. He told me he too had studied at the Royal Academy and, although he was seeing a candidate from the Royal College at 10.30am the next morning, I'd better come at 10am.

Jack Lanchbery met me at the stage door of the Sadler's Wells Theatre. He was a tall man with a high forehead and a pointed imperial beard who resembled an amalgam of his two heroes, Tchaikovsky and Ernest Ansermet. I played something at sight, told him about conducting a Masque for dancing for BBC TV, *The Fair Queen of Wu*, danced by Sonya Hana, and of being Felicity Grey's Musical Director for her BBC TV series, *Ballet for Beginners*.

'I don't think we'll bother with the bloke from the Royal College,' he said. 'You've got the job!'

I was called back a couple of days later to be vetted by the director of the theatre, Norman Tucker, a good-looking man with a charming manner. 'Call me Norman,' he said, and introduced me to his general manager, Stephen Arlen.

Stephen was careful with money (he and his wife rode to the Wells on a tandem) and he offered me a three-month probationary contract as Company pianist. I would be required to play for all ballet classes and rehearsals, to cover Jack for all performances, and to conduct my own performances twice a week.

The salary was £15. Stephen was *very* careful with money.

But, what the hell, I'd have worked for just bed and board. At last, I had been given that pearl without price: the opportunity to become a professional conductor.

I was to start with the Company in three weeks' time, and, as Roger seemed to be coming round less often, I began to tickle Elizabeth's ivories again, reviving all the happy memories of John Osborne's flat. She forgave me the broken promises, and after a romantic tryst in the depths of Epping Forest, we became engaged. Sadly, the romance amongst the trees didn't survive the bus trip back to Hammersmith. On the top deck we looked the truth in the eye – that my new job would mean constant separation or her giving up singing – and when we left the bus, we were no longer engaged. She fried an enormous supper of sprats – our favourite dish – and we said farewell.

Elizabeth and I had been together, on and off, for three years, but now we'd made a final choice and it was time to part, this time for good. But to go where?

Once again, fate took a hand when my pianist friend from the RAM, John Burn, invited me to dinner at his flat and happened to mention that the old lady who lived in the basement had shuffled off this mortal coil and that her flat was now free. Not only free, she'd also had the kindness to pay the rent of £66 a year in advance the day before she died! Did I know anyone who might be interested?!

Two days later I walked from Brook Green to No 54 St George's Square, Westminster, a few hundred yards from the Thames, carrying my few worldly possessions. I had to walk, for it was the weekend of the great smog of 1952 when the air was so foul – a real 'pea-souper' – that no Tubes, trains, buses, cars or even taxis were able to move, and over four thousand Londoners breathed their last, polluted breath.

The walk took over three hours. I had to feel my way, reading the street names by the sickly yellow light of the street lamps, asking directions from people whose replies were muffled and who resembled wraiths from an Edgar Allen Poe horror story. It was worse near the Thames, and when I opened the door of my new basement home and switched on the lights, the 60-watt bulbs left the corners of the rooms in darkness. But even though I had only a tin plate and mug, and my furniture was a damp bed and sofa – it was mine!

But it was a sad place, and not just because the old lady had died there a few days before but also because of something which I later learned from Beatrice Godfrey-Faussett, who lived across the passage in the other basement flat. In the 19th century, before the Thames Embankment had been built, the river had overflowed and the servants who lived in the basement of No. 54 in my flat had all been drowned.

This was a rather depressing introduction to what was to be my home for the next ten years, but with a new suite of furniture, a dry bed, cheerful curtains and the assistance of Dr Music, the gloomy spirits departed, and I got down to learning something about my new workplace, one of the most famous theatres in the world.

Mr Sadler was the owner of a common music hall in Islington. His chance discovery of a pure well in its garden in 1683 meant that, by 1685, London's most fashionable people were samplers of Mr Sadler's water, which he claimed was 'a sovereign cure for dropsy, jaundice, scurvy, green sickness, distemper and other ailments to which females are liable, ulcers, fits of the vapours and virgin fever' (whatever that is).

Although the entrance to the well can still be seen in the theatre stalls, no one drinks the waters these days, but for over three hundred years Londoners came to see Aqua Shows (where boats sailed the stage), the Shakespeare of Sarah Siddons and Edmund Keen, the clowning of Grimaldi and the music hall stars, Marie Lloyd and Harry Champion.

Sadler's Wells Theatre

In 1931 the Theatre went onto the world map when Ninette de Valois formed the Sadler's Wells Ballet. Already famous by 1939, it toured the country at war, but in 1947 it returned to the Wells as the country's national ballet. As such, the Royal Opera House invited Ninette de Valois to Covent Garden, but this left Sadler's Wells without dancers. De Valois then formed the Sadler's Wells Theatre Ballet, to provide not only dancers for the opera but, as a touring company, a performing experience for young dancers in the classics and new ballets by choreographers and composers.

This was the energetic company that I was joining, run by Peggy van Praagh. It was an exciting prospect.

On my first day I was thrown in the deep end when I played two classes for Peggy. I thanked the Lord that, although I'd never been a regular ballet pianist, as the Musical Director of *Ballet for Beginners*, I knew enough about the steps to play the right sort of music. Over the next couple of days, I met all the thirty-six dancers, notably: Svetlana Beriosova from Latvia; Nadia Nerina and Patricia Miller from South Africa; Maryon Lane from Zululand; Elaine Fifield from Australia; and Anya Linden, Annette Page, Margaret Hill, Stella Claire and Sheila O'Reilly, who were all home-grown.

Among the twelve men were: two South Africans, David Poole and Johaar Mosaval; Pirmin Trecu, a young refugee from the Spanish Civil War who, for a while had been an art student in Croydon; Miro Zolan, from somewhere in central Europe via Australia; and the very English Stanley Holden, David Blair, Michael Bolton, Donald Britton and David Gill. Dancing small parts were two future directors of the Royal Ballet, Sir Kenneth MacMillan and Sir Peter Wright. Quite a cast list for a company christened for the leading grocery chain of the time: with so many dancers from the Commonwealth and the Colonies, it was known as 'The Home and Colonial'.

Although these dancers were known as the 'Second Company', they had the talent and determination to show that they were second to none. They even had their own initiation ceremony. All new boys had to prove their strength, balance and nerve by walking the narrow parapet of the Theatre forty feet above Rosebery Avenue. Fortunately, being music staff, I was excused. In spite of being a pilot, I have no head for heights.

Those first weeks with the Company were very exciting. I loved the music, the friendly company and, in particular, a pretty dark-haired girl with a cheeky manner who'd made her ballet debut at fourteen as a monkey in John Cranko's ballet *Children's Corner* – Annette Page.

Annette wanted to leave her family home in Hatch End and move into London, so I suggested she might like my old room at

Elizabeth's. From that time onward, we became very close, and she gave up plans to move to America.

**The Company I joined: Peggy van Praagh with the
Sadler's Wells Theatre Ballet, 1952**

I'm sure she'd made her decision before we met, and that I was not the reason, merely the catalyst. Certainly, Ninette de Valois must have been pleased that, perhaps, I had helped Annette to decide on what was to be her future great career at Covent Garden.

Although it had not been going long, the Company had accumulated a large repertoire of the standard romantic ballets:

Act Two of *Swan Lake*, *Les Sylphides* and revivals from the 1930s
– Frederick Ashton's *Les Rendezvous* and *The Haunted Ballroom* –
but following de Valois' remit, it had also presented new ballets
with specially commissioned music from leading British
composers.

Anthony Hopkins (who could play Beethoven's *Für Elise*
standing with his back to the keyboard) wrote the music for
Rodrigues' comic ballet about a cycle race, *Café des Sports*, and
John Addison provided the score for Walter Gore's light-hearted
romp about nothing in particular, *Carte Blanche*. Addison had
been very successful as the composer of the music for the
Richard Attenborough film, *Brighton Rock*. John eventually went
to Hollywood to write for films and won an Oscar for *A Bridge
Too Far*.

One of the most difficult orchestral scores to reproduce at
the keyboard was John Gardner's music for Cranko's *Reflection*.
Although the dancers were quite at home with modern music,
they found a lot of Gardner's music almost incomprehensible.
One particularly complicated section we christened 'the mess'
and, at Cranko's suggestion, everyone ran about for a bit until it
was all over. However, at the first orchestral rehearsal, when
John Gardner suddenly leapt to his feet and roared 'Second
violins should be playing B flat!' we knew that at least one person
knew what it should sound like.

I'd had no chance so far to conduct. I had to prove my
worth as that overworked and often undervalued servant of the
dance: the ballet pianist. Toscanini declared that conducting is
simply a matter of tempo – an oversimplification in the concert
hall, but it is often the case in the ballet theatre. In the absence of
the composer or conductor at rehearsal, the pianist has the sole
responsibility of playing rehearsals at a speed which avoids
difficulties at orchestral performance.

However, on rare occasions, the choreographer may get it
wrong. In 1946, when Andrée Howard choreographed *Assembly
Ball* to Bizet's *Symphony in C* for the opening of the first season by
the Sadler's Wells Opera Ballet, she created a problem which was
still with us in 1953. Bizet marked the last movement *saltando*,
which means the violins must bounce their bows. This is only
possible if the music is played quickly. Andrée gave the *corps de*

ballet some *brisé volés*, being little travelling jumps which have a top speed slower than the minimum speed for bouncing bows. The conductor must compromise, and so Bizet's sparkling finale merely plods.

Happily, this kind of in-built difficulty is very rare, and it was certainly not found in John Cranko's and Charles Mackerras' *Pineapple Poll*, the comic ballet set to Arthur Sullivan's music about sailors' girls who decide to go to sea on *HMS Hot Cross Bun*, masquerading as 'Jolly Jill Tars'. It was an enormous success, and John and Charles decided to collaborate again, this time to the music of Verdi.

What a lively and productive place the Sadler's Wells Theatre was. As well as rehearsing our own ballets, the Company was still dancing in the operas, so after a full day's hard work, some stayed on to dance in the evening.

Finally *The Lady and the Fool* was completed, ready for its first night in Oxford, and with the other ballets all rehearsed, and Annette and I established as an 'item', I left London for my first provincial tour. I was now an accepted rehearsal pianist, but was still to be tested as a ballet conductor.

Jack decided that, rather than a short ballet at a matinée, I should have a whole evening to myself, and he chose Delibes' *Coppélia*. I would be making my first-ever appearance with a professional orchestra at a live performance without rehearsal and, there being no full orchestral score, conducting from a piano part.

That night in 1952 at the New Theatre, Oxford was to be a 'do or die' experience. One serious mistake in handling the orchestra, a stage cue or speed, and my dream would be shattered. I'd be back to a basement in abasement, with no job and no Annette.

The house lights dimmed, and from the dusty world under the stage where theatre ghosts are said to live, I climbed the two steps into the orchestra pit and raised my baton for the very first time in a theatre – that magical world where young men fall in love with beautiful dolls, and dreams come true.

That night mine did, for, at the final curtain, Annette led me on stage to acknowledge the heady sound of applause from the audience.

But to me, the sweetest sound of all was the applause of friends: the dancers. At last, at the age of twenty-seven, I was a professional conductor – and the fun began.

Annette Page

'To Ken, who conducted my first
and many happy Coppélias'

CHAPTER 20

TRAINS, BOATS AND PLANES

Oh, Mr Porter!

My debut that night at the New Theatre, Oxford was the first step on the road, but now it was trains, boats and planes that were to take me around the world again – this time, not alone but in that warm-hearted family that was to be my home for the next five years, the Sadler's Wells Theatre Ballet.

Unlike most touring productions, which were usually not good enough to rate a season at a major theatre and so were 'forced to tour', the SWTB was a *tour de force*, bringing London standards of performance to the many theatres starved of first-class productions during the war. Our week would start with the Sunday 'train call'.

> *Oh, Mr Porter, what shall I do?*
> *I want to go to Birmingham,*
> *But they've taken me on to Crewe!*

J. Edgar Bruce – at 90, the oldest member of the cast of my first musical, *The Crooked Mile* – told me that he'd spent many hours on Crewe station in the required dress of a Victorian touring actor: grey striped trousers, black shoes with white spats, a frilly shirt with cravat and a frock coat. He carried all his worldly goods in a carpet bag because no actor worth his salt would sully the dignity of 'the profession' by carrying a brown paper parcel. It was accepted wisdom that, sooner or later, every actor would meet all his fellow thespians on Crewe station on the way to their next theatre.

> *J. Edgar Bruce's joke – one Victorian actor, on encountering another carrying a brown paper parcel: 'Hello, old chap. Moving?'*

I too was to spend many hours at Crewe, but we dressed for comfort, and there was always the warm station buffet to provide curly sandwiches made with yesterday's bread, Camp coffee from a bottle, tea from a large brown enamel pot, and sugar and milk stirred with the solitary spoon chained to the counter.

But there were the occasional lighter moments. One Sunday, as we waited for the slow train to Southport, which was already an hour late, Ted unpacked his clarinet and began Gershwin's 'Lady, Be Good'. Some of the other players joined in and, not to be outdone, Jack Lanchbery borrowed a fiddle and, although no Stéphane Grappelli, led the jazz quite tidily. It was the only time in all the years I knew him that I ever saw Jack play an instrument of any kind.

When our slow 'slam-door' finally pulled in, we were glad to get aboard and make the cold and cheerless carriages our home for the next few hours, some to sleep off the two Saturday performances, others to read the papers or burrow into a book, and a few to join in the orchestra in its favourite pastime: poker.

When we finally arrived at Southport, it was dark and raining. There is little more depressing than an out-of-season seaside town with wet pavements. The taxi dropped off Annette and Sarah Neil at their digs and then Walter Trevor and I began a search for somewhere to put our heads down for the week. Finally, the taxi driver ran out of ideas and dumped us at our last hope. The painted horror that opened the door said she could take us, and led us to a damp dark ground-floor room with a small double bed.

'It's the only one left, dear. Just put a bolster down the middle, and you won't even know he's there!' she said with a suggestive leer.

We did just that, and were both rescued the next day by Annette and Sarah and moved in with them. But in the 1950s, unmarried couples didn't share bedrooms, and Peggy van Praagh, who was responsible for her dancers' welfare (and the reputation of England's national ballet), would have put a stop to it anyway.

Although the lack of privacy, the living out of a suitcase, the landlady lottery, the rehearsals in cold halls and the five hours a day of playing an out-of-tune piano with no breaks for coffee had downsides, each evening I walked through the stage door into the magic world of the theatre, where everything in the ballet was beautiful and where, to the sound of glorious music, fairy tales were on offer.

Ballet girls on tour: everything was (not always)
beautiful in the ballet

We performed eight times a week, and I was there for all eight. Two were mine to conduct, and for the other six, I was on standby in case Jack was ill. Each performance was a conducting lesson, for he was a solid technician with a very clear beat, and known in the trade, from the authoritarian flick of the wrist, as a 'cuff-shaker'.

As his assistant conducting without orchestral rehearsal, it was vital that I used the same basic signals. If I changed the way he beat, I might produce an orchestral hiccough, and conductors are not allowed to make mistakes, especially young ones who might seem to be trying to be better than their master.

As Stephen Arlen's budget (and the size of the orchestra pit in the smaller theatres) limited us to a maximum of thirty-six, we got up to a few dodges to try to give the impression of having a much bigger orchestra. If Stephen said the orchestral budget could only pay for two horns, one dodge was to stuff a roll of cartridge paper into the barrel of the bassoon to lengthen its tube. This extra length produced the missing third horn note, vital in the overture to *Coppélia*. I doubt whether musicians today would be so co-operative, but all our musicians had to be flexible. Most of them had been unable to afford professional training at a full-time school of music, but had been taught by fathers who made their living in the many small orchestras up and down the country.

The last 'family-trained' musician I encountered was only a few years ago. A young viola player, taught by his famous uncle, was good enough to go straight to the first desk of the BBC Concert Orchestra.

Our tight little band had three players from one family, and all had been taught by their dad: Tom was the principal viola, brother Jack the first cello, and sister Elsie played the flute. They were very strong musically, but the brothers had a weakness: beer. They started drinking around 11am with a couple of pints of best bitter. Before the performance, they steadied their nerves with another couple, and afterwards relaxed with another two.

Their playing was, if anything, better for their bitter, but I once had to share a bedroom with Tom, and six pints a day do not make one a pleasant roommate.

Stanley, the principal trombone, was taught by his father, a member of a small seaside orchestra. Dad had a simple rule: no practice, no food. Too many wrong notes produced a cuff around the ear. However, Stanley sent his own son to the Royal Academy of Music, and he eventually played trombone in what I considered to be the finest orchestra I ever recorded with: the Philharmonia.

Our principal trumpet, Eddie, had been taught by the Salvation Army, and like all Salvationists, he was equally at ease playing on the pavement or collecting money in the pub. But he was happiest of all with us in the theatre pit.

Our only drummer, Jimmy, was a little weak on the xylophone, and sometimes a little too strong on the timpani – a common danger in small orchestras – but was otherwise very deft and able to play all the percussion parts in Walton's *Façade*, usually divided between two or three players in those orchestras that could afford them.

Keith and Ron were our clarinettists. Keith had been a Royal Marine bandsman and Ron a former medical orderly in the American Medical Corps, where he'd assisted in delicate operations under fire. So it was understandable that the rest of the woodwind trusted him to apply his skill to repairing their instruments.

The harpist, Peggy, was frequently with the Hallé, but since that orchestra gave most of their concerts in the winter season, she was free to work with us during the summer.

Our oboist, John, like all who struggle with that beautiful but capricious instrument, worried constantly about the reeds that he'd personally cut in the marshes of the Camargue and which he kept in a jam jar.

The thirteen string players were led by Garth, a very large and florid Australian. In his hands, his fiddle looked only half-size, but his solo in the second act of *Swan Lake* was as good as I ever heard. He'd been a War Reserve policeman in London, and one of his duties during the Blitz was to patrol the West End 'cottages' – public lavatories where gay men sought consolation.

I do not believe that Garth arrested anyone for what, in those days, was a criminal offence. On one occasion, he claimed to have slapped the bottom of a well-known actor, saying, 'Go home, you naughty boy. You'll never get your knighthood that way!' Garth loved being with the ballet boys, but never crossed the line (and the actor did get his knighthood!).

I remember my first orchestra with great affection and gratitude because they taught me so much about our mysterious art.

Unlike most touring companies, we enjoyed a varied musical

repertoire, and so there was less chance of that curse of the touring musician – boredom. Our most popular ballet was a full-length *Coppélia*, which always meant that Wednesday and Saturday matinées were packed with children and their mums. I had the special pleasure of conducting Annette's debut as Swanilda. She was perfect, and I got all her personal speeds right (I didn't dare do otherwise). The other programmes were mixed bills, starting with a 'white' ballet, so-called because of the short tutus used in the second act of *Swan Lake* and *Les Sylphides*. After the interval would come a story ballet, perhaps de Valois' own *The Rake's Progress* or *The Haunted Ballroom*, and, to end the performance, something light-hearted with good tunes, spirited dancing and comedy.

Easily our most successful finale was the Cranko-Mackerras adaptation of Sullivan's music, *Pineapple Poll*, commanded by Captain Belaye, and brilliantly danced by the handsome David Blair. *Poll* always brought the house down, especially when 'Auntie' is gloriously enthroned as Britannia (as seen on the back of an old penny) whilst the orchestra thunders out the overture to 'The Yeomen of the Guard'.

This repertoire was great fun, both to conduct and to play for piano rehearsals. I managed Ravel's *Valses Nobles et Sentimentales*, *Adelaide*, *Ma Mère l'Oye* and *La Belle et la Bête* and Debussy's *Isle des Syrènes* quite comfortably and to make recognisable Schumann's *Carnaval* (not an easy piece for those deficient in the finger department). Easier was Geoffrey Toye's *The Haunted Ballroom* (in which de Valois gave the young Margot Fonteyn her first role as the boy Young Treginnis) and de Valois' masterpiece *The Rake's Progress*, composed by the Sadler's Wells opera singer, Gavin Gordon. Add to all this Mozart's *Divertimento No 2 in D* for the ballet *Pastorale* and a new ballet, *Harlequin in April* (both choreographed by John Cranko, and the second one set to music by Beecham's protégé, Richard Arnell), and I was kept very busy.

In April, the Company was scheduled to tour Europe, but meanwhile the February train calls took us, as ever, to Crewe, and then onwards to Leeds, Birmingham, Manchester, Hanley and a town that nearly put paid to my blossoming career: Wolverhampton.

The view from my piano:
in rehearsal with Svetlana Beriosova

The theatres we played rarely had a room big enough for a full company rehearsal, so the assistant stage manager's first job on arriving in a town was to find us somewhere to rehearse.

In Wolverhampton, he found a church hall which, it being February, was cosily warmed by a coke stove and free of draughts. The ballet mistress, Barbara Fewster, took the morning class and rehearsals. All was normal, except that one or two of the girls didn't feel too well. As was often the case, I played straight through without a break until lunch-time, when Peggy van Praagh arrived to take over the rehearsal of *Swan Lake*. I'd had no lunch, but I carried on until, suddenly, the Swans began to silently collapse, rather like the soldiers in the scene in *Goldfinger* when Pussy Galore's girl pilots drop their nerve gas. Only one spoke, Doreen Tempest, who informed us in a shaky voice that she couldn't feel her legs or arms, but that she was all right. All right she was not. Peggy rang 999, and within minutes the fire brigade, ambulances and police arrived.

The stove was doused, all the windows opened and oxygen administered to the dozen or so pretty dancers by enthusiastic firemen until the ambulances, lights flashing and sirens screaming, removed everyone to Wolverhampton Hospital – everyone, that is, except me. I was still sitting at the piano.

'What about him?' the fire chief asked Peggy.

'Oh, don't worry about him,' she retorted. 'He's only the pianist!'

Fortunately for me, the chief ignored her, and off I went to hospital too.

Carbon monoxide poisoning has no symptoms except that sometimes the face turns cherry-red. However, the accepted wisdom is that, if you are red, you are almost dead. It was thought afterwards that the dancers collapsed so soon because they were physically active. I, on the other hand, was the only person to be in the hall for the whole day, so I was slowly absorbing the gas, and was very severely affected.

Nevertheless, it was my turn to conduct the evening performance, and so I got on with it. The near-tragedy was in all the papers, and we were mentioned on the BBC's 6 O'clock News, so the theatre was packed. The programme included *The Rake's Progress*. That night, the brothel was a bit short of girls (some had headaches, which is rare in real brothels, I imagine), but filling in for the sick dancers were two old tarts: the tall and elegant ballet mistress, Barbara Fewster, and, in a dress that showed magnificent cleavage, Peggy van Praagh, who danced her socks (and very nearly her top) off. They both joined the younger tarts and, to the accompaniment of our Salvation Army trumpeter, mimed the traditional words of bawdy song, 'Oh, deary me, I do want a pee, and I don't much care if the audience see!'

That night, Wolverhampton saw something very special. However, there was a lip-reader in the audience, who later wrote to de Valois, and henceforth the mimed words were changed to 'Oh deary me, I do want my tea.' Hardly the thoughts of a bawdy tart!

When the results of my hospital tests appeared the next day, it seemed that I had been more than halfway to a sudden and fatal collapse, so I was sent home where, for the next two weeks, I was bedridden and injected twice a day with penicillin by the district nurse. My arms and legs swelled so much that I resembled the Michelin Man, and I had to be fed by from my old tin plate by the kindly ladies of the meals on wheels service.

I recovered in time to put my new-found conducting skills to the test in the refining fires of my first encounters with the orchestras of Europe's leading opera houses.

CHAPTER 21

BOATS AND TRAINS

Mayhem in Munich

In 1940 the Sadler's Wells Ballet had escaped from Holland and the advancing Germans by just thirty minutes. If the Company had not got away by the skin of its teeth and had been captured, I've often wondered what the Nazis might have done with – or to – Frederick Ashton, Margot Fonteyn, Robert Helpmann, Constant Lambert and Ninette de Valois. I doubt if the Sadler's Wells Ballet as we know it would have survived.

The Hague, 1940

Left to right: Madame van Beek, Ninette de Valois, Robert Helpmann, Mary Hohner, Margot Fonteyn, June Brae, Frederick Ashton and Pamela May

But it did, and even under the difficult wartime conditions, the Company managed to add no less than seventeen new productions to its repertoire: Frederick Ashton's *Dante Sonata*, *Façade* and *The Wise Virgins*; Robert Helpmann's *Hamlet* and *Miracle in the Gorbals*; and Ninette de Valois' *Orpheus and Euridice*.

In the post-war years of 1946 to 1954, the dynamic de Valois had masterminded no less than fifty-four revivals and new ballets – an achievement greater than Diaghilev's.

At the end of the war, Sadler's Wells Ballet returned to tour the Low Countries and northern Germany, but in April 1953 it was the Junior Company's turn, when the Sadler's Wells Theatre Ballet sailed for Holland, Belgium and (for the first time since the war) southern Germany and those cities closely associated with the Nazi movement: Nuremberg and Munich. It was to prove a tough assignment.

As we often gave only one or two performances in each city, and considerable distances were involved (always by train), the schedule meant that, for the first time, I had the opportunity to take total musical responsibility for almost half of our performances: a big leap forward in my career. I would be sent ahead to the next theatre to rehearse its orchestra in advance. Those musicians would get to know me at rehearsal, but the actual performance might then be conducted by Jack – a stranger to them. Meanwhile, I would have moved on to the next city. Occasionally, I conducted an orchestra prepared by Jack, and sometimes the orchestra which I had rehearsed.

It was a great experience to conduct the orchestras of Europe's finest opera houses and to hear, for the first time, the glorious sound of the original orchestrations, and not the watered-down versions of our touring band.

Then, as now, The Hague, Amsterdam and Rotterdam Opera House orchestras were happy to rehearse in English, which was a language forbidden during the German occupation. In Belgium, my French proved adequate for the Orchestra of the Theatre de la Monnaie in Brussels, in Antwerp, and at the Liège Opera House, where I was both to rehearse and conduct the performance.

On the afternoon before my Liège rehearsal, I set off from Rotterdam to cross the border into Belgium. Our manager, Peter

Banks, had given me an allowance of five pounds to cover my return rail journey of a hundred and fifty miles and the cost of a room and meals at the hotel, but nothing for porters or taxis, and I was expected to manhandle the large wicker basket of music myself.

A suspicious Belgian Customs Officer insisted I unpack the skip. He inspected the music and asked me what instrument I played. Proudly, I showed him my little white stick.

'You won't play much with that!' he said.

'No,' I replied, 'but it's a magic stick – I wave it and it makes *other* people play!'

He let me into Belgium.

My rehearsal next morning was at 9am, and from the window of the Hotel Angleterre opposite the Opera House, I watched the orchestra stub out their cigarettes and disappear into the theatre, leaving the square empty except for me, my basket, and an anxious-looking orchestral manager who, looking remarkably like Hercule Poirot, was pacing up and down nervously.

I dragged the basket across the square over to him, sat on it and spoke to him.

'Bonjour, Monsieur. Ici la musique pour la répétition.'

'Oui, oui, oui,' he responded impatiently, 'mais où est le chef d'orchestre?'

Straightening my aching back and mopping my sweating brow, I replied:

'Ici! Moi! Je suis le chef d'orchestre!'

I'm sure that under his breath he murmured 'Merde', but with great courtesy he led me to a plush dressing room and, viewing my sweating brow, tactfully asked if I would like a shower. This was the first time I'd encountered the consideration afforded to conductors in Europe.

The orchestra of the Liège Opera House included many professors from the Conservatoire, where the great violinist Ysaÿe had founded his school of string playing and where César Franck, Vieuxtemps and many international musicians had received their first training.

It was a red-hot band.

One must remember that, in these post-war years, real

conductors had white hair and did not lug large baskets about; nevertheless, the director introduced me as the conductor of the '*bien connu*' Sadler's Wells Theatre Ballet, and from the very first notes, the professors showed their worth.

I began with *Pineapple Poll*, and it will come as no surprise that they sight-read Sullivan's music perfectly. Delighted, I asked the leader of the orchestra if they'd played *Poll* before. He smiled and gently put me down with the comment: 'This is not the sort of music we usually play.' However, I believe the players let their hair down and had fun with Charlie Mackerras' brilliant arrangements, and when we tackled *Harlequin in April* and Bizet's *Symphony in C (Assembly Ball)*, respectability was restored and we parted good friends.

The librarian packed the music – which was vital for that evening's performance in Antwerp – and took me to the station. Now I was on my own again, and because what was left of the five pounds did not cover even a second-class fare, I travelled with the farmers and their poultry on their way to market, sitting on the wooden slatted seats of a Belgian third-class compartment. Once again, I was an English conductor: below the salt.

In 18th century Salzburg – in common with the custom of the times – its Prince Archbishop sat at the head of the communal dining table, with easy access to valuable salt. But he seated Mozart well down the table: a lowly position, and a reminder to Mozart that he was only a servant.

At Antwerp station, and with the help of a porter who spoke English like a Cockney, I arrived at the Opera House twenty minutes before the performance, still dragging my skip, where Jack was anxiously awaiting the music.

'Where the hell have you been?' he demanded.

'What have you done with the five pounds?' said Peter Banks, as he paid off the taxi.

I remembered the lovely sound of the Liège Orchestra and held my peace and my temper – something I found almost impossible in my first encounter with a German orchestra in Munich, one of the RAF's prime targets.

The Bavarian National Theatre had been bombed by the

Allies. On the way to the rehearsal room, as I picked my way through the burnt-out shell of a once-beautiful auditorium, now open to the sky, its red plush seats soaked with rain and the gold decor stained with smoke, I felt some regret. But remembering how, in Croydon, I'd been able to read a newspaper by the light of London ablaze, not too much!

Munich had seen the birth of the Nazi party, and I was the first English conductor with whom the orchestra had worked since well before the war, so I steeled myself for a rough ride. As is the continental custom, the orchestra stood for my entrance. Most of the players were of an age where they might have been members of the German Forces, and as I was obviously of military age myself, to say that the atmosphere was icy would be to exaggerate its warmth.

The syllabus of my wartime education did not include studying German. Indeed, it was considered to be defeatist to do so. The Germans, on the other hand, were taught English, probably the better to control their planned occupation of Britain. My only German, apart from the numbers and 'Yes' and 'No', had therefore been gleaned from wartime films in which the evil Nazis spoke English with heavy accents and there was frequent use of 'Jawohl!' (Yes indeed!).

Although conducting is the art of gesture and few words, explanations *are* sometime necessary, and these proved impossible to convey to this sulky band. I avoided English, but used a cocktail of very basic German, and some Italian and French. But my tact was misinterpreted, and the orchestra's unhelpful attitude remained the same. There was much chit-chat in German and a 'go-slow' policy, so that I soon realised there was little chance of getting the music ready for the performance.

We lumbered our way through the Bizet *Symphony in C* and I announced the next music for the ballet *Pastorale*: Mozart's *Divertimento No. 2 in D*.

As I raised my baton, suddenly a horn player stood up. In perfect English, he said, 'I have no music. May I go home?'

Every eye was suddenly on me. Perhaps all the rumours that I'd heard of 'How to handle a German' affected the way I reacted, but I was worried, and now angry.

In my best authoritarian English I declared, 'No, you may

not. You are German and you know that your great composer wrote this divertimento for four horns.'

I paused and, looking around, went on: 'If you all think we have any chance of a performance together, you are mistaken, and I have no intention of even trying!'

With that, I broke my baton in two, threw it down and stalked out, on my way to God knows where.

Now I had the orchestra's full attention.

I had hardly reached the door when the leader caught up with me and, in English, asked me to return with a promise that 'things would go better'.

They did!

There's no doubt that my outburst produced results. I could understand the orchestra's initial hostility towards this Englishman, who might have been the pilot of the Lancaster that dropped the bomb on their opera house. At the end of a now very good rehearsal, the principal cellist asked my opinion of his instrument, bought for him by the local villagers when he had been a prisoner of war in England.

Music won that one!

But it was in Nuremburg that the artistic direction of the Sadler's Wells Theatre Ballet expected too much – not of the German orchestra, but of the audience. Like most of my generation, Nuremburg represented to me the heartland of the National Socialist Republic, with its mass rallies of tens of thousands of uniformed Nazis flying swastikas and responding to the increasing exhortations of Adolf Hitler with roars of 'Sieg Heil' and the threatening 'Deutschland Über Alles'. A chilling sound: once heard, never forgotten.

The evening began well with Frederick Ashton's charming 1933 ballet to the music of Auber, *Les Rendezvous*. It was followed by the mysterious and serious *Harlequin in April*, which takes place in the ruins of a theatre, and symbolises the frustrating struggle for life in spring. It ends unhappily, and its symbolism of decay gripped our German audiences, always producing lengthy and serious applause. Not so our finale, calculated to send the audience home in high spirits: *Pineapple Poll*.

Oh dear!

This frivolous tale of sailors' girls who, tired of being left ashore, sail as stowaways on *HMS Hot Cross Bun* produced a few laughs, but when *Poll's* Auntie is 'gloriously enthroned as Britannia' to Sullivan's patriotic 'Yeomen of the Guard' and the Union Jack is unfurled (a moment which always produced applause at home), a chill spread through the house, and we ended the ballet in total silence.

The audience left the theatre without a sound – not even a word of protest – and who could blame them? Imagine that the Germans had won the war and had brought to a defeated England a ballet of swastika-waving Nazis, dancing a homage to Hitler to the music of Wagner.

Fifty years later, the American actor and writer Mel Brooks capitalised on such an unthinkable idea with 'The Producers', in which a chorus line of jack-booted girls in black leather swastika armbands and whips are partnered by gay Nazi storm troopers in the big production number, 'Springtime for Hitler'. Accused by some of tastelessness, Brooks replied that the best way of coping with evil was to ridicule it, and who was more entitled to make fun of Hitler than a Jew?

In Frankfurt, the bombed theatre having not yet been rebuilt, we played in a vast sports stadium with an orchestra of freelance musicians. In Hanover, the theatre orchestra played very well, and there was even some applause for *Poll*. After all, Britain had long been ruled by Hanoverians, and we all thought of George Handel as British.

The theatre in our next stop, Hamburg, had been almost destroyed during the war, and so we performed in the re-built Hagenbeck Zoo. All of the animals had been killed on the night of 24th July, 1943, but some of the cages of their successors had been turned into dressing rooms, which were rather smelly. The performances were well-received, and it was only during the quiet music that one could hear the distant sound of the displaced animals' objections. The orchestra was pretty good, but it was a different story in Bremen, where I encountered a strange band of musicians. They were quite willing, but after a few bars of *Casse-Noisette*, the leader informed me that our music was much too hard for them. They were a light orchestra, and all at sea with music as difficult as Tchaikovsky! But I had to press on until, with 'The Dance of the Sugar Plum Fairy' (which sounded more like a 'Victoria Plum Fairy'), we ground to a halt. Every celeste player in the world knows it – every player except, it seemed, in Bremen. This chap was the Les Dawson of the celeste world, who kept playing one very obvious and funny wrong note. I pointed it out and when, after he'd got it wrong for the third time, I eventually played it for him, he replied vigorously, 'Ja! Ja! Ich verstehen!' and continued as before.

I thought he might have been mocking this young English conductor, but at the performance it was no better, and Elaine Fifield giggled her way through a travesty of the famous music. Elaine was a great giggler and was married to Jack Lanchbery, who had a well-developed sense of humour. Sometimes I had to share a dressing room with them, but on the last night of the tour in Cologne, Jack and Fifi had the Opera House's star dressing room to themselves. It had been occupied the night before by a large Wagnerian soprano, who had left behind her blonde wig and a bottle of brandy.

It is customary on the last night of a long tour that performers let their hair down a little, but on her entrance in Ashton's ballet, *Les Rendezvous*, it was revealed that our perfect, small-boned ballerina Fifi had concealed her dark locks beneath the large Wagnerian wig and – not to put too fine a point on it – had drink taken! She only managed one giggling arabesque before falling flat on her face for, as every toper knows, balance and booze are incompatible.

It says much for ballet discipline that not one of the eight couples on stage showed any signs of anything being amiss, but down came the curtain, up went the house lights, and the theatre manager made apologies for the sudden indisposition of Miss Fifield.

We were now a thirty-minute ballet short, so I passed around the orchestral parts of the Mozart *Divertimento*, the lights dimmed, and we finished the evening with Cranko's unrehearsed *Pastorale*. A remarkable ending to a memorable tour, which gave me the chance to conduct and speak for myself – priceless experience, which I was to put to good use over the coming years.

Fifi's lapse that night in Cologne was unique, and during my many years of conducting ballet, I never saw its like repeated. To be truthful, I think Jack's earthy sense of humour had got the better of him and he had led his poor wife astray. In the following year, 1954, Madame moved Elaine Fifield on to the Sadler's Wells Company at Covent Garden, leaving husband Jack with the Theatre Ballet.

CHAPTER 22

AND PLANES

Entebbe

Although it was good to get home to St George's Square and to unpack my suitcase, the Company was back to sharing the theatre with the Sadler's Wells Opera, and was only giving two or three performances a week, all of which Jack conducted. But there was no let-up in my workload. I was still the only Indian in Jack's tribe, so I played everything: classes, repertoire rehearsals and all the new ballets that de Valois had planned for this young and energetic company.

The role of the ballet pianist was becoming increasingly difficult. The dear old 'maid of all work' – the piano – could deal adequately with the music of Tchaikovsky, Delibes, Chopin and the like, but since Stravinsky's ground-breaking *The Rite of Spring*, ballet music had changed for ever. The piano was becoming much less effective at giving a workable impression of the modern music which we were using.

At rehearsals of *The Rite*, the Diaghilev Company had the benefit of Stravinsky and conductor Ansermet sitting at one piano, using all of their twenty fingers to produce a recognisable impression of the music, but here was I trying to do the same with only nine.

The first new ballet which I had to get to grips with was by choreographer Alfred Rodrigues with music by Welsh composer Denis Apivor: *Bodas de Sangre* ('Blood Wedding'). Based on Lorca's story of the love between a runaway young Spanish bride-to-be and an older married man, it was the perfect subject for Rodrigues, who had a real feel for the Latin passion. However, Dennis Apivor deliberately avoided music with a Spanish flavour (castanets were out), and he brought a native Welsh gloom to his score. Much of it was without a recognisable key-centre (atonal) and relied on texture, rather than tune. A pianist can't create much effect with only one note, but the overture to *Blood Wedding* begins with just that – a B natural played as quietly as possible by the full orchestra, which then crescendoes to pain level as the curtain rises. On the first night, it became so loud that a lady horn player slid to the floor in a dead faint.

However not all of the new ballets scores were as dramatic. *The Great Detective* was a brave try at transferring the cerebrations of Sherlock Holmes and his arch-enemy, Moriarty, to the dance. This music was by Richard Arnell, and it was comparatively simple in texture. How could it be anything else, for he was the recommendation of Sir Thomas Beecham, who, when asked if he'd ever conducted any music by Stockhausen, replied: 'No, but I once trod in some.'

The choreographer was a former Sadler's Wells dancer, Margaret Dale, and she gave the role of Sherlock Holmes to the young Kenneth MacMillan, who, wearing a deerstalker and smoking a curly pipe, leapt about in knickerbockers, showing his long legs to advantage. Maggie included a scene in a mortuary, a *pas de deux* of deduction and a dance for boxers and gorillas. It was fun, but not destined for a long life.

Margaret Dale found her true calling as the BBC's first Director of Ballet. She told me that her one televised performance of 'Sleeping Beauty' was seen by more people than the total of all the theatre audiences since 1890.

I enjoyed the challenge of coping with the new music, but I was desperate to get back on the rostrum – particularly when I shared a pint in The Shakespeare with Alexander Gibson, who was conducting *La Bohème*, and Charles Mackerras, who was conducting *Carmen*. I asked the Musical Director, James Robertson, if there was any chance of joining the opera staff. After all, I had already coached Britten's *Albert Herring*, but he, in a somewhat patronising manner, told me that opera was packed with traditions of performance – something which I would need a lifetime to learn.

Never mind, I thought, the ballet needs me, and so I settled down to wait for my next appearance on the rostrum, which, strangely, was linked to a game I had played during the war at a party in Manchester whilst awaiting flying training.

With so many having 'gone on ahead' in the war, there was a lot of interest as to where they'd gone, and our game was a half-serious attempt to contact the other world. We sat at a table with the letters of the alphabet arranged in a circle. The lights were dimmed and, resting our fingers lightly on an upturned wine glass, someone whispered: 'Is there anyone there?'

The glass moved to 'Yes'.

To the second question, 'Who is our spirit guide?' it slowly spelt 'G… O… D.'

That was too much for some, who wanted to give up, but when I pointed out to whoever was moving the glass (strongly denied by all) that 'god' was a palindrome of 'dog', we continued.

Then I asked whether I might ever become a conductor. The glass nearly shot off the table as it answered 'Yes', and to my 'Where?,' it raced round the letters spelling out 'A… F… R… I… C… A.'

We laughed at this nonsensical answer, and yet, ten years after that game, I was on my way down to the small Surrey airport of Blackbush to conduct in Africa.

1953 was the year of Cecil Rhodes' centenary, and to commemorate this great man (who, it is said, won a great slice of Africa by curing King Lobengula of toothache), the Rhodesians had organised an international exhibition. We were to be part of the celebrations which had included performances by the Covent Garden Opera and concerts with the Hallé Orchestra, conducted by Sir John Barbirolli. The good news was that most of the Hallé were staying on to play for us. The Rhodesians were then still very loyal 'colonials'. Their new hotel and a theatre were named after Queen Victoria, and the exhibition had been opened by the Queen Mother.

The flight out by Dakota meant an overnight stop at Entebbe, where we were taken to the Victoria Falls, but after a walk through the mists of the rain forest, we came back to find the bus had been invaded by baboons – most of them with their young, and very dangerous. That sorted, we flew on to Buluwayo, where I joined Annette and the dancers in an old colonial hotel, staffed by genial Africans who, entirely overwhelmed by the prospect of feeding forty at a time, stood by smiling as we took over the kitchens and cooked for ourselves.

It was as well that we didn't go to the new Victoria hotel, for the lifts didn't work, and the English Tea Garden was delightful, as long as one didn't encounter the resident black mambas, reluctant to give over their habitat to the visitors' afternoon tea and cucumber sandwiches.

The new theatre was very well built, but it had to be checked nightly for snakes, rats and spiders – particularly frightening to our girls, most of whom felt threatened by even the small and entirely innocent English spiders which they might find at home in the bath. But when the house-lights dimmed and the music began, Dr Theatre again worked his magic, and the perils of backstage were forgotten.

Our programmes had been completely sold out well in advance, and two young men who'd ridden a motorcycle for nearly three hundred miles, only to be turned away at the box office, were so disappointed that I arranged for them to watch from the wings – a pleasant surprise, which turned out to be more than they expected.

At the afternoon orchestral rehearsal of *Pineapple Poll*, we ran into a technical problem. The finale begins when one of the sailors' sweethearts mistakenly fires a cannon and the jolly 'Jill Tars' shake with fear. The exploding thunder-flash had not been permitted aboard the aircraft, and without the big bang there, the finale would merely fizz.

'Don't worry,' said the Rhodesian assistant stage manager. 'I'll give you the bang tonight!' And so he did. Right on cue, he fired a gun big enough to kill an elephant into a huge barrel of sawdust. There was an enormous explosion, and the ASM and the two motorcyclists disappeared in a yellow fountain, which then slowly descended, covering everyone on stage. In the pit, the Hallé Theatre Orchestra and I battled our way through bravely as the dancers gradually began shaking, not with fear but with laughter, and hoisted a sawdust Britannia. The audience knew that something out of the ordinary had happened, but the sight of the Union flag produced tremendous applause.

The significance of this anecdote is apparent when one remembers that in 1965, the ex-RAF fighter pilot and Rhodesian Prime Minister Ian Smith declared independence from the 'Mother Country', and the Union Flag never flew again.

The exhibition was a great success, and on our last night, the beautiful Princess Margaret came to see us. She was a great friend of the ballet.

The next morning, we boarded the Airwork Dakota, bound for Blackbush. But I wasn't to make it. Bulawayo is on a dusty plateau over four thousand feet above sea-level, and, when the sun goes down, the sudden and massive drop in temperature, combined with the red dust, can produce 'Bulawayo throat'. I made it as far as Entebbe, where I consulted the hotel doctor – a useless fellow who, without bothering to examine me, offered to syringe my ears. I knew from bitter experience that would only make matters worse, so I refused, and his revenge was to declare to the captain that I was fit to fly. Being stranded in Entebbe in the care of that same doctor, at my own expense, was not an option, so I had no choice but to board the Dakota. The captain promised to climb and descend very gradually, but what young pilot could resist the temptation to show his young and pretty passengers (and that's just the girls) the wonders of the wild at close quarters? His first dive to within a hundred feet of the ground scattered herds of elephants, wildebeests and giraffes and produced cries of wonder.

It was a wonderful experience for all – except me, for I'd popped an ear drum. When we landed at our next stop – Khartoum – I was taken to hospital, leaving Annette and the Company to their trip back to London and a month's holiday.

Khartoum is where the White Nile from the desert and the Blue Nile from the mountains meet to form the shape of an elephant's head – in Arabic: 'Khartoum'. I've frequently felt lonely, but Khartoum was something else. The daytime temperatures were around 130-140°F, and in my hospital room, a mere 102°F. I only obtained some relief by spending most of the day in a lukewarm bath (the water wouldn't run cold).

I was looked after by a Scottish doctor who taught at the Kitchener School of Medicine, and he introduced me to his friend, a professor of English at the Gordon Memorial College. As my ear gradually improved, I was taken under the wing of the Bishop of Khartoum, Agostino Baroni, whose cathedral was, surprisingly in this land of Islam, built in the Byzantine style. Being a walking patient, and the Bishop speaking fluent Arabic, he took me to Omdurman – the only completely 'native' city, where the daily temperature averages 150°F and where it never rains.

My only knowledge of this part of the world was the story of General Gordon's death at the hands of a 'whirling dervish'. But here I was at the scene of the great, final Battle of the Nile where, in 1898, a classic cavalry charge by the 21st Lancers was led by Lieutenant Winston Churchill and where, finally, the Mhadi's army was defeated with the loss of twenty thousand men.

In 1961 I conducted Frank Cordell's excellent music for the film 'Khartoum' with Laurence Olivier and Charlton Heston. Remembering how hot I'd been there helped a lot, having lived on the actual location of the film.

As my traveller's cheques were not valid in the Sudan, I walked everywhere – a dangerous business, for in these extreme temperatures, if the body runs out of potassium, one is prone to sudden heart failure. The three attractions in Khartoum were the cemetery, which had a few patches of grass, the open air cinema (which I couldn't afford) and the zoo. It was a very unusual zoo. Many of the animals wandered about freely, with no fear, including shoe-billed storks, and a puma and his companion: a tiny mouse-deer, a full eighteen inches tall. Newly-captured in Ethiopia and on his way to a European zoo was a lion, who paced up and down a small cage, exhibiting great rage. He fixed me with angry eyes, turned his back, lifted his leg and missed me by a whisker with a stream of steaming urine – his only weapon. He was magnificent, and I was sad to think that he'd probably end his days in a cage, toothless and without dignity.

I was now fit enough to fly home, but Sadler's Wells had closed for a month's holiday, and here I was in the hottest city in the world, with no money and no one to turn to. I asked Bishop Baroni (what a nice fellow he was) to take me to the airport, and there I presented myself at the British Overseas Airways Office as the Musical Director of the Sadler's Wells Ballet. This was a desperate lie, but as I was accompanied by a bishop, my statement that, as a senior official of the Company, I could authorise my own flight, was accepted (and no one is going to lie in the presence of a bishop, are they?). I was booked on the next afternoon flight on the BOAC Comet G-ALYP from Khartoum to Heathrow.

At last, I was on my way.

I waited for the Bishop to drive me to the airport, but everything changed when he arrived earlier than planned to tell me that the very last charter Airwork Dakota flight back to Blackbush was expected in an hour, and that there was sure to be room for me if we hurried. Hurry we did, but we arrived to see the G-AMZD taxiing out for take-off. I waved frantically at Maryon Lane, who'd stayed on to meet her family in Zululand. She smiled and waved back, and what I did next can only show the depth of my desperation.

I ran out in front of the Dakota and gave the international signal to stop engines (arms crossed and waved above the head – my RAF training again). I stood my ground, the pilot throttled back, and after a radio message from the Bishop, he opened the door and I was hauled aboard.

I was lucky not to fly home in a Comet, for the aircraft which I'd booked myself on later crashed into the sea off the Island of Elba with the loss of all on board.

There had been a couple of unexplained Comet disappearances, but after G-ALYP, exhaustive underwater tests carried out, and it was discovered that, under the enormous pressure differentials found at high altitudes, the window seals gave way.

Back from holiday, the Company got busy on *Carte Blanche*, a ballet by Walter Gore who'd been the original Rake in de Valois' *The Rake's Progress*. We'd worked together in *Ballet for Beginners*, but *Carte Blanche* – a 'fantastical burlesque' about nothing in particular – perfectly suited his piquant personality, and was great fun.

Anything went. Tutus descended on wires, three 'zanies' brought on a statue, which they took to pieces, and ancient

Egyptians appeared, carrying vases and looking lost. Then a full-blown circus arrived: clowns, tight-rope walkers, trapeze artists, a pantomime horse, and a puzzled looking male dancer in white tights appeared, tinkled a little bell and left the stage looking for someone or something.

It was a great success, and with two new ballets in our repertoire, we began the last tour before what promised to be a lonely Christmas, until Annette invited me to the Page family home for Christmas Day.

CHAPTER 23

BOATS AGAIN

A night with the Mother Superior

Christmas Day at Hatch End with Annette's charming family was fun. Her sister, Gillian, numerous cousins and her aunts, together with her bank inspector father and sporty mother, made for a very jolly day. It was a great contrast to the Christmas before, which I spent alone in my basement flat roasting a pigeon – all that was left on the Dolphin Square butcher's slab late on Christmas Eve. When I wished my fellow shopper, Bud Flanagan, the compliments of the season, spying the pigeon, he'd said, 'Hello Ken. Having a party?'

The New Year saw me hard at work. Always on the look-out for new talent, de Valois had given her blessing to the 'Sunday Experimental Group' where, on Sundays, choreographers and composers could show their work to private audiences at the Sadler's Wells Theatre – critics, balletomanes and other leaders of the world of dance.

An aspiring choreographer at Covent Garden and dancer, Gilbert Vernon, asked me if I'd like to write the score for a ballet called *Chiaroscuro* in which Annette was to dance the leading role. *Chiaroscuro* became a labour of love in every sense.

I was pleased with my music for her romantic *pas de deux* with David Blair, a 'Soldier's Dance' for Donald Britten, and a 'Dance for Puck' for Johaar Mosaval – a small man with great speed and precision, the Wayne Sleep of his day. Although *Chiaroscuro* went well, it was simply a set of dances to the music of two pianos, and was quite overshadowed by a ballet from Kenneth MacMillan: *Laiderette* ('The Little Ugly One'), which was danced by Maryon Lane to an orchestral recording of Frank Martin's *Petite Symphonie Concertante*. *Laiderette* is the story of a young girl, Pierrot, an ugly duckling, who, envying some young and beautiful people on their way to a masked ball, borrows a mask, gate-crashes the party and dances with a handsome young man. But in a *coup de théâtre*, she is unmasked, revealing that, not only is she ugly, she is also completely bald.

The following year, *Laiderette* was taken into the repertoire of the Ballet Rambert. 'Mim' Rambert had obviously been in the audience that Sunday afternoon.

My music was well-received, and Dennis Apivor told me I should write more – high praise indeed, for composers are not given to complimenting their colleagues (Benjamin Britten considered Puccini a bad composer).

But there was no time for any private work, for I was involved for several hours a day in *The Lady and the Fool*.

The 'Lady' was the gorgeous Svetlana Beriosova – quite simply one of the most beautiful women ever to grace the ballet stage. She was perfectly cast by Cranko as the aristocratic La Capriossa who, in spite of having the world at her feet, is a bit daft, and falls in love with a tall and impoverished clown, Moondog (Kenneth MacMillan and his long legs again).

Moondog has a tiny pal: the sad clown, Bootface (Johaar Mosaval), who is abandoned when the lovers run away together. But all ends well, for the lovers return, and all three curl up together on a park bench – a *ménage à trois* not to everyone's taste.

Unlike Sullivan, whose orchestrations were always on the thin side and benefitted from Charlie's augmentation, Verdi's had to be reduced to fit our touring band. The orchestra did its best, even with the 'Grand Adage', which Charlie had marked *Quasi Melachrino* ('extra schmaltzy'). To successfully sound like George Melachrino's sixty string players when one was only fielding fifteen would have been an accountant's dream. Nevertheless, on 25th February, 1954 in Oxford, Mackerras conducted our small band on the first night, and everyone came up from London to see if this new ballet could rival the success of *Poll*.

I took over the second performance, a matinée – traditionally, a difficult occasion when, with the tension of first night over, everyone relaxes, and sometimes too much. But all went well, and looking back, I'm very pleased to have worked so closely with John and Charles on a ballet which, as I write over fifty years later, is still in the Royal Ballet's repertoire.

During the weeks following *Lady*, we were busy with yet another new ballet, *Café des Sports*, which was to be given its first performance on the coming tour of South Africa. This time, Rodrigues had moved away from the atonal music of Dennis Apivor to someone known more for his chatty and entertaining talks about music than as a composer: Anthony Hopkins. The story, such as it was, was based on a cycle race, the Tour de France. It centred on the reactions of the patrons of a café to the competitors who, led by the traditional yellow jersey, try to create all the excitement of the real thing without actually moving. Not exactly a great theatrical moment.

At least *Café* was colourful and designed by the 'in' young artist, Jack Taylor. Tony Hopkins showed his party trick again and played Beethoven's *Für Elise* with his back to the piano. Unfortunately, his tuneful and witty score has not survived.

At this point in my career, provincial touring was still fun, but those of us in relationships had a tough time and would go to almost any lengths to get some privacy. That winter of 1954, we had a week at the Stratford Memorial Theatre, and I was determined to get away somewhere with Annette – so determined that, after the performance, I hired a clapped-out Morris for the weekend, and we drove through heavy falls of snow to Birmingham.

The secret escape from Peggy's watchful eyes at Stratford and the drive through the beautiful snowy Warwickshire countryside were very romantic. On the way back to Stratford, I stopped the car in the snow to talk about 'us'. I would have liked to have asked Annette to marry me, but I was tremendously aware of how little I had to offer – no family, no home, no relations, and a job dependent on the next contract. How could I match her rich family life and promising future? The moment came and went, killed by my silence.

The snows melted, spring blossomed and in April, the Sadler's Wells Theatre Ballet embarked the *Edinburgh Castle* for a three-month tour of South Africa.

The last time I'd been at sea had been on the *Rangitiki* in a six-berth cabin, but on this trip I shared with the Czech dancer Miro Zolan. Miro was multi-talented, and when I mentioned a troublesome tooth, he opened a small, sinister-looking case to reveal a set of dental instruments. He assured me that, when he had been in a Russian prison camp, he'd carried out successful dental work on his fellow prisoners.

My tooth improved dramatically.

Dancer and dentist – quite a combination for a man who had also choreographed a ballet to his own music for the Borovansky Company in Australia.

Life aboard was great fun, and, compared with our usual tough schedule, the voyage looked like being a two-week holiday. But dancers must be kept in top form physically, and Peggy wasn't going to let anybody stiffen up. As the *Edinburgh Castle* was not a pleasure cruiser but principally a cargo carrier, the only place to rehearse was on the boat deck. Lifeboats not being equipped with pianos, as the ship rolled and pitched, the dancers held on to davits and rails and stretched to the music of 'Life on the Ocean Wave', 'High over the Waves', 'The Sailor's Hornpipe' and any other nautical music I could remember, played on a 120 bass Soprani Piano Accordion, which I'd borrowed from one of the ship's crew. Rehearsals of *Pineapple Poll* took on added reality as the cast of *HMS Hot Cross Bun* staggered about trying to keep their balance. It was a little dangerous, but very entertaining, and we soon had an audience of passengers and crew enjoying watching make-believe girl sailors dance to Sullivan's jolly music, played by a piano accordion on a real ship.

Although our tourist-class area should have been off limits to the first-class passengers, the captain turned a blind eye to the 'toffs' spending their evenings with a famous ballet company. We all mixed very well, and one night the SWTB put on a cabaret and sang an opening number, cobbled together for the occasion:

How do you do, everyone. How do!
How do you do-do-dee-do.
We're glad to see you here. Well rather!
Hope you're feeling in the pink and –
How's your father!!
(Shades of Ralph Reader's 'Gang Show')

Our fellow passengers included the South African concert pianist, Albie Louw, on his way home to play the Tchaikovsky

Piano Concerto with the South African Broadcasting Orchestra, and Sir Francis Dashwood, a descendant of the aristocrat who founded the 'Hell-Fire Club' of Medmenham, where the aristocratic libertines of the 18th century (including American President Benjamin Franklin), masquerading as monks, caroused with prostitutes and thrill-seeking high society ladies dressed as nuns.

Francis came to our fancy-dress dance as half-man, half-woman. From the front, complete with dark glasses, a white stick and chequered pantaloons, he portrayed a blind Venetian. From the back he wore a dress covered in white slats – a Venetian blind. Although he was unable to dance in this peculiar get-up, he eyed the girls, but, not surprisingly, without success.

The crew, particularly those under the wing of the 'Mother Superior' (the leading gay sailor), were very happy to serve us in every way. One good-looking and married blond waiter had a brief encounter with one of our male dancers (later to rise to a very high rank in the Royal Ballet), but said he felt no guilt because, the affair being with a man, he remained faithful to his wife.

On the last night of the voyage, the 'Mother Superior' hosted a great party in the crew's quarters, and so ended a voyage to remember on a very happy ship.

Three weeks after sailing from Southampton, and with the newly-formed South African Broadcasting Corporation Orchestra in the pit, we opened in the Alhambra Theatre, Johannesburg to a great welcome from a first-night audience, which included Danny Kaye. His new film *Knock on Wood* (about a ventriloquist who loses control of his dummy) was showing at the Coliseum, and he was rehearsing his one-man show at His Majesty's Theatre, just across the road from us. He'd had great success with Frank Loesser's *Hans Christian Anderson*, in which Renée Jeanmaire and Roland Petit had danced a seven-minute ballet based on *The Little Mermaid*, so he must have wanted to see what we were like.

He came to our first-night party and became a Company friend, often slipping across the road to our theatre and watching from the wings. I think he'd taken a fancy to Annette, for he always seemed to be there when she was on.

The Company was fêted royally each night: flowers at the curtain calls, and after each performance, parties under the stars, 'vlees brie' (barbecues) and the ubiquitous brandy and ginger ale.

But soon, a few of us grew tired of the constant round, and Maryon Lane, 'Scatty' O'Reilly, Annette and I went back to supper each night with Sue-Anne and Denny and their husbands at their beautiful house in fashionable Hyde Park. They were obviously immensely rich, and when I asked how the family came to Africa, Sue-Anne told us the story of her great-grandfather.

At the age of fourteen he'd left his Welsh village to become a cabin boy on a sailing ship. These were the days when merchant captains wore top hats, and in the West Indies, when the ship was sailing off-shore, a sudden squall blew the captain's top hat overboard. He sent the young cabin boy in a small boat to retrieve it, but the squall was the beginning of a violent storm, and the ship, being too close to a lee shore, foundered with the loss of all hands. The young man managed to get ashore, but now alone, the captain's top hat was his only possession. He eventually found his way back to his village. It was Sunday, and he sneaked in at the back of the chapel to hear prayers for 'the repose of the soul of the cabin boy, lost at sea.'

Saved from a watery grave by a top hat, he went back to sea and became a captain and the owner of a fleet, sailing the East African coast with cargoes of coal, ironware and pig-lead. He became rich enough to sail his own yacht against King George V's *Britannia*.

Danny Kaye invited Annette and me to a matinée of his one-man show, and it was a great experience to watch an international star work his magic on the audience. He could act, sing, dance and clown, but most of all he had heart – that quality not given to many, and certainly absent from so many of today's comedians. On stage, he was the perfect family entertainer, but we found him relaxing afterwards in his dressing room with a large whisky and using some surprisingly strong language; both are releases from the stress of performance and are common to many performers. It's a pity that some of our contemporary entertainers don't save their bad language for after the show.

Unlike our trip to Rhodesia the year before, we were never

aware of any overt racism; we lived, worked and played in a European island, and Africa began outside the city limits. We weren't aware that Johaar Mosaval from India and David Poole, a 'Cape-coloured', had received special government permission to allow them to share the stage with us. The audiences were all white, the Company was of mixed race, and none of us at that time believed that black Africans would want to come to see us anyway. How wrong we were. I'm sure that the young Nelson Mandela (often in Johannesburg during the 1950s) would have loved to have come to *Swan Lake* to hear his favourite composer, Tchaikovsky.

After a couple of weeks where we were the toast of the town, it was time for me to take the train south to rehearse the Durban musicians. They were nothing like as good as the SABC Orchestra, being an amalgam of the barely competent, the mediocre and the excellent. Inevitably, my rehearsals were slow and frustrating. The first-class players had to wait while their less competent colleagues battled with the notes. Apart from the uneven quality, a major problem was keeping in tune. Musical instruments are manufactured to produce the correct international pitch when the temperature is 68°F and the relative humidity is 30 per cent. If these vary a little, some minor adjustments are possible, but the Durban City Hall was not air-conditioned, and we were working in a temperature of over 80°F and a humidity of 90 per cent. The music didn't sound very good, and the long afternoon rehearsals were a great trial for us all.

Jack and the Company arrived, but I didn't stay, as I had to take the train down to Cape Province to rehearse the Cape Town Municipal Orchestra. I was looking forward to an easier ride because, in the 1930s, they had given concerts in London under their young English conductor, Leslie Heward. They were a very friendly lot, and I was invited to stay with the principal bassist, Blanche Gerstmann, a lady of middle years who had a lovely flat with a superb view of Table Mountain.

Compared with frenetic Johannesburg and sleepy Durban, Cape Town had a relaxed but lively atmosphere, and we were made to feel very much at home. Indeed, some of the Company *were* at home: Patricia Miller had been a pupil of Dulcie Howes at

Cape Town University, and Pat's mother was a typical 'ballet mum' to us all and strengthened the feeling of family, which was always a feature of our tight little company.

The orchestra, although underpowered, was very competent, but it seemed that they had to recruit musicians from overseas, and Blanche told me that this had produced some unusual problems. Some years before, a string bass player had been sent from London to fill a vacancy in the orchestra, but without being auditioned. When Blanche heard him play, she was horrified to discover that he'd only played in amateur orchestras, but as he was already contracted for three years, and it would cost too much to buy him out, she relegated him to a special desk at the back of the orchestra with instructions not to play anything but to follow the other players' bows without touching his strings. He gradually added a few notes each year until he became quite competent, and eventually retired to England with a pension.

His replacement was again contracted in London, this time after an audition. But somebody had got it wrong again. The vacancy was for a double bass but they sent a cellist. The poor man had severed all his roots with England, and was desperate to start a new life with his family in this beautiful part of the world, so Blanche lent him a double bass, which he soon played well enough to join the section. He got the best of both worlds when, at a concert, he surprised the audience by leaving the double bass section to come forward as soloist in the Dvorak *Cello Concerto*.

One morning Blanche and I cycled to meet her friend, the famous Russian soprano, Oda Slobodskaya. She was giving a singing lesson and was taking her student through Tatiana's letter song from *Eugene Onegin*. (She was in her seventies, and I was reminded of how thrilling her voice was, even then, when I recently listened to her singing the song on YouTube.) We took tea, Russian style, and she talked about her days in St Petersburg at the Mariinsky, where she had sung Liza in *The Queen of Spades,* and about working with Diaghilev when she created the role of Mavra in Stravinsky's opera.

There were many questions that I would have liked to have asked, but her next pupil arrived, and as we cycled back in the shadow of Table Mountain, I asked Blanche how this great

Russian singer had come to be giving singing lessons to untalented pupils in what some might call a musical backwater.

'Ah,' she said. 'It might be something to do with Albert Coates.'

Blanche had played under Albert Coates when he conducted the Cape Town Orchestra, and she told me something about a composer and conductor of whom I had very little knowledge. Coates was born of an English mother and a Russian father in St Petersburg in 1882. He was sent home to get a degree in engineering at Liverpool University, but then changed tack completely and studied conducting in Leipzig with the great Arthur Nikisch. Coates had found his true vocation and, aged only twenty-six, Nikisch invited him to share the Wagner Season at the Royal Opera House, Covent Garden. His career led him back to Russia, where he became the principal conductor of the Mariinsky Theatre in St Petersburg during Slobodskaya's time there. After the Revolution, he escaped from Russia, and Slobodskaya followed him two years later. Back in London, in 1936 he conducted his opera *Pickwick* at Covent Garden (*Pickwick* was the first opera ever shown on BBC Television and includes a fugue for cricketers). The previous year, Slobodskaya had sung with Sir Thomas Beecham in his production of Delius' *Koanga*, so they had shared some unusual experiences.

When the war began in 1939, Coates' career went on hold. After the war he was still only in his sixties (no age for a conductor), but instead of continuing his very successful career, he left Europe to live in Cape Town. He conducted a little and taught composition at the University. In 1952, the year before he died, he wrote an opera prophetically called *Tafelberg se Kleed* ('Cloud over Table Mountain').

Albert Coates and Oda Slobodskaya were both at the Mariinsky, both escaped from St Petersburg, both worked at Covent Garden and both died in Cape Town.

The Sadler's Wells Theatre Ballet tour was an unqualified success. Our most popular ballet continued to be *Pineapple Poll,* and when Britannia appeared and the Union Jack was hoisted, both were cheered to the echo. On our last night, the orchestra presented me with a recording of Stravinsky conducting his *Symphony of Psalms* with their 'best wishes for my successful professional career'.

We sailed for home and a year which was to bring great changes to the Sadler's Wells Theatre Ballet, and would give me my first opportunity to conduct music by the greatest of all ballet composers since Tchaikovsky: Igor Stravinsky.

CHAPTER 24

TRAINS AGAIN

Ninette de Valois strikes!

After a very comfortable and exciting three months in one of the most beautiful countries in the world, and now back at home, the Sunday train calls, living out of a suitcase, and the lottery of the landlady began to pall.

To add to my twenty-five hours a week at the keyboard and conducting two performances, I'd also been given the job of checking that there was enough room in the pit for an orchestra of thirty-six players. We'd always send word ahead, warning the theatre managers that they would probably need to take out two rows of the front stalls and raise the level of the pit floor, but on the previous provincial tour, we had turned up late one afternoon at a theatre for the routine seating rehearsal to find that the front two rows had been sold, and there was no way that we could all get into the pit. The manager declared that there was plenty of room and 'only last week I had forty musicians in the pit'. My riposte – that they must have all been piccolo-playing midgets – fell on deaf ears, and it was a stand-off until, with a sorrowful smile, I explained that as ballets need music, if there was no orchestra, there was no ballet.

That did the trick. With only a couple of hours to go before curtain-up, some hastily-summoned burly men with screwdrivers and hammers began tearing out red plush seats and carpets that been there for many years. We finally shoe-horned the orchestra into the pit, and, five minutes late, the doors were opened. Excited balletomanes, dressed up to the nines in dinner jackets and long dresses, swept down the red carpet to the most expensive seats in the house to find them gone, and, in their place, violinists, flautists, clarinettists, a bassoonist and a friendly but slightly tanked-up viola player, and his similarly tanked-up cellist brother. When those who'd booked the stage boxes opened their little doors, they encountered a smilingly regretful harpist in one and a less-than-happy burly drummer and his kettle drums in the other. Jack and I could only control this dreadful set-up by balancing on a couple of beer crates.

It was a very uncomfortable week in the theatre, but a most exciting time was had in the local church hall, where I had my first encounter with Stravinsky's *Danses Concertantes*, the ballet which signalled Kenneth MacMillan's transition from *Somnabulism* and *Laiderette* at the Sunday Choreographers' Club to becoming the principal choreographer of the Royal Ballet.

When MacMillan was dancing with us in the SWTB, and as good as he was at acting (the Burgomaster in *Coppélia*, the Duke in *Swan Lake* and Sherlock Holmes), there was little in our repertoire to suit him, for he had neither the sex appeal of David Blair nor the athleticism of Michael Bolton, Harold Turner or Donald Britten. I remember (somewhere in the darkest North) conducting a matinée of *Les Sylphides* with music by Chopin and thinking how Ken's dancing lacked poetry; but had he been a *danseur noble*, he might have spent too much time propping up ballerinas to have created some of the world's finest ballets.

Danses Concertantes was his first major work, and a very brave one, for it invited comparison with the original 1944 version created by George Balanchine for the Ballet Russe de Monte Carlo. Ken's version of this 'ballet for orchestra' (as Stravinsky described his music) was for fourteen dancers, led by Maryon Lane, Annette Page and Donald Britten. I was to conduct it on many occasions – in fact, it became my ballet. I took the orchestral rehearsals as well as all performances.

In May, Ken produced his second ballet for the SWTB, *The House of Birds*, based on the Daphne du Maurier short story *The Birds*, to the music of the Spanish composer, Federico Mompou. Originally for the piano in a style that Mompou christened 'primitivista' (no bar lines or key signatures), Jack Lanchbery added both, and then orchestrated the lot. Mompou, dressed in a black cloak lined with red satin, and looking every inch the world-famous composer (which he wasn't), came over from Paris for the first night at Sadler's Wells.

The House of Birds had the sinister flavour of the Daphne du

Maurier story and it preceded the Alfred Hitchcock film version by a full ten years. Once again, Ken was showing his originality of scenario and choreography – first *Laiderette's* bald heroine, then the spiky angularity of *Danses*, and now sinister black birds.

Under Peggy van Praagh's direction, and with our interesting new repertoire and the skill of dancers who'd polished their techniques while performing eight times a week, loud whispers began around town that the SWTB was becoming more exciting than the Covent Garden Company. This was not entirely to Madame's taste, and when Annette Page and Pirmin Trecu brought the house down during our season at Sadler's Wells with a glittering performance of *Jota Toledano*, complete with male and female castanets, she spoke privately to Peggy about the Company getting to be too 'showy'.

Madame dealt with any problem in her own highly effective way, and when she decided that henceforth the SWTB would become a permanent touring company, she transferred pretty well all of our leading dancers to Covent Garden: David Blair, Maryon Lane, Annette Page, Svetlana Beriosova, Kenneth MacMillan and Jack Lanchbery's wife, Elaine Fifield.

It could have been a death blow to the Company. My personal loss was Annette, but it was a great career move for her. She was a very pretty girl whose warm personality, sense of humour and great talent, would, under the keen eye of de Valois, soon take her to the top of the tree at the Garden.

What a hole they all left. Peggy was not long in moving a long way away from Madame to take over the Australian National Ballet. The denuded company had a new director, John Field, and a new ballerina, Anne Heaton, who was his partner.

The re-vamping and promotions of soloists to leading dancers began, but in the spirit of the old Company, we got on with another new ballet by the *Blood Wedding* team of Alfred Rodrigues and Denis Apivor. This time, Rod had crossed the border into Portugal during the Moorish occupation. It was called *Saudades* – the story of a beautiful blonde Portuguese princess, about to marry a Moorish Caliph, who is overcome with longing for her homeland, where cool breezes stir the snow-like tree blossoms, beautiful unveiled women openly wear priceless jewels and exotic birds fill the air. The scenario suggests music in the style of Rimsky-Korsakov's *Scheherazade*, but romance was dead to mid-20th composers, and Dennis gave it the full atonal treatment, with some rhythms even more complicated than Stravinsky's. One ensemble dance was written in the rhythm of eleven quavers to the bar – 11/8 – one note short of the easy 12/8. It meant that the dancers had to jerk rather than flow, and everyone (including Rod) had a problem, until I came up with an eleven syllable phrase, which all shouted as they danced: *'We don't like Lanch-be-ry, we don't like Al-wyn!'* (Count them!)

I found their enthusiasm to be a bit too heartfelt, but it worked.

The Company began to recover from de Valois' drastic culling, but now banished permanently to the provinces, I began to think that, after three years of playing and conducting much the same music, my career had stalled. When I received an offer to become Musical Director at the Bristol Old Vic for their Christmas pantomime, I asked Stephen Arlen and Jack to release me for a few weeks. They agreed, provided I return for one day during the Bristol run to conduct *Danses Concertantes* at Princess Margaret's Sadler's Wells Gala.

This was the change of scenery I needed. I was to make lifelong friends and to extend my musical life in a way that I could hardly have imagined when I caught the fastest train in the country - the 'Bristolian' – to my new home, the Bristol Old Vic.

CHAPTER 25

THE BRISTOL OLD VIC

*Moira Shearer sings Puccini
and Peter O'Toole is late – again!*

The Bristol Theatre Royal dates from 1766, when Bristol was a thriving port but lacked a theatre, and so, against fierce local opposition (and without royal permission), a group of merchants built their own. In spite of a supporting opening night speech from the famous actor, David Garrick, it was not until twelve years later that King George III granted the building a royal charter, and it became the Theatre Royal in – appropriately – King Street.

Over the following years the Theatre Royal had many ups and downs, and was often threatened with closure until, in 1946, it became state-subsidised, with a resident repertory company and a theatre school. As it shared its repertoire with the London Old Vic, the theatre became known as the Bristol Old Vic.

It is a jewel: comfortable and cosy, with great atmosphere and a ghost.

There are those who claim to have seen Sarah Siddons wandering the theatre. Late at night, when all is silent save the creaking boards of the ancient stage, and the only light is a single 60-watt bulb casting mysterious shadows, anyone with an ounce of imagination can feel the presence of Sarah and those long-dead actors and actresses who, for nearly two hundred years, brought the theatre to life each evening.

The Theatre Royal also possesses a 'thunder-run', a device for creating a 'virtual reality' storm. Concealed in the ceiling is a metal trough which runs from the back of the theatre over the auditorium to the stage. When, as in Act Three of *King Lear*, a stage instruction calls for a storm, a cannon ball is rolled down the trough over the heads of the audience to the stage where it strikes metal plates with an almighty crash – an 18th century Dolby system.

Having worked with the silent stage of ballet for three years, I was really looking forward to not only to directing and arranging the music for the theatre's Christmas attraction, *Dick Whittington*, but also to all the robust fun of one of England's oldest (and strangest) theatrical entertainments and to its jokes – rare in the highly-disciplined world of the dance.

The Old Vic's 'Dick' was not going to be a 'commercial' pantomime with a cast of television 'stars' and 'pop' singers, but would be played by the resident Old Vic Company – actors all.

The book was by an Oxford Professor of English, V. C. Clinton-Baddeley, and the music was by Gavin Gordon, composer of the ballet *The Rake's Progress,* which was already well-known to me.

The cast list was heady stuff:

Dick Whittington - Betty Huntley-Wright
Alderman Fitzwarren - Derek Godfrey
Fitzwarren's cook, Dame Sarah - Eric Porter
Fitzwarren's servant, Simple Simon - Edward Hardwicke
Simon's friend, the kitchen maid - Phyllida Law
The Ship's Mate - Peter O'Toole
Neptune's handmaiden - Moira Shearer

Director - Owen Reed
Musical Director - Kenneth Alwyn
Choreographer - Elizabeth West

Except for one of Neptune's handmaidens, Moira Shearer and the principal boy, Betty Huntley-Wright (who reputedly possessed the best legs in the business) and Lally Bowers as Fairy Snowflake (with Joyce Grenfell overtones of 'No! Don't do *that*, Mr Rat!'), the cast were all at the beginning of their acting careers.

Because of the worldwide success in 1948 of Hans Christian Andersen's *The Red Shoes,* in which Moira co-starred with Marius Goring, Anton Walbrook and Léonide Massine, she was very well-known as a film star. However, there was a down-side, for although she had created the title role in Frederick Ashton's 1948 production of Prokofiev's *Cinderella* and richly deserved her success as a dancer, *The Red Shoes* had made her more famous in America than Margot Fonteyn.

At the first night of the Company's American tour in 1949, a member of the New York audience was heard to remark, 'Where's the red-haired chick, and who's this Margie Fountain?'

Ninette de Valois was determined to preserve Fonteyn's position as *prima ballerina assoluta*, and so, in 1950 Moira left Sadler's Wells to concentrate on her acting career. She was welcomed with open arms at the Bristol Old Vic, and had already played Cordelia to Eric Porter's Lear, but now for our Christmas show – with the true democracy of a resident company – she was to be a mere handmaiden of the Lord of the Sea.

In another of those invisible patterns of life, thirty years after working with Moira at Bristol, I received the German Critic's Award for my recording with the Philharmonia of 'The Red Shoes'.

The resident Musical Director at Bristol was Julian Slade. He and Dorothy Reynolds had written a musical about a magic piano called *Salad Days*, which had done so well in Bristol that it had transferred to the Vaudeville Theatre in London. Julian went with it, leaving Christmas 1954 to us. There was no room in the pit for even a small orchestra, but we managed to squeeze in a second piano and a drummer, who provided the required Christmas effects: sleigh and church bells, slap-sticks, cymbals for the pratfalls, a squeaker for the pussy, and, of course, the Bells of Bow.

Rehearsals were great fun. Owen Reed gave the cast their basic stage moves, then left the dancing and singing to Elizabeth West and me. There were only two of the cast who had ever sung professionally, and I was viewed with justifiable caution, even suspicion. Eric Porter, our Dame and future Soames Forsyth on BBC television, had a fine robust voice (he used to go at night to Clifton Park and declaim Shakespeare at the top of his voice.) But when I told him that he had to sing bass in my barber shop arrangement of 'It always pays best to be honest', he pleaded tone deafness. But I won him over, and his quartet with a couple of sweet melodious tenors (John Cairney and Edward Hardwicke) and a rich resounding baritone (Derek Godfrey) became one of the high spots of the show.

The crew of the pirate ship (under the command of Peter O'Toole), the citizens of London and the lovely and lightly-clad harem girls and sea-nymphs all came from the Theatre School. One of them, Ingrid Hafner, caught my eye, for she was a particularly good dancer, and pretty with it.

We included in the cast a couple of students from the Bristol School of Dancing, an establishment run by the gentle Mary Carpenter and her chain-smoking partner, Muriel. They were the best teachers in Bristol, and their school was to become the first home of the Western Theatre Ballet, later the Scottish National Ballet.

We rehearsed in the theatre all day. Lunch was either a pint and a sandwich at the Llandoger Trow – the pub across the road where Daniel Defoe had met the real-life castaway who inspired him to write *Robinson Crusoe* – or two doors down at a 'greasy spoon', nicknamed 'Hell's Kitchen', which even the most impecunious could afford. I moved into a very small flat with Edward Hardwicke, and after rehearsals, we were joined by Peter O'Toole.

We three had great conversations, which went on too far into the night. I slept on a settee in the living room, and I had to wait until Peter had gone before I could go to bed. After rather too many nights of Peter reciting great chunks of Dylan Thomas, and Ted Hardwicke's stories of his father Sir Cedric's life in Hollywood, I would have dark shadows under my eyes. One night, in desperation, I reminded Peter that I'd called him for rehearsal at 10am the following morning and would he please get the hell out of my bedroom.

I made sure I was at the piano at 10am sharp the next morning. At 10.20am, looking rather the worse for wear, Peter strolled onto the stage. I gave him a long hard look, and after a long silence, he said, 'Sorry, me old darlin'!'

He was never late for me again.

After the show opened, our flat became the scene of nightly parties, fuelled by white wine, pretty girls and the buzz that one gets from a good performance. Life with these easy-going and attractive people made me wonder if I should have ignored Gypsy Rose Lee's advice on Eastbourne Pier and chosen an actor's life.

I spent Christmas Day at the Bristol School of Dancing, and I got to know Elizabeth West really well. She was a bundle of energy and new ideas (she wanted to write an operetta about a circus) and told me of her dream – a dance company which would take dramatic ballets to the small towns and villages of the West Country. It would be called the Western Theatre Ballet – a title which combined her name and the company's origin. Over that Christmas lunch, we discovered that we shared many ideas, and later, when her dream came true, I was to become the first Musical Director of her company.

But meanwhile I was still contracted to Sadler's Wells, and so, under the terms of my loan to Bristol, and leaving Courtney Kenny on one piano (which he could always make sound like two anyway), I caught the 'Bristolian' back to Sadler's Wells to conduct *Danses Concertantes*.

It was a great evening, with that almost-hysterical excitement that only ballet and pop stars seem to produce. The young and beautiful Princess Margaret Rose made a charming speech, showing her enthusiasm for all things theatrical. She was a great party-goer, and those who'd heard her sing were of the opinion that, if she hadn't been in line for the throne, she'd have certainly been in the chorus line, at least!

After a month or so, *Dick Whittington* still had a freshness that good actors bring to each performance, but now unscripted jokes began to appear. The best are those that the audience can also enjoy. In the dénouement, Alderman Fitzwarren, dressed in a long red cloak, fur-trimmed medieval hat, buckled shoes, a brass-bound, richly-decorated belt, hanging just below his ample paunch, and looking very like Holbein's portrait of Henry VIII, confronts Dick (framed by Idle Jack) for stealing money. He thrusts his thumbs into his belt and dismisses the boy from his employment with the words, 'Dick, I am grieved to see that my trust has been displaced.'

However, one night Fitzwarren thrust a little too forcefully, his belt opened and the buckles hung down in the vicinity of his wedding tackle. Quick to take advantage he changed the lines.

'Dick, I am grieved to see my *truss* has been misplaced.' Then he inspected himself more closely, and leering at the audience capped it with, 'However, since I have lost nothing... I shall not send for the police.'

Everyone laughed – not true of Peter O'Toole's unscripted running gag: an inability to remember the name of the newest member of his crew, Dick Whittington. At each performance he'd try a different variation. 'Here you, Boddington, or Tittington, or Waddington – or whatever your name is.' After several nights the list got longer, until Betty Huntley-Wright, who was getting fed up with standing there with egg on her face, said 'Try again, Sir!' but Peter couldn't think of a single new name and in the embarrassing silence, from the gallery was heard a solitary, chilling and mirthless 'Hah, Hah, Hah...' No one else laughed.

I heard later that the ironic laughter came from a drama student at the Old Vic School.

Although Ingrid was still with her career all before her, and I was a few years her senior, we were very close, and our nightly trysts after the show meant a lot to us both. I was eventually invited to her home for tea and parental inspection.

Flying and music once again walked hand in hand when I met her father, Raoul. He was cleaning his swimming pool and was totally naked except for a baseball cap given to him by his American friend, the helicopter designer Igor Sikorsky. After cucumber sandwiches and Viennese pastries, and now wearing an embroidered velvet jacket, Raoul sat at his Steinway Grand (what else?) and played *The Blue Danube*. Daughters are inclined to look towards their fathers as role models, and he was a tough act to follow – aircraft designer and concert pianist!

Raoul built his first helicopter in 1929, but being Jewish, with the rise of Hitler, he emigrated to Britain. On the outbreak of war, the government branded him an enemy alien, and under Regulation 18b, they sent him to be interned in Canada. His ship was sunk by a German submarine, but he survived and was returned to England, where the government, realising their mistake, employed him in the design of secret weapons.

The day went well, and later in the year, I spent a holiday with them on their yacht in the Mediterranean.

Meanwhile, it was back to Dick.

After a good deal of thought, Owen Reed, Liz West and I decided that, although Moira Shearer was willing to be a sea-nymph, there was nothing for her to do, and so, rather than disappoint the audience, it was better to leave her out of the cast. I think she was quite relieved, for she had no confidence in her singing voice, and after we had opened, she asked if I'd give her lessons.

I thought she'd look wonderful as Puccini's coquettish Musetta who, in *La Bohème*, 'wanders through the streets merrily', but first we had to find her singing voice. We started each morning with breathing exercises. Dancers are accustomed to snatching breaths to fuel great physical effort, and women do so rapidly, from high in the chest, whereas singers of both sexes need to breathe deeply, and then only when the musical phrasing allows. This change of technique is something that Moira couldn't expect to acquire fully in the short time that we had together, but she was always in tune, acted very well and, although vocally underpowered to rise above a full Puccini orchestra, made a delightful Musetta.

Dick Whittington had been a show to remember, but I was glad to get back to the ballet and the orchestra. Yet after five years of changing at Crewe, living out of suitcases, dodgy landladies and playing the same ballets at the same theatres, I decided I'd had enough and that it was time to make a move. Where to, I had no idea.

I interviewed for a BBC Music Producer job and, although the selection board liked my Radio Malaya experience, when they asked if I was willing to give up conducting forever, the thought of a job for life and a pension couldn't tempt me to give up following my star. Meanwhile, I had been invited back to the Bristol Old Vic to direct *The Two Bouquets* by Eleanor and Herbert Fargeon.

As John Field knew I was getting restless, he released me, but not before taking me to aside to promise me the Chief Conductor's post when Jack Lanchbery left to go to the Garden. I didn't know Jack was leaving (and, apparently, neither did he), although events were later to take an unexpected turn.

The Two Bouquets went well, but it was not very interesting musically, and as Ingrid was now at the Norwich Repertory

The Two Bouquets, Bristol Old Vic

**Phyllida Law (fourth from left), Annette Crosby (fifth from right)
and Edward Hardwicke (fourth from right)**

Theatre, it was no great hardship to return to touring.

A few weeks later, I was back in Bristol with the ballet. I had friends in both theatres (we were playing at the Hippodrome), and at my invitation, after our performances the ballet dancers joined the Old Vic actors at a lovely rented Georgian house in Clifton, where I slept in its disused private chapel.

Our nightly parties when we'd cook supper, swap stories and listen to records were very entertaining, and it was there that I heard for the first time the New York cast recording of *My Fair Lady*. Although the songs were wonderful, it was the stunning orchestral arrangements by Robert Russell Bennett that appealed to me even more. So when Ted Hardwicke (whose father Sir Cedric had sent him the record from New York) told me that the Musical Director, Franz Allers, was paid a royalty for each performance, plus a whacking weekly fee, I began to speculate that, with such well-written and well-performed music, London's musical theatre scene might be my next step, from the restless suitcase into a more settled world.

The late-night coming-together in this beautiful house of

young actors and dancers made for a great atmosphere. When Peter O'Toole heard that I was sleeping in the private chapel, he gathered us around to listen to him – in true Irish style – tell of the night that he too slept alone there.

It began, he said, when at around midnight he was awakened by the sound of a thunder storm. Lightning, flashing through the stained glass windows, threw horribly-distorted images of the Saints and Apostles onto the chapel's cold, grey walls. He shivered and drew the bedclothes closer around him. Gradually, the storm rolled on, and the only sound now was the distant thunder and squalls of rain on the window panes. Then there came a tapping (and here Peter gave us a little of Edgar Alan Poe's *The Raven*), tapping on the window: 'tap-tap-tap, tap-tap-tap'. Something, or someone, was trying to get in. Summoning all his courage, Peter threw open the window and looked out into the white face of... a policeman. He fixed Peter with cold eyes, but no words came from his colourless lips. The rain ran down the helmet, the shining black cape and the narrow black trousers to where one shiny policeman's boot was matched by (and here there was a shattering roll of thunder and a flash of lightning) a cloven hoof.

Being the great actor that he is, one young dancer was too frightened to go home, and at bed-time sought his personal protection. In later years, when Peter had become a world-class star, she remembered fondly how he had protected her that night from the ghastly, ghostly policeman.

Peter O'Toole

Back on tour, I was conducting and playing much the same repertoire for the second (and sometimes third) time around in Stockton-on-Tees, Hanley and similar small towns. The music never lost its magic, but the train calls and the landlady lottery began to lose their charm. It was in Bradford, where I had previously stayed at the Wedgewood Hotel, formerly the home of the Delius family, that the rot set in.

I turned up at the hotel to find that it had been demolished and replaced by a petrol station. I was so appalled that, when a car drew up close to where I was standing, I demanded to know from the driver what sort of people lived in Bradford who could destroy the birthplace of one of our greatest composers.

'Ah,' said the Mr Jaffe, a Public Analyst for the city, 'but he wasn't born there. Mrs Delius felt unwell and crossed the road to her friend. I'll show you where Delius was born,' and he led me upstairs to his laboratory, crowded with test tubes and evil smells. Mr Jaffe had two sons who were both professional musicians. He had written a book on Gabriel Fauré and he had met Rachmaninov, so I had no reason to doubt his knowledge.

I finished up with a Bradford landlady whose menu was dominated entirely by the chickens that ran loose in her back garden. As I ate my after-show meal of scrambled eggs and chips, I was viewed with understandable suspicion by an Alsatian, whose coat was threadbare – the result of being thrown into a cement mixture by someone who believed that a puppy was only for Christmas.

Things got worse in Cardiff, which was the last week of a miserable tour. I stayed in an old house where my bed was so damp that I had to douse my pillow with eau-de-cologne to kill the musty smell. In the corner of the room was a cupboard which contained old and dusty grave decorations – glass cases of pallid artificial flowers dedicated to the long-since dead.

One night, I was sitting with my solitary supper in the dining-room when the oak door to the kitchen swung open, and I glimpsed a figure hunched in a chair before the fire: human or animal, I could not tell. Each night as I lay trying to get to sleep, I listened to the creaks and groans of this deserted and decaying house, and wondered who, or what, was the occupant of that chair and why my bedroom cupboard was filled with flowers stolen from cemeteries. The week finally ended, and not wanting to spend another night in the house of horrors, and being the proud possessor of my first car – a 1937 Morris Series E convertible – I decided to drive back after the performance to my Westminster flat. Being very old, the engine was on its last legs, and the dynamo brushes were almost worn out, but Peter

Wright (who'd surprised and delighted us all by marrying Sonya Hana, the beautiful Queen of Wu in my BBC production), was anxious to get back to his new bride, and so in the dark and the rain we set off for London.

The drive went well until the headlights began to dim and the windscreen wipers started to slow. Clearly, the dynamo was failing, but using only side-lights, and the wipers only occasionally, I was able to keep going at about fifteen miles an hour. Not being able to see properly, I drove over a level crossing rather too fast. The passenger door burst open, and Peter disappeared on to the railway line. We finally arrived in London as the dawn broke, at about the same time as the first train from Cardiff.

That dreadful weekend journey proved to be the last straw, and on Monday I rang Jack to tell him I was leaving the Company.

'Where are you going?' he asked.

I had no idea. On 23rd June I conducted the matinée and evening performances of my debut ballet, *Coppélia*, at the old Brighton Hippodrome.

After the performance, clutching the silver cigarette case presented to me by my friends in the orchestra, I walked through the stage door and into an unknown future.

Programme for 'Coppélia', Brighton Hippodrome.

The programme advice reads: 'Patrons are requested to either retain or destroy their Programmes after the Performance and NOT to give same to the paper boys in the streets as it only tends to get them into trouble with the Police.'

CHAPTER 26

THE ROYAL BALLET BEGINS

Claire Bloom and I meet in the afternoons

That night I drove home through Croydon, past the familiar places of my childhood: the Davis Theatre; the flat in Thornton Heath where my mother had died; Winterbourne School, scene of my athletic prowess; and Streatham Common, with its memories of Sir Oswald Mosely and his Blackshirts. I wondered where the road which had brought me thus far would now lead. Would I ever again don the 'tails' that were strewn across the back seat of my little Morris, or ever again open my baton case?

As I picked my way down the dark basement steps of 54 St George's Square, a cloud of depression descended with me, but then I remembered that there was a farewell party that night at Covent Garden for the ballerina Violetta Elvin. Christened Violetta Prokorova, she had been a star of the Bolshoi in Moscow, but she had married a British architect and had for the past ten years been dancing ballerina roles with the Sadler's Wells Company. Now, once again, she'd fallen in love – this time with a rich Italian – and was leaving the make-believe world of ballet to live in a real palace as a real-life countess. To celebrate her last performance that evening, the Count had invited us all to champagne and lobster in the Circle Bar of the Royal Opera House.

I was still contracted to the Company until midnight, and I knew that some of my friends would be there, so I climbed back up to the street and drove my little Morris along the Embankment, through Trafalgar Square and along Long Acre to Floral Street where, opposite the stage door, I parked next to one of the many Rolls Royces.

I was not dressed for a formal party, but I introduced myself to Sergeant Martin, the legendary Major Domo, as the conductor of the Theatre Ballet. He somewhat doubtfully indicated the regal staircase, and its mirrored walls reflected back my crumpled suit as I joined the glitterati on their way to the Circle Bar. Not just any old bar, but a grand, ballroom-like chamber, where the jewellery and decorations of the distinguished guests sparkled in the light from the crystal chandeliers – a scene that even Hollywood would have found hard to equal.

Searching the crowded tables, I saw the familiar faces of my friends from the early Theatre Ballet days: Kenneth MacMillan, David Blair and Maryon Lane. There was room at their table, but as I grappled with my lobster, I felt that I was unkindly being shown by the Devil the riches of a world far beyond me. Tomorrow, I would be that most useless of musicians: a conductor without an orchestra.

Then Ken turned to me and, against the background of the cocktail pianist's tinkling 'A Nightingale Sang in Berkeley Square', he said: 'I'm glad you've joined us.'

'I'm glad you had room at your table,' I replied.

With a puzzled look, Ken said, 'No, I'm glad you've joined us at Covent Garden.'

It was possibly the greatest moment of my life, and I was hearing this staggering news… at a party! That one short sentence changed my life forever, and I looked around the Circle Bar in the knowledge that, not only had I been shown the high places, but (totally unexpectedly) I was to dwell among them. The party ended, the Countess departed, and I descended my basement stairs, this time in a buoyant mood.

But in the still small hours, when doubts and fears rule, I awoke, and was to sleep no more. Could it really be true that I was to conduct at Covent Garden?

After the longest of Sundays, the phone rang late in the afternoon, and I heard for the first time the kindly tones of the Sadler's Wells Ballet's Principal Conductor.

'Kenneth Alwyn? This is Robert Irving. How would you like to come to Covent Garden?'

It was true!

The next day I went to his flat in Gloucester Place, and Bob (he was always 'Bob' from the word go) told me that, as his associate conductor, I would be in charge of the two Company pianists. One of them, Hilda Gaunt, was immensely experienced, having toured as second pianist to Constant Lambert during the war years. She was of tough North Country stock, with a voice cracked and roughened by years of chain-smoking. Her colleague was quite different, a charming and pretty Canadian, Jean Gilbert, who had been a violinist in the orchestra until someone had dropped a glockenspiel on her hand.

Bob saved the best till last. Although I was required to play for some rehearsals, I would also conduct my own performances at Covent Garden, even for the occasional press night.

I left Bob's flat walking on air.

I imagine that my years with the Theatre Ballet had convinced de Valois and Bob that I could be trusted with the great occasions. Indeed, in his autobiography he described me as 'a very efficient young man who had been unhappy with the Theatre Ballet'.

And so I was the latest to join the ranks of conductors who (again from Bob's book) 'existed in the brilliant world of the ballet and the treacherous quicksands of the Royal Opera House'.

Many disappeared beneath those sands, including Constant Lambert, who it was thought was drinking so heavily in 1947 that Margot Fonteyn had to help him with his meals. He went down so rapidly that, after a disastrous performance of Tchaikovsky's *Hamlet*, it was generally accepted that Lambert was too ill to continue conducting.

His performances were then taken over by Warwick Braithwaite – a reluctant ballet conductor whose real interest was the opera.

There was now a real shortage of conductors, and so a nameless protégé of Sir Thomas Beecham was tried out. This young man's audition was a performance of *La Boutique Fantasque* at Croydon. It was a disaster, and for the very short time he was with the Company, he was known as 'Dolly Dullbeat'.

Braithwaite was increasingly anxious to get back to the opera, and so another young conductor was given a chance. He was an Edward (his last name is lost in the depths of incompetence, for he proved to be even worse than Dolly Dullbeat).

The effect on the dancers of these performances by

conductors with no knowledge of the special demands of the ballet can only be imagined. But in the nick of time, Robert Irving, who was Ian White's assistant with the BBC Scottish Orchestra, became available.

Irving had been a pupil of Lambert, and was welcomed by him with 'I'm so glad you've come! You've no idea what's been going on here!' (which was a bit rich from the man who'd caused the chaos).

Bob soon fitted comfortably into the ballet world, for he was a conductor with that rare gift of understanding the moment in the music when the dancers' feet should hit the ground. With Bob's arrival, matters quickly improved. The Company was giving seven performances every two weeks, but in spite of occasional guest conductors, including William Walton, Arthur Bliss and Ernest Ansermet, Bob still needed someone with whom to share the routine programmes, and so the search continued.

The first to be tried out was John Hollingsworth, well-known for his work in the film studios. He was a charming man, who had an unfortunate experience in New York, indulging too freely in dry martinis in the lunch-time 'Happy Hour' (two for the price of one) at the Algonquin Hotel. He was probably unfamiliar with the American 'Dry Martini' (a very large gin over which the bartender quickly passes the Martini bottle), and Bob was quite unable to wake him in time for the evening performance. John was popular with the Company, but nevertheless Sir David Webster replaced him with Anatole Fistoulari, known to us as 'Fisty'.

Although hailed as a great Russian conductor, Fistoulari's exact nationality was something of a mystery, for he spoke Russian with an accent. The many linguists in the Company said he spoke *all* languages with an accent. Musically, he was excellent, and had conducted for Léonide Massine's Ballet Russe, but perhaps his Ballet Russe tempi gave our dancers some problems, and so when he telephoned to enquire about future performances, it was left to Bob to tell him that he had none.

To replace Fistoulari, two names were proposed: Hugo Rignold and George Weldon. Rignold had earned the gratitude of de Valois when, at a performance of a very early Ashton ballet in 1936 (*Nocturne*, set to Delius' *Paris, Song of a Great City*), the conductor fell suddenly ill, and Hugo stepped up from the first desk of the violas to the podium and saved the day. Now Hugo's playing days were far behind him, and he was the Musical Director of the City of Birmingham Symphony Orchestra. It was decided to wait a few months until he had more free time, but meanwhile George Weldon was offered a job.

Bob described Weldon as 'a well-to-do young man who drove a Frazer-Nash sports car and conducted amateur orchestras' (Bob had actually played the cello in one of them). However, a limp meant that he was unfit for war service, and he'd had the opportunity to become a professional, giving successful concerts of the popular classics.

To quote Bob again: 'George was very enthusiastic and agreeable, but had serious rhythmical deficiencies such as I have noticed in other lame conductors.'

(Surely not true of Victor de Sabata, the Musical Director of the Scala Milan, who limped onto the stage of the Davis Theatre, Croydon when I saw him conducting a performance of the Royal Philharmonic Orchestra in 1946.)

This is where I entered the shaky scene. To quote Bob's autobiography: 'We appointed a very capable young man, Kenneth Alwyn, who had been very unhappy with the junior ballet company at Sadler's Wells.'

It is only at the distance of fifty years that the Machiavellian manoeuvring being carried out in 1956 has been revealed. After seven highly successful years, Bob's good reputation was fading. He was accused of rushing the dancers off their feet. His answer was that he was trying to maintain the original tempi of the first performances. This is a perfectly valid point, and is, indeed, the duty of the conductor, but the damage was done, and it was decided to replace him.

The original, secret plan was for Jack Lanchbery to go to Covent Garden and for me to take over the touring company. Then, when Hugo arrived in the spring, he would take over most of the conducting and Bob would be 'kicked upstairs' to the position of Musical Adviser. However, I scuppered this plan by resigning, and, with it being extremely difficult to find an experienced ballet conductor who could, at a moment's notice, take over the Theatre Ballet and a thirty-eight-week tour, Jack instead had to stay where he was for the next two years, and I went to Covent Garden.

I was to begin with the Senior Company in August, but meanwhile I had one last commitment to the Theatre Ballet as pianist for their visit to the Granada Festival, held in the beautiful gardens of the Alhambra Palace.

The dancers were apprehensive about performing in the open air, and rightly so, for after they had warmed up, General Franco kept them and the audience waiting until he'd finished dinner. Finally, an hour late, he arrived. All went quiet and an oboe, which seemed to come from somewhere out in space, sang the opening bars of Tchaikovsky's *Swan Lake* as the Prince and his hunting party entered, not into a painted forest glade under a make-believe sky but perhaps the most beautiful garden in the world, lit by a full moon.

When I returned to London, there were still a few weeks before I started at Covent Garden, and a need to earn some money. So when the Musical Director of the Old Vic Company, Fred Marshall, asked me to step in for him for a week or two, I thought it would be fun. At that time, Michael Benthall ran the Company, and his partner, Robert Helpmann, had directed two of the productions which were shortly to be toured in the United States, *Romeo and Juliet* and *Richard II*. Bobby was still with the ballet, but was by now acting in films and directing.

To discuss my future function, I met Fred at the pub next to the stage door to the Old Vic, where the Company was giving *Macbeth*. I noticed that he kept a sharp eye on his wrist-watch, and suddenly he put down his unfinished pint with 'Time for the bloody bagpipes!' and disappeared into the theatre.

He reappeared after a few minutes. 'I hate tuning bagpipes,' said Fred, and finished his pint.

All I can remember about the performances of *Richard II* is a very young Judi Dench and John Neville, who was a handsome Romeo to the sweet-voiced Juliet of Claire Bloom.

One afternoon on tour, Claire Bloom arrived early at the theatre and heard me playing Tchaikovsky's *Sleeping Beauty*, the ballet which Bob had told me was to be my first performance at

Covent Garden and which I would have to know backwards, since I would not have an orchestral rehearsal.

It was four years since Claire had starred as the young ballet dancer in Chaplin's *Limelight*, and when I told her that I was to conduct *Beauty* at the Royal Opera House, she asked if I minded her listening. Every day I started my practice a little earlier, so that when she arrived, I had a new section ready for her. For the next few days, we sat together in the romantic company of Tchaikovsky. What higher motivation could a musician have than the presence of a beautiful woman who was also a famous film star?

At night it was an exciting experience to watch such fine actors in the wings as they prepared to take the few steps from the reality of a provincial theatre into Shakespeare's world of 14th century England, Verona and Glamis. 'The Scottish play' (as I learnt to call it, for fear of offending superstitious actors) gave me Fred's former task of tuning the 'bloody bagpipes' each evening before the performance. I am an admirer of bagpipes in the open air, but to be imprisoned with them in a tiny off-stage room was more than one should have to bear!

The last performance before the Old Vic production left for America took place in Manchester. Being somewhat taken with Claire Bloom, I particularly noticed when Richard Burton spent the whole time between the afternoon and evening performances in her dressing-room, but I judged it an inopportune moment to remind him of our time together in the Royal Air Force at Bridgnorth.

There were still a couple of weeks to go before I began at Covent Garden, and so when Ted Hardwicke (who was by now a very good friend) suggested that we spent a few days with a friend of his mother's in Monte Carlo, I jumped at the chance. Lady Hardwicke, whose maiden name was Helena Pickard and was known as 'Pixie', had met her Cedric when they acted together. Pickard was a very famous name in flying circles, for it was her brother, Percy, who was the pilot in the Crown Film Unit's documentary of a real-life raid on Germany by the Wellington bomber, *F for Freddie*, and, in 1944, the leader of the low-level Mosquito raid on the prison at Amiens to release members of the French underground.

Pixie's friend in Monte Carlo, Betty, was the former wife of another famous actor, Raymond Huntley, but now she was the secretary to an American millionaire named Lynch.

Mr Lynch (no one in Monte Carlo appeared to know his first name) was highly connected with Coca-Cola. He and Betty spent their evenings in his beautiful house on Cap Ferrat and their days in the exclusive Sea Club, where, accompanied by his stockbroker and a long-distance telephone, Mr Lynch moved his millions around, making enough money to keep his hangers-on fed daily on France's finest cuisine.

There were usually twelve at table, and whilst we lunched like royalty, Mr Lynch, cursed with the millionaire's ulcer, toyed with a little fruit and Vittel water. He sat with his pale face almost entirely concealed by a Quentin Crisp hat and his small, round body covered by a large white napkin, occasionally murmuring to Betty. He never spoke loudly enough to talk to his guests directly, but always through the clear, cool English voice of Betty. At the third lunch which we had together, he finally looked in my direction and mumbled something to her.

'Mr Alwyn,' she called down the table, 'Mr Lynch would like to know what you do.'

All eyes turned in my direction. I was the guest of an American millionaire in Monte Carlo, and this was no time for false modesty, so I plunged in.

'I conduct at Covent Garden.'

All eyes now turned back to Mr Lynch. Then followed, 'Mumble, mumble, mumble', and everyone looked at Betty, eagerly awaiting Mr Lynch's response to this exciting news.

She spoke. 'Mr Lynch says that Frank Sinatra is the greatest conductor in the world.'

Well, here I was cracking Mr Lynch's lobster, so I paused and thought before I replied to this extraordinary statement. Sinatra always knew inside out the wonderful orchestral arrangements made for him by Nelson Riddle, so that when they were rehearsed with other conductors, Sinatra would move from section to section, encouraging the players to make the sort of sound that Riddle had intended. Finally, at a charity concert, he himself conducted the Nelson Riddle Orchestra – and very well too, by all accounts.

All eyes were now in my direction and, with a knowing smile, I replied:

'Nelson Riddle' (which must have itself been a riddle to those unfamiliar with Sinatra's backing orchestra).

Down the table the word was passed from one guest to another: 'Riddle!' 'Riddle!'

Unlike the request sent back by an Army General from the front line ('Send reinforcements, we're going to advance!', which was received at the rear as: 'Send three and fourpence, we're going to a dance!'), when Betty repeated it to Mr Lynch, my reply seemed to please him, for that evening Ted and I were invited to dinner at his house. It resembled a movie set, which indeed it was. It was here that *The Monte Carlo Story* had been filmed, and at dinner I learnt that my chair had once supported the beautiful undercarriage of Marlene Dietrich.

The next night, our generous host invited us to dinner and cabaret at the Sea Club where, after Eartha Kitt's one-woman show, there was to be a grand firework display.

With Ted Harwicke at the Sea Club, Monte Carlo

The evening began well with champagne, but it was not Mr Lynch's usual vintage, and he had it removed by white-gloved waiters, mid-glass. Dinner was now delayed, so when in her famous song, 'An Old-Fashioned Millionaire' Miss Kitt reached the line about the 'slurping' of oil wells, six feet away from her, a real-life millionaire and his guests were slurping champagne, rudely and noisily enjoying our delayed dinner.

In spite of being a very big star (Orson Welles described her as 'the most exciting woman in the world'), she persevered until, suddenly and ahead of schedule, her song was drowned by rockets and Catherine wheels.

All heads now turned the splendid spectacle in the bay and, finally defeated by the cacophony of cutlery, chatter, whizz-bangs and rockets, Eartha Kitt turned her eyed to heaven, muttered 'Shit!' and stalked off.

Practically no one but Ted and I noticed.

A tough audience, the Monegasques.

Our last night in Monaco was even more memorable. Mr Lynch knew of Ted's famous father, Sir Cedric, but also knew that Cedric's son, like all young struggling actors, was short of the ready, so this generous American gave us each fifty francs 'for incidental expenses'. Perhaps we'll have a flutter on the tables ourselves, we thought, but when our party was admitted to the exclusive Salon Privé, where admission was by invitation only, we knew that fifty francs wouldn't even get us a drink at the bar.

The Salon Privé's golden columns reached to the high, frescoed ceilings and the walls hung with splendid paintings. Under a crystal chandelier, as the centrepiece of all this magnificence, was a *chemin de fer* table, around which sat Aristotle Onassis, M. Dubonnet and a couple of anxious-looking Americans. Before each of them was a stack of colourful plaques, the larger of these representing ten thousand francs and the smaller being the minimum stake of five thousand francs.

Once again, I'd been shown the riches of the world, but, remembering how my mother had had to sell the furniture to keep us fed, I found it appalling to see these people lightly losing the equivalent of a house and a car.

However, I took a sip of champagne and held my peace.

My fifty francs came in very useful the next day for the hotel bill. Ted and I had just enough money to get back to England: he to Bristol and me to the Opera House for an occasion which proved to have all the makings of a disaster.

CHAPTER 27

PASTURES NEW

Benjamin Britten brings Bali to Bow Street

My first work with the Company at Covent Garden was *The Prince of the Pagodas*, the first original full-length ballet ever commissioned by the Royal Ballet. The choreographer was the young South African, John Cranko, who, with Charles Mackerras, had had outstanding successes with *Pineapple Poll* and *The Lady and the Fool*. But these were one-acters, and now he was to be trusted with the whole evening: an enormous undertaking that required not only good story-telling but also great choreographic invention.

For this one, Cranko moved from Charlie to the composer of the opera *Peter Grimes:* Benjamin Britten. Ben had proved his ability to write full-length operas, but was initially reluctant to follow in the steps of Tchaikovsky, whose *Swan Lake*, *Sleeping Beauty* and *Casse-Noisette* (*The Nutcracker*) each occupied a whole evening. However, he was persuaded, and wrote a brilliant score. It was inventive and colourful, with strong rhythms vital to the dance matching the exotic plot of *Pagodas* (described as a mixture of *King Lear*, *Beauty and the Beast* and *Cinderella*) with transformation scenes, travel music and a happy ending to a great final waltz.

By the time I joined the Company, *Pagodas* had been in rehearsal for some weeks with a pianist who'd been prepared by Britten himself. But when I appeared, he was fired to save money, and I had to take over from him. The accountants were at work.

When one is in at a ballet's beginnings, the music is choreographed a few bars at a time, so the pianist has the chance to learn the notes and the all-important cues. But *Pagodas* was already at an advanced stage, and one dreadful morning I found myself at the grand piano in the orchestral pit of the Royal Opera House playing for a run-through of the first act, some of which was entirely new to me.

To make matters worse, sitting at the orchestral rail was Britten himself. In the theatre were Ninette de Valois, Sir David Webster and Frederick Ashton, who had all come to see how well Britten and Cranko had succeeded in this unique venture. I could see nothing of the stage, nor was anyone conducting, and so on the word 'And!' from an invisible John Cranko, I began.

It is difficult to describe my feelings as, in what is appropriately named the pit, I struggled with Ben's very difficult piano transcription of his brilliant score. I was entirely in darkness except for a single, wobbly angle-poise lamp. I could see nothing, and could only hear the sound of the dancers' feet and incomprehensible shouts from the stalls.

The first act of *Pagodas* is nearly forty minutes long, but before it ended I began to crack. It became clear from the shouts from the stalls that I had no idea about cues, and very little about the tempi. The rehearsal was becoming a disaster when two palely-illuminated faces appeared at the orchestral rail: Britten and Bob Irving. A puzzled Britten looked at me, realised that I wasn't his pianist, and said to Bob, 'Haven't you got someone else?'

Dear Bob, ever the kind man, descended into my pit of shame and reprieved me with: 'I'll play, Kenneth.'

I have never previously drunk to drown my sorrows, but I went through the stage door for what I was sure was the last time and took the few steps across Floral Street to the Nag's Head where, at eleven-thirty in the morning I proceeded to down strong ale until the memory of my disgrace was clouded, and my only thought was how to get back to my basement home and comfortable bed.

The next day, with the mother and father of all hangovers, I went to ground in my gloomy basement, wondering what was going to happen to me now that my short-lived career at the Royal Opera House had ended in disgrace. I was not accustomed to failure, and I was hit hard. Late in the afternoon, I reluctantly answered the phone for a call from Robert Irving. His tone was kindly.

'You weren't at rehearsal today, Kenneth.'

'I don't think I'm much good to you," I replied.

'Nonsense! We're going to bring back Ben's pianist, and I want you to start work on our revival of *Petrouchka*.'

My career was reprieved in this most positive way, but there was a lesson for us both in what had happened. Firstly, at such a critical phase of the mounting of *Pagodas*, the management should not have changed horses mid-stream to save money; secondly, I should not have been so eager to please that I agreed to be the replacement horse.

When next I met Ben, it was at the first orchestral rehearsals of *Pagodas*. He was quite agreeable to me, and I sat, if not at his feet, at least behind the rostrum, listening as, under his direction, the black and white piano version of the score which I had struggled with became clothed in beautiful orchestral colours. It was all splendid, but it was his music for *The King of the East* which erased for us both his earlier 'Haven't you got someone else?' After a few bars, I exclaimed in delighted surprise, 'A Gamelan Orchestra!'

In 1956 there were not many musicians who recognised the sound of an orchestra from the island of Bali, but I had heard one when I was a Colonial Officer in Singapore. Ben told me that he and his partner, Peter Pears, had gone all the way to Bali to hear one first-hand. As many of the Gamelan instruments were not in the Covent Garden orchestra, Ben had an expert, James Blades, make instruments which copied the perfumed sound of the Balinese percussion, chimes, bells, gongs and woodblocks. The Balinese tunes were played by the orchestral flutes, and the two-string Arab violins – the *Rebab* – were imitated mainly by violas.

It worked perfectly. Ben and Blades brought Bali to Bow Street.

Each rehearsal brought to life music for the kings of the North, South and West. Gustav Holst's daughter, Imogen, assisted Britten's at rehearsal, and we sat together. When a harpist declared something he'd written to be 'unplayable', Ben sent Imogen to show her that it wasn't. Such was Britten's skill and knowledge that not one note in over two hours of music needed to be changed.

In 1956 Britten was at the height of his powers as a composer, but, as yet, he had not found his feet as a conductor. The orchestra had great respect for him, but he was very nervous and was inclined to over-conduct, a failing of the inexperienced.

In Act 2, Ben had written a waltz ('Clouds, Stars and Moon'). Each bar of three beats is followed by another containing four, but taking the same amount of time as the one of three. The way to conduct it is to beat one in a bar and trust the orchestra to fit in the four notes themselves. Ben correctly beat the first bar in one, but trying to be helpful, he beat the four-note bars in two, which made those bars a bit too long, and he spoilt his own idea. I yearned to say something, but wisely kept my counsel.

Ben never seemed relaxed on the rostrum, but his five performances went very well. As always, when I took over, it was without rehearsal (quite an undertaking), but by this time, I knew the music very well, even drawing a rare compliment from Ninette de Valois.

Although our 1957 production looked wonderful, sometimes Cranko's fantastical confection faltered, and it was thought that he'd not been creative enough for his beautiful ballerina, Svetlana Beriosova, and her handsome prince, David Blair. When Belle Rose and her prince finally get together, perhaps Ben's own temperament did not inspire him to a great romantic *pas de deux*, where we yearned for music with the sort of warmth and intensity which Tchaikovsky (even though also gay) was able to bring to the moments of love between a man and a woman. At this point, Ben's music was generally felt to be lacking in romance.

In 1989 'Pagodas' was re-choreographed by Kenneth MacMillan. Even so, the ballet is very rarely performed, but there is an excellent recording conducted by Britten in 1958, and there are occasional performances of a concert suite.

Whilst Ben's pianist had been completing the piano rehearsals, as Bob had promised, I found myself very busy with our revival of *Petrouchka*. Here, unlike my first encounter with *Pagodas*, I scored heavily, for I played from a version written for four hands at one piano. This meant combining four lines of music, giving emphasis to the most prominent orchestral sound. This on-the-spot adaptation suited both my somewhat limited piano technique and my well-developed orchestral sense.

The revival was in the hands of Serge Grigoriev, who had been a member of the committee with which Diaghilev sometimes consulted, comprising composers, artists and the odd prince or two. His background as a leading character dancer at the Mariinsky meant that Diaghilev trusted him to hire and fire the small soloists and *corps de ballet*. It was Grigoriev who hired the little Irish girl, Edris Stannus, who was to become the mother of English ballet: Ninette de Valois.

At all our rehearsals was his wife, Lubov Tchernicheva, who had been the Company Ballet Mistress, had danced The Ballerina in the first performance of *Petrouchka* in 1911.

To work closely with such a pair was like a step backwards in time. Grigoriev, though now well into his seventies, was still hale and hearty, with a perfect memory of every step of Fokine's original production, and he remembered precisely the tempi agreed between Stravinsky and conductor Pierre Monteux. In the Shrovetide Fair scene, when he instructed our male *corps* to *tour en l'air* (pirouette in the air), our boys, who could easily pirouette in the air twice, did so. Grigoriev protested: 'No, no, no!' In the Diaghilev Company, only principal dancers were allowed a *double tour en l'air*. Otherwise, the principal dancers could be mistaken for ordinary *corps de ballet*.

Rehearsals were very intensive, and there was little opportunity to ask my many questions about Diaghilev, but when one day I dropped in for a meal at Lyons Corner House, there sitting at a table were Grigoriev and Tchernicheva, two glittering stars of the past, sharing a roll and butter and a pot of tea. It was a self-service restaurant, so I suspected that must be all they could afford. I decided that this was neither the time nor place for questions about their great days.

Although I never did find the right moment to ask for their personal reminiscences, working with these two key figures from the greatest of ballet companies gave me confidence when I moved from the piano to conducting my own performances. Bob was at rehearsal daily and was scheduled to conduct the first night of the revival – or so we both thought, until one Sunday evening, when I was going through the score with him at his flat, the phone rang.

'Good evening, Robert,' said Sir Malcolm Sargent. 'I expect you know they've asked me to conduct *Petrouchka*, and I thought we might discuss rehearsals.'

The fact was, Bob *didn't* know.

As he said to me at the end of what must have been a very difficult phone call, although he was quite used to distinguished guest conductors – Ansermet, Bliss, Walton, Britten, Arnold *et al* – how could his friends and colleagues of many years put him in a situation where he had to pretend to knowledge which he didn't have?

The treacherous sands of the Opera House were beginning to shift – again!

At the time, Ernest Ansermet was with the Company, directing the ballet he'd conducted at its first performance in 1919: Manuel de Fallas' *The Three-Cornered Hat*. At the dress rehearsal, although the dancers muttered that the music was much too fast, no one dared rebuke such a great man. But came the performance, when Ansermet delivered exactly the same tempi, the dancers came off stage raving about the exciting music. After Ansermet's last guest appearance, I discovered that he'd left behind one of his batons. It was light, about a foot long and beautifully balanced, and I used it on 25th February 1957 in Coventry to conduct *Sleeping Beauty* with Margot Fonteyn and Alexis Rassine. Afterwards, we all went to dinner at the Leofric Hotel, and for the first time I really felt a member of this world-class company. Henceforth, I conducted all my performances with Ansermet's baton, or with copies which I had specially made by Guiviers of London and known as 'The Ansermet No. 1'.

I still have the original.

The Company had been invited to perform in Russia. The Bolshoi Ballet, which had had great success in London, was considered at that time to be the greatest company in the world, if a little old-fashioned. It was decided not to play them at their own game by competing with their splendid versions of the great classics, but instead to take a repertoire of contemporary English ballets. These included *The Lady and the Fool, Daphnis and Chloé, Checkmate* and, to commemorate the 25th anniversary of the Sadler's Wells Ballet, Frederick Ashton's *Birthday Offering*. We rehearsed very hard and felt that we'd show the Russians a thing or two, but on 4th November, 1956, Russia invaded Hungary. Budapest was bombed, there were tanks in the streets, and to reflect a violent wave of anti-Russian feeling, the government cancelled our visit.

As the year drew to a close, there was a great feeling of anti-climax in the Company, which had really been looking forward to visiting Russia – even though we'd heard there were no plugs in the bathroom. Worse still, there were rumours of poor quality and badly-served food in hotels staffed by people with neither knowledge of nor interest in the comfort of their guests. I didn't mind too much, for I became busy conducting the bulk of the repertoire and, most interestingly, Stravinsky's *Scènes de Ballet* and *Firebird*.

Another lonely Christmas was avoided when I was invited by one of our soloists, Meriel Evans, and her husband, Luke, to Christmas lunch with most of the surviving Asquith family. The Asquiths had always been in the front rank of the English elite, producing a Prime Minister (Edward, known in the family as 'Squiffy'), and at Christmas lunch, there was the director of many successful English films, Anthony (known as 'Puff'). In the war, Luke Asquith had fought in the very long Italian campaign and had been one of Churchill's aides. He told of how the old man kept an oxygen bottle under his desk to revive him after the very long nights, when he planned the next step in the war and drank his Generals under the table. Churchill always offered Luke 'a sniff' on their first meeting of the day. The oldest Asquith at lunch was a lady simply referred to as 'darling'. She was well over eighty, but she seems to have been protected from the rough edges of this world. In spite of there being twelve at table, conversation did not split up into those irritating duologues, so we all heard the old lady addressing Luke: 'Lukey, darling, I'd like to ask you something.'

We paused, mid-turkey, and then in the cultured tones of the English upper-class, she spoke.

'What does 'f***' mean?'

All eyes turned to Luke, who had not worked for Churchill without learning a thing or two.

'Well, darling, it's a common slang word for what Meriel and I do in bed together.'

'Oh, that!' she said, in a tone that made me wonder if this Victorian lady had enjoyed making babies as much as her Queen.

CHAPTER 28

1957: A GREAT YEAR

Sir Malcolm Sargent sends me to his tailor

My new life at the Royal Opera House was exciting, stimulating and demanding. But I missed the intimacy of the Theatre Ballet: those Sunday journeys when the Company would take over the cold, damp trains and bring them warmth and laughter; the determined silence and serious drinking of the orchestral poker school; chomping one's way through stale buffet sandwiches and bitter coffee; sleeping off the exhaustion of the two Saturday performances; and then, usually in the rain, looking for digs and an affordable meal in an English town where the only restaurants open on Sundays were Chinese and the only people walking the streets were policemen.

Mostly, I missed having a warm and exciting place to go each evening. Even in the provincial towns, theatres were oases of red plush, rich ornamentation and romantic lighting, designed to bring a touch of luxury to an audience who lived and worked in drab buildings dedicated to industry. The luxury didn't extend to backstage, where we shared pokey little dressing rooms and the one lavatory.

Happy days.

But I'd taken the decision to leave all that behind me before I was promoted to Covent Garden, and so it was time to grasp the future. Although the main Company rehearsed daily, it took place at the studios in Barons Court, a few miles from the Opera House. I now saw Annette again every day at class and, as of old, I could always make her giggle when I played silly tunes for serious exercises. *Battement en cloche*, when the dancer must swing a leg like the clapper of a church bell, requires a lot of physical effort which, in my view, is helped along by light-hearted music. Annette had quickly became popular, amusing her new friends with wicked impersonations of imaginary conversations between Margot (whom she strikingly resembled) and who possessed a somewhat 'cut-glass' voice and 'Madame, whose soft Dublin accent had a upward inflection, as though everything were some kind of unwelcome surprise.

Annette now was with a fine-looking young dancer of romantic appearance, Ronald Hynd. They married, and when they eventually left the Company, Ronald became one of the English *Maîtres de Danse* that de Valois provided for companies throughout the world. He became the Director and choreographer of the Bavarian State Ballet, and his ballet *The Merry Widow* has been given by sixteen international companies. With Annette always at his side, they are widely respected throughout Europe and the Americas.

I was now sharing my flat with Courtney Kenny, my second pianist in Bristol, who had become a great friend. He was Irish, and the nephew of song-writer, Percy French, of 'Phil the Fluter's Ball' fame. Courtney's great love was opera, and he ran a small festival in his home town of Ballinrobe, Co. Mayo, but he was also a fine classical pianist.

I was down to conduct three of our four performances of Balanchine's *Ballet Imperial* (set to Tchaikovsky's *Second Piano Concerto*). Bob had conducted the opening night, when the solo pianist had been Shura Cherkassky, but Shura wasn't free for the remaining three, and so, at my suggestion, Courtney, being well up to playing the Tchaikovsky, auditioned for Bob. We also needed another rehearsal pianist, and he agreed to join the team, bravely making his debut with Tchaikovsky under my baton.

On 16th January our manager, the august Michael Wood (rumoured to be a distant cousin of the Queen) called the Sadler's Wells and Covent Garden Companies together on the stage of the Royal Opera House and announced that the Her Majesty had granted a Royal Charter, and that henceforth we would be called the Royal Ballet. It was a dignified occasion, but it was lightened by us singing a few lines from South Pacific in praise of Ninette de Valois, the Irish dancer who had brought Sadler's Wells so far: 'There is nothing like a Dame'!

Petrouchka was now in the regular repertoire, and I sometime shared a mixed bill programme with Sir Malcolm Sargent. I found him a friendly man, who had the kindness to compliment me on my conducting, and so I was not at all inclined to join in some strange mockery, some of it led by his rival, Sir Thomas Beecham. I am reminded of Shaw's preface to *Androcles and the Lion*: 'When a lion meets another with a louder roar, the first lion thinks the last a bore.' Beecham never lost an opportunity to score against the immaculate and old-fashioned Doctor Sargent, nicknamed 'Flash Harry'. When Doctor Sargent was knighted, Beecham expressed surprise with the line, 'I knew the fellow had been doctored, but I didn't know they'd knighted him!' (This innuendo about Sargent's marital state produced a cheap chuckle from his Royal Philharmonic Orchestra.)

Beecham continued to refer to 'Doctor Sargent', presumably considering him unworthy of the title that Beecham himself only bore because his grandfather had made a fortune with his patented 'Little Liver Pills'.

It is said that after Beecham's grandfather, a music lover, had paid for a new set of hymn books for his church, a well-known carol now read:

Hark the herald angels sing,
Beecham's pills are just the thing.

On another occasion, when told that Sargent was conducting in the Far East, he stroked his beard and responded with, 'Ha! A Flash in Japan!'

Sargent was frequently the butt of mindless humour. He was even mocked for arriving by Rolls Royce at the artists' entrance of the Royal Albert Hall, when his flat in Albert Hall Mansions was just across the road, but it was far enough away for him to be overwhelmed by autograph-hunters if he walked. I asked the elderly and gentle Archie Campbell – the greatest bassoonist of his generation, whose career had grown with Sargent's – why the man did not receive the orchestral affection lavished on Beecham. Archie had no real answer, but told me that when he first played at the 'Proms' in Henry Wood's time, the orchestra, like head waiters, wore black ties with tails, but Sir Malcolm's association with the Royal Family raised the profile of orchestral musicians, who now all wore white ties, like 'real gentlemen'.

Unlike Beecham's free and easy way with his musicians, Malcolm kept an old-fashioned discipline.

At one of his orchestral rehearsals, the two flutes were having a problem with a duet. They tried it again, but it was no better, and the principal flute suggested that Sargent leave the passage for them to practise on their own without the pressure of a waiting orchestra. Sargent refused, and insisted they play it for the third time. In his turn, the principal flute refused, so Sargent ordered him to leave the platform. It was an extraordinary move, for the player was not only the most famous flautist of his day, he was also a personal friend of the conductor.

Sargent was an autocrat, but then all the great orchestras were in the hands of what became known as the 'last of the great dictators': Toscanini in New York; Stokowski in Philadelphia; George Szell in Cleveland, John Barbirolli with the Hallé *et al*; and, unlike today, neither conductor nor player used first names.

One evening at Covent Garden, when I'd conducted the first two ballets and Sir Malcolm was waiting to conduct *Petrouchka*, we got to talking about the sheer physical effort of rehearsing and conducting four Proms in a week.

We calculated that he moved his right arm something in the nature of a hundred thousand times. It was another reminder to keep my wrist loose, in the best traditions of fencing.

He was very nice to me and suggested that I could do with a new set of tails, recommending that I went to his own tailor, an elderly gentleman who'd been with Moss Bros for many years. When the old boy measured me, he remarked, 'Yes, just like Sir Malcolm. Your right shoulder is higher than your left!'

I found it a very sad sight when, some years later at the Last Night of the Proms, Malcolm, who was dying of cancer and was only a shadow of his former self (but looking as immaculate as always), made a brave and funny speech of farewell.

Then, in the sad silence that followed, a lone voice called out, 'Good old Flash!', and that great audience responded with the affection that his musicians had denied him for years.

Bob and I were still keeping the curtain up, but finally the Royal Ballet's new Musical Director, Hugo Rignold, arrived.

Bob wrote later:

Hugo duly arrived in the spring with the title of Musical Director, and this was to prove something of a milestone in my life. After a few months, I took stock of the situation and began to feel it was time for a change.

The conducting situation at the Sadler's Wells Theatre Ballet was not healthy after I left. Jack's only assistant, one of the violins, stepped up for a couple of performances each week, but was not thought capable of conducting a short tour of Spain, so I went back temporarily to my old Company. It had changed a good deal, but the pioneering spirit was still there.

In May, I re-joined the Royal Ballet for the Dublin Festival in a programme which included Ashton's *Birthday Offering*. Glazunov's music had been put together for Fred by Robert Irving, and so he had conducted the first performance that very month.

During a performance, one of the dancers had fallen on stage – a very rare occurrence – and at a curtain speech, Ninette de Valois (with her Irish accent stronger that we'd ever heard it) explained to the audience about 'an old theatrical tradition that if someone falls on stage, it means that they will be coming back'. I suspect that it was a tradition that she'd just invented, a piece of pure Irish blarney, but the place went wild.

On 21st June I dusted off my old organ shoes to play for Ted Hardwicke's wedding to Anne, an actress from his Bristol days. The reception was at Checkendon Manor, now the home of his mother 'Pixie', who, having divorced Sir Cedric, had married an elderly millionaire financier. He was a charming man, obviously delighted with his new actress wife and her many famous friends. Ted's best man was Ronnie Corbett and the guests, included Sir Ralph Richardson, Ernest Thesiger, Clive Dunne, Sam Wanamaker and Peter O'Toole.

The happy couple left for their honeymoon and I for the Company's annual month's holiday. As usual, I was at a loose end and, having already spent Christmas with the Asquiths, Meriel suggested that I might like to join her and Luke at a small hotel in Italy. There were to be several of the dancers and our pianist, Jean Gilbert. Luke had bought a brand new green Morris van for the trip, but there were only two front seats, and so Jean and I sat on the floor in the back, bumping over the streets of

France and Italy with no sight of the outside world for nearly a thousand miles. Our hotel in Praiano, perched high on the rocks, was run by a former English prisoner-of-war, Luca. It had a wonderful view of Capri. All the rooms opened onto a balcony, from which two hundred steps led down to the sea and from where, under the black water, one seemed to be flying next to a submerged mountain.

One of our party was Mary Drage, who danced the beautiful Tsarina in *Firebird,* and she had come on holiday with her father, Commander Charles Drage R.N. Charles was a great scholar and biographer. He recommended that a young man like myself should emulate the ancient Greeks and once a year take part in an orgy. The nearest we got to that was when we visited Pompeii and, spotting this elderly gentleman and his young companion, the guides showed us the erotica normally kept under cover. During his service with naval intelligence in Hong Kong Charles had become friendly with a young Jewish Cockney who was a General in the Chinese Army. Inspired by Cohen's incredible life, he wrote his biography. Charles gave me a copy: *Two-Gun Cohen* is a great read.

This holiday with my new friends was colourful, but once back home, it was becoming increasingly clear that the 'treacherous sands' of the Royal Opera House were on the move again, and it was time to look ahead.

I invited the BBC Head of Light Music, Frank Wade, to a performance of *Swan Lake* which I was conducting for Margot Fonteyn. He was sufficiently impressed to invite me to lunch to tell me about his new Concert Orchestra and to play its recording of Wagner's *Meistersinger Overture* on an electric turntable using a thorn needle!

This new BBC Concert Orchestra had only seventy musicians. Nevertheless, with some expert balancing of the reduced string sections, for the first time the BBC had an orchestra that was dedicated to performing the popular classics of Franz von Suppé, Wagner, Strauss, Tchaikovsky, Puccini and Verdi in their original form.

He raised the orchestra's profile by inviting conductors from the concert hall and the world of ballet and opera. Charles Mackerras and I were among the first.

In the days when Friday night was when the ladies washed their hair ready for the week-end, the enterprising shampoo manufacturer Anami coined the slogan 'Friday Night is Anami Night'. Frank gained a lot of free publicity for his orchestra by naming the orchestra's flagship programme, *Friday Night is Music Night*.

Anami is no longer with us, but over fifty years later, 'Friday Night is Music Night' is the longest-running live radio programme in the world.

When I met the BBC Concert Orchestra for the first time, I sensed that they were determined not to be regarded as a second-class symphony orchestra but as the best concert orchestra in the world. On the first run-through of Vaughan Williams' *Sea Songs*, Delius' *Walk to the Paradise Garden* and Malcolm Arnold's *Scottish Dances*, it was immediately obvious that the players possessed both that particular skill of British musicians – almost perfect sight reading – and, because they were reaching upwards together, a strong sense of family. The timpanist and first percussion were father and daughter.

They were a pleasure to work with, both then and for the next fifty years which we were to spend making music together.

It had been a great year for me so far, and I was looking forward to the Company's fifth American tour. On 5th September, we trooped aboard a Constellation aircraft, bound for New York.

CHAPTER 29

NORTH AMERICA AGAIN

*Frederick Ashton takes a pill
and Alfred Hitchcock spills the beans*

Fred Ashton, who was terrified of flying, took a pill and curled up in a sleeping berth for the entire flight. I sat next to Bob, and was surprised when he seemed very nervous as the four engines came to full power and we began the take-off roll.

'God, I hate this bit,' he said.

'But Bob,' I replied,' in the war you flew Beaufighters, and the Royal Air Force gave you a Distinguished Flying Cross – twice!'

'Yes,' he replied, 'but I know what goes on under the bonnet, dear. This is a very dangerous moment!'

He was right to be more than a little apprehensive, for the *four*-engined Constellation Starliner was known in the trade as the best *three*-motor airliner in the world. In the two months before our flight, all four engines of one Constellation had failed and it had come down in the sea. Another time, an engine had simply dropped off, and it had force-landed in the desert.

Luckily, ours did neither, and fifteen hours later, it delivered us safely to New York for the first of our hundred and forty performances throughout America and Canada on a five-month tour.

My first impressions of New York were of a city trying to catch up with itself. Everyone was in too much of a rush to pause long enough to hold a swing door open but would instead let it slam in one's face. This 'city of canyons', with steam coming from whatever hell was below the streets, was hot, noisy and claustrophobic. Sinatra may have sung of a 'wonderful town', but a friendly town it was not. Even after many visits in subsequent years, my first impressions remain unchanged, and I can't wait to get out of the place. However the *Algonquin*, an Edwardian hotel just off Times Square, frequented by actors and writers such as Douglas Fairbanks, John Barrymore, Robert Benchley and Gertrude Stein, was quiet and the staff courteous. It was a haven of peace in the war of the streets, and it had the reputation of being the best hotel in New York. It certainly served the best dry martinis, mixed by the oldest barman in America.

As on the previous American tours, our impresario was Sol Hurok. Although Hurok was short in stature, like many small men, he had a fiercely dominant personality, and he insisted that a member of his family join us as the required American member of our conducting staff. The guest might have been useful, but there was a rumour that, on a previous tour, Hurok's protégé had fallen out with a violinist, had snatched his instrument out of his hand and had threatened to beat him with it. True or false, he did not conduct one note on the whole tour.

The American Union had a rule that the size of the orchestra was dependent on the audience capacity of the venue, and they gave Hurok a quota of musicians which he had to pay, even though they were not required musically. An ice rink with a capacity of five thousand would mean that, as well as paying our touring orchestra of about ninety players, Hurok would have to pay for an extra twenty, whether they played or not.

It fell to me to go ahead and take a rehearsal of these compulsory 'extras'. To rehearse twenty players of various odd instruments in Stravinsky's *Firebird* is almost comic, except that it is so difficult to do, and I did a lot of singing of missing parts to try to hold things together.

If I decided that I could trust a few players, I let them play at the performance. Otherwise they watched the performance, were paid off, and went home!

Although Bob wrote in his autobiography that he didn't remember feeling resentful at being promoted downwards from the post of Musical Director to Musical Adviser (and so, conducting fewer performances), the relationship between him and Hugo was cool, and then there came the occasion which was the subject of this book's Prologue.

In his autobiography, Bob explains all:

No one had asked me to conduct the second night of 'Birthday', and I had a suspicion that Hugo had not realised he was down for the whole programme, but I was not going to volunteer uninvited. Sure enough, when I got back to the hotel after a pleasant night out, Dennis Maunder, the stage manager, asked anxiously, 'What happened? Did you forget? I thought you'd been run over by a bus!' There had been a minor panic, and Kenneth Alwyn had been pushed into a white tie and thrust into the pit to save the day.'

I had a loyalty to Bob, the man who'd given me my job, but I nevertheless found myself increasingly attracted to Hugo's expertise.

Bob and Hugo were so different. Bob was the son of a Master of Winchester public school and had read music at Oxford, whereas Hugo was from a family of professional musicians and had come from Canada to study the violin at the Royal Academy of Music.

Although a fine classical violinist (he played the Beethoven *Violin Concerto* under the baton of Sir Henry Wood), when Hugo left the Academy, he initially earned a living in Jack Hylton's Dance Orchestra playing the violin, and, as was the custom in those days, the saxophone and also joining in the vocals. He left to form his own band, and to the names of Mantovani, Joe Loss, Billy Cotton and Charlie Kunz was added Hugo Rignold and the Kettner Five.

As I mentioned at the close of the Prologue, Hugo was described in *Melody Maker* as that 'super jazz artist' and was acknowledged as one of the three greatest jazz violinists in the world, alongside Joe Venuti and Stéphane Grappelli.

When war broke out in 1939, Hugo joined the Royal Air Force and was posted to Cairo, where he put his classical background to good use conducting the Cairo Symphony Orchestra (later, the Israeli Philharmonic) in concerts for the troops. At the end of the war, and having no job, he became the principal viola of the orchestra of the Royal Opera House. But this was no dead-end, for one day the conductor fell ill and, as mentioned earlier in this book, Hugo stepped up from the first desk of violas to save the day by conducting – without rehearsal – Delius' *Paris, Song of a Great City*.

It was a move which was to have far-reaching consequences. His old boss, Jack Hylton, who had sponsored classical music concerts during the war and had a great deal of influence, suggested that he become the conductor of the Liverpool Philharmonic Orchestra, and his career really took off. He moved on to join the City of Birmingham Symphony Orchestra, and he was still there when he joined us – no longer as first viola of the orchestra but as Musical Director of the ballet.

By the time he got to us, his light music career was long forgotten, but I have a recording from pre-war days called 'Calling All Keys' in which he plays on both viola and violin and demonstrates how well he deserved his reputation as an outstanding jazz violinist.

I naturally gravitated to him and his delightful daughter, Jennifer, who had been one of the first announcers on BBC Children's Television. Jen was pretty, with a wonderful smile that lit up the small screen. But now she was following her own ambition and dancing with the Royal Ballet.

All the girl dancers had been provided with a free wardrobe by the London fashion houses, which were keen to promote the British look. They wore the clothes like models and were very popular with the New York balletomanes.

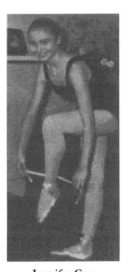

Jennifer Gay

One very rich enthusiast invited us all to lunch at his palatial home on Long Island. His guests of honour were Margot and her fiancé, Roberto d'Arias, known as Tito. After a splendid lunch, done full justice by the ever-hungry dancers, most of us decided on a swim in our host's private lake. But Georgina Parkinson was no swimmer, and, not to be outdone, held onto a small rowing boat and thrashed about a bit until she lost her grip. It was almost too late for her when Tito noticed that she had disappeared. He dived in, unravelled her from the weeds, and brought her to the bank, where she lay in a scene which resembled the death of Ophelia. Tito saved her life.

Thanks to Tito, Georgina survived to dance leading roles at the Garden, and eventually to become Ballet Mistress of the American Dance Theatre Company.

En route to see the Old Sequoia in Yosemite National Park

Left to right: Hylda Zinkin, me, Margaret Hill, the driver, Maryon Lane, Georgina Parkinson, Ronald Hynd, Pirmin Trecu, Annette Page, Bryan Ashbridge and Dorothea Zaymes

The tour was a great experience, and we spent a great deal of time, both day and night, on our private train. Cast your mind back to the special train of the all-girl band in *Some Like it Hot*, and the goings-on behind the curtains of the sleeping berths of Tony Curtis, Marilyn Monroe and Jack Lemmon, and you'll get some idea of the intimate but innocent atmosphere of a night on the Royal Ballet's special train.

As we steamed our way across the wide open spaces, the evocative train whistle warning the cattle and cowboys to clear the line ahead, I half-expected to see Indians galloping alongside and arrows flying. Having a private train meant that we could ask the driver to stop so that the dancers could stretch their legs – vital if they were to be on top form when we arrived. The journey took three days. After arriving in Los Angeles, the day was spent rehearsing, but the next day Hugo and I lunched at the Brown Derby at the invitation of an old friend of his, Dave

Raksin. Raksin was well known to me as the composer of 'Laura', my signature tune on Radio Malaya.

Perhaps Raksin's most intriguing success was making elephants dance the polka! The Barnum and Bailey Circus had commissioned Stravinsky to write music for their elephants. The choreographer was George Balanchine and the piece was called *Circus Polka*. Unfortunately, the elephants didn't like the music, and the story goes that Balanchine sent a telegram to Stravinsky: 'Elephants won't dance.'

Back came the reply, 'Send more money.'

Balanchine obliged and the composer sent back a revised version. But the elephants didn't like this one either, so Balanchine sent a new telegram: 'Elephants still won't dance.'

Back came the same reply: 'Send more money.'

Stravinsky's third version failed again, but this time Balanchine passed the problem to Dave Raksin.

Finally, the elephants danced the polka to everyone's satisfaction – not least Stravinsky's, who had made a deal of money out of a three-minute piece (elephants, like ballet dancers, find a three-minute dance quite long enough!)

From Dave, we heard of the lifestyles of the Hollywood musicians. Even the lowliest second violin could afford a big house and swimming pool. Actually, there were no lowly violins in Hollywood, for film music was very big business, attracting not only the best players from all over America but also European composers like Erich Korngold, Max Steiner and Miklós Rózsa – many of whose film scores I was later to record.

At the Shrine Auditorium, Stravinsky came to the performance of *Firebird*. Bob conducted, and we were all anxious to meet the great man, but afterwards he went straight home. Bob was particularly disappointed. However, he should not have taken it too much to heart, for Stravinsky hardly ever had a good word for any conductor, and was particularly critical of all performances of *Firebird*.

The last scene of this wonderful ballet is the wedding of Prince Ivan and the Tsarevna in a gold and silver palace, with the courtiers in magnificent costumes and everything that suggested the splendour of a Russian Court. There is initially no movement on stage but just a wonderful tableau, matched by a broad, noble theme, which is begun by a solo French horn and taken up by the full orchestra. Then, as the theme changes to double speed, the tableau comes to life.

However exactly doubling the speed, as Stravinsky instructs in the score, makes it all look and sound a bit of a rush, so most of us do it a tad slower – something that apparently infuriates the composer. Perhaps that's why he left after Bob's performance. However, when some years later I heard Stravinsky conduct it himself, did he double the speed? He did not!

By halfway through the American tour, it had become increasingly clear that the relationship between Robert Irving and Hugo Rignold was not a happy one.

Fortunately, the situation resolved itself when Bob heard from a friend of his in the New York City Ballet that its conductor, Léon Barzin, was leaving. He flew to Toronto for a meeting with George Balanchine, who welcomed him with open arms and immediately appointed him Musical Director to take over from Barzin the following May. It was the perfect solution, and Bob was to remain a great friend and adviser to Balanchine for the next thirty years.

Before I had left New York, Cedric Hardwicke had suggested that I call in on his second wife, Mary, at his Hollywood home in Beverley Hills. Ted said that his father had met Mary when she was working as a hat-check girl. Maybe that's what she was when she met the great star, who was also an English lord, but now it was Lady Hardwicke whom I invited to the ballet. Afterwards she took me to supper, and when Alfred Hitchcock sent over a message to her ('Who is he?'), I realised that she was Mary Scott, an actress who had worked for Hitchcock many times He was alone and invited us to join him.

The conversation began curiously when I turned down his suggestion of oysters, for I'd heard that the gin in my martini would harden them and cause a dangerous blockage.

'Nonsense!' said Hitchcock, and he instructed the waiter to bring a glass of gin, into which he popped a large one.

Here I was dining with a genius of the cinema, so I listened and learnt.

I'd heard that Hitchcock believed that the cooler a beautiful woman seemed, the more passionate she was likely to be, and the hidden fires of brunettes were not as hot as those of cool blondes. Here he took an amused look at Mary – a very pretty brunette!

We found some common ground when I told him I'd met his most famous blonde, Grace Kelly, when I conducted the Royal Ballet in Monte Carlo, where she was now a princess, and that his fellow Englishman – her co-star and lifelong admirer, Cary Grant – had come backstage at our performance of *The Two Bouquets* at the Bristol Old Vic on a visit to his home town.

The conversation turned to the Hays Office, a board of censors which set the rules as to what was allowed to appear on screen before issuing the required certificate for public showing. When I played for the Gaumont Chelsea's children's club, even Mickey Mouse needed a U (universal) certificate. Children were not allowed to see A ('adult') certificate films, and even those films had thirty-six 'don'ts'.

You were not allowed to show how to commit a murder and not get caught; the mockery of a church of any denomination, the institution of marriage or the clergy were forbidden; and you could not show sexual relations between black and white.

Even a screen-married couple could not be seen in bed together unless one had their foot on the floor, and 'tongue kissing' was forbidden. Romantic kisses could last no longer than three seconds.

Hitchcock smiled, for he had found his way around the Hays Office. His film kisses were only three seconds long, but there were a lot of them, and words spoke almost as well as actions.

In the scene in his 1959 film *North by North West* when Eve Marie Saint and Cary Grant meet in a train dining-car, Grant gets right to the point with: 'How is it that when I see a beautiful woman, I always want to make love to her?', which leads us in our own imagination from dining to sleeping car. The Hays office changed her original answer, 'But I never make love on an empty stomach', to 'But I never discuss love on an empty stomach'.

But it really didn't make a scrap of difference – we were already there!

About fifty years later, this scene was used as an advert by Virgin to demonstrate that anything can happen on one of their trains.

Hitchcock was rumoured not to like actors, but he obviously liked Mary, who, though not a blonde, starred in *Mr Blanchard's Secret*. It was one of the best in his television series, *Alfred Hitchcock Presents,* with its bizarrely comic but still sinister signature tune, Gounod's *Funeral Dance of the Marionettes*.

It was a great evening. Conducting for Margot Fonteyn and dinner afterwards with a pretty actress and Alfred Hitchcock were the highlights of that American tour. And Hitchcock was right. The oyster stayed soft!

Now it was time to get back to the East Coast. From the warmth of California, our Company train took us right back across America to a cold Christmas in Chicago, where I took a room in Al Capone's old headquarters, the Lexington Hotel.

Capone had taken over the whole of the fourth floor, and, protected by an army of bodyguards, it was here that he'd planned the St Valentine's Day Massacre. The hotel was very much as it had been during his day, and there was an atmosphere of mystery, which I learned wasn't just the product of my imagination. Twenty years later, a hotel chain, hoping to restore its faded fortunes, discovered a hidden shooting gallery and dozens of secret passages leading into tunnels connecting with the whorehouses and speakeasies on the Levee.

Our tour was coming to its end when we moved up to Detroit, where I had the great pleasure (mixed with not a little pride) of staying just across the border in Windsor with my cousin Roy, where I'd been at school and where he'd given me my first piano lessons.

The last music he'd heard from me was 'The Chapel in the Moonlight' in 1937, but now, twenty years on, he and his wife Anne were my special guests when I donned white tie and tails to conduct Toscanini's old orchestra in a Royal Ballet performance.

There is a destiny which shapes our ends and it hadn't finished with me …yet!

CHAPTER 30

DECCA'S FIRST STEREO

I go to war with the London Symphony Orchestra

Portrait by Juliet Pannett MBE

Back in London, Bob's imminent departure meant that I became very busy. Looking through the 1958 Annual Report of the Royal Opera House, I find that I conducted more performances there than the house Musical Director, Rafael Kubelík. Suddenly I was in the limelight: Cranko's *The Lady and the Fool* and Britten's *Prince of the Pagodas* with Beriosova; Vaughan Williams' *Job* with Helpmann; Stravinsky's *Firebird* and *Petrouchka*; and Adam's *Giselle* with Fonteyn, Nerina and Beriosova. But it was when I conducted Frederick Ashton's full-length version of *Sylvia*, danced by Fonteyn, that I received a notice from Noel Goodwin in the *Daily Express*:

'Where has Sir David Webster been keeping Kenneth Alwyn? This young conductor, sparing of gesture, produced the sort of colour and rhythms heard too rarely now from the Opera House Orchestra.'

Now the publicity department of the Royal Opera House began to take some notice. Angus McBean was commissioned to produce my official photograph, and Juliet Pannett, whose subjects included Edward Heath and Yehudi Menuhin, was asked to prepare a large charcoal drawing. I seemed to be on my way, certainly in the theatre. But my career took a giant leap forward when, during a rehearsal on Tuesday 29th April of a ballet divertimento for an ITV programme *Chelsea at Eight*, I received a surprise call from John Culshaw of the Decca Record Company. Culshaw told me that he'd had good reports of me from the Royal Opera House and he wondered if I might be interested in conducting Decca's first stereophonic record, Tchaikovsky's *1812 Overture* and if so, what was I doing this coming Friday, three days hence. Although I knew not a note of the *1812*, I was sure that this was not the right time to mention it. However, as it happened, I wasn't free that Friday, as I was conducting Nadia Nerina's *Sleeping Beauty*.

'Don't worry,' said John, 'We'll call the London Symphony Orchestra and the Grenadier Guards Band between 3pm and 6pm, so you'll be able to get to the Garden for 7.30pm.'

I said I'd confirm in the morning and went back to the *Chelsea at Eight* rehearsal.

When I got back from the studio late that night, I located a recording of *1812*, and for the only time in my career, I stayed up all night, playing it over and over again.

In a contemporary 'Gramophone' magazine article, Charles Mackerras, who was then at the beginning of his long career, shook the purists by admitting to using recordings as being a perfectly sensible way of making a quick study of the increasingly wide repertoire demanded of conductors.

The next morning, red-eyed and with the sound of the Franco-Russian war still ringing in my ears, I phoned John to confirm – but then he moved the goalposts. The Grenadier Guards Band wasn't available after all on the Friday, so we were to record the flip side of this all-Tchaikovsky disc: *Capriccio Italien* and *Marche Slave*. Again, I knew neither, but I wasn't going to miss a once-in-a-lifetime opportunity, so I took a chance and asked for the conductor's scores. They arrived by motorcycle messenger within the hour (the Decca offices on Millbank were less than a mile away from my flat in St George's Square). After a quick visit to the record department of the Army and Navy Stores in nearby Victoria Street, I got down to learning two of Tchaikovsky's most popular works.

Recordings help a quick study of the notes, but no two conductors ever interpret music in the same way, and by the time I walked up the steps from Kingsway into the Methodist Church Hall two days later, I had very clear ideas of how I wanted to present Tchaikovsky's music.

So... the oily student from the Royal Academy of Music, who'd arrived late to conduct for BBC TV because his motorbike had broken down, had smartened up a bit and was about to conduct one of the finest orchestras in the world in the first-ever stereophonic recording by the leading record company of the day: mighty Decca. Life don't come much sweeter.

Before the session, John warned me about the 'Kingsway Rumble', caused by underground trains on the Piccadilly Line running directly beneath Kingsway Hall, and then introduced me to the London Symphony Orchestra. When he told them I was a ballet conductor from Covent Garden, I caught one or two knowing smiles. Was I a protégé of someone either in Decca or at Covent Garden who had 'the weakness' (the euphemism for the still-illegal homosexuality)? Certainly, there were plenty of them around in both organisations, but my tatty pullover and rolled-up shirt sleeves indicated I was buying my own clothes, so perhaps I was straight. John went back to the recording desk, and I mounted the small and dangerously high box which passed for a rostrum. It had no rail, and a careless step back could mean a bad fall.

I announced *Marche Slave* and all speculation ceased. I would not have chosen to make my recording debut with a funeral march, but from the first notes of 'Come my dearest, why so sad this morning?', the Serbian folk song which Tchaikovsky chose to represent the oppressed Serbian Christians, the orchestra showed their mettle, and I was transported from a church hall in

Kingsway to the blood-stained Balkans and the horrors of the Serbian-Turkish war.

It was long held that British orchestras, unlike Russian orchestras, couldn't play fast music. I'm not a slave to speed for its own sake, but a Tchaikovsky presto must be just about as fast as one can go without losing clarity. The LSO showed me that afternoon that they could match any orchestra in the world for both. I had a few personal friends in the orchestra: a fellow student from the Royal Academy who was the leader, Hugh Maguire, and, from my BBC TV days, the principal oboe, Roger Lord, and first clarinet, Gervase de Peyer. They all came to talk to me afterwards – always a good sign. It had gone well.

I walked, on air, from Serbia into the comparative peace of Kingsway, with just enough time to get to the Opera House for a shower, sandwich and to make a complete change of mood to the fairy tale world of *Sleeping Beauty*.

To conduct the London Symphony Orchestra in the afternoon and the Royal Opera House Orchestra in the evening is a pleasure given to few conductors, something I mentioned to Valery Gergiev at lunch when we received our Fellowships from the Royal Academy of Music (a day revisited in the Coda to this book). He told me that he conducted every day and that, after our lunch, he had a rehearsal and performance at the Garden. The next day he was to be with his Rotterdam Philharmonic. The day after that he was with the Vienna Philharmonic Orchestra – and so on. No wonder he sometimes seemed to have had hardly time to shave.

The next afternoon I was with the LSO again, this time to record Tchaikovsky's souvenir of his visit in 1880 to the Carnival in Rome: *Capriccio Italien*. Tchaikovsky loved his holidays, and the *Capriccio* is a delightful and brilliantly orchestrated record of brooding gypsy music, lively tarantellas (said to be the only way of countering the fatal bite of the tarantula) and folk dances – all pure entertainment, free of any political significance. That night at the Garden, and back in front of the Opera House Orchestra, the sleeping beauty was Rowena Jackson. During the next few days I conducted *Les Sylphides*, Robert Helpmann's first *Petrouchka* and *The Lady and the Fool*, until, at last, it was back to the war of 1812 and the battle of Borodino.

The recording session started at 6pm. To my horror, a rather weary-looking LSO arrived with only a few minutes to go. John told me that they had been recording since 10am that morning at Abbey Road or Watford Town Hall (I forget which). But he told me not to worry: 'They always play better when they're tired'. It was a case of the old orchestral complaint about overwork that I first heard during my Theatre Ballet days – 'same old horse, different jockey'. The horse was tired, but I was in the saddle, and this wasn't the time to spare the whip.

Tchaikovsky wrote *1812* in a week for an open air performance in Moscow, but that turned out to be too difficult to organise, and it was moved into the cathedral. The critics hated it, and Tchaikovsky himself didn't view it highly. Nevertheless, its popularity and style made it a perfect choice for Decca's new stereo. They spared no expense, and the hall was brimming with musicians. On the floor level were the hundred-and-twenty-strong LSO; in the gallery, the fifty Grenadier Guards Bandsmen; and, scattered around, there were extra players with tubular bells, tam-tams, bass drums and cymbals – close on two hundred musicians. John was right: they all played with great intensity and enthusiasm, mixed perhaps with a little desperation. It was a wonderful noise, and if the Piccadilly Line was rumbling, I didn't hear it.

The musicologist Percy Scholes defined conducting as 'generalship on the battlefield of music'. Under the High Command of John Culshaw, his *aide de camp*, the legendary sound engineer Kenneth Wilkinson and my Field-Marshall baton, the recording proved a resounding victory for Tchaikovsky, the Russians and, above all, Decca.

The recording has now been on sale continuously for over fifty years, and is still used by many hi-fi enthusiasts to evaluate their equipment.

As part of those extraordinary seven days, my friend from the Bristol Old Vic, Ted Hardwicke, had persuaded me that I was just the man to conduct the spoof 'Yorkshire Symphony' at the actors' annual charity show at the Adelphi Theatre.

Recording Tchaikovsky's
Capriccio Italien with the
London Symphony Orchestra,
Kingsway Hall, London, 1958

The caption reads: 'Quite frankly, I'm beginning to think it was an error of judgement inviting Tchaikovsky to entertain the troops...'

The original drawing was kindly gifted to me
by the artist, Ray Lowry

So one afternoon I found myself facing a collection of kazoos, bells, whistles, spoons, sandpaper blocks, biscuit tins filled with cutlery, swanee whistles and ocarinas, which were played by ballet dancers, music critics, choreographers and actors, including a tasty blonde who was playing the lead in Agatha Christie's *Mousetrap* in the West End and the biscuit tin for me.

Her name was Mary Law. Luckily for me, she married me and is still rattling my biscuit tin!

Bentley Archive/Popperfoto/Getty Images

Agatha Christie cuts the cake, watched by Mary Law and Sir Peter Saunders, to mark the 6th anniversary of The Mousetrap, London, 1958

In May the Royal Ballet was invited to the World Festival in Brussels. Our performances at the Théâtre Royal de la Monnaie included Ashton's ballet to celebrate the coronation of Queen Elizabeth II (*Homage to the Queen*), *Sleeping Beauty* and *Firebird*, which must have gone well, for de Valois decided that I was to conduct the return of Beryl Grey to the part of the Black Queen in her most famous ballet, *Checkmate*.

For years, the piano rehearsals had been played by the redoubtable Hilda Gaunt, but I decided that a fresh look at the music called for another pianist: in this case, Colin Kingsley. The ballet room sessions had gone well, but the piano dress rehearsal on stage was a different matter. De Valois sat on stage with her back to me and called 'And' (the choreographer's equivalent of the conductor's downbeat), and we were off.

Colin gave an account of the piano score which was far better than both the dancers and de Valois were used to hearing. The usual shouting and clapping which was heard at all of de Valois' piano rehearsals increased, and the rehearsal ground to a halt. De Valois, looked over her right shoulder and said in her best Irish accent: 'I didn't recognise a note of it!'

My initial reaction was to defend Colin, but then I remembered the Company story that had caused much mirth in America when de Valois had visited the Ringling Circus to see the famous waltzing horses. The conductor of the circus band had practically stood on his head to make them appear to be dancing in time. Some bars were three and a half beats long, others two and a bit, but de Valois had exclaimed, 'Just look at those horses. All perfectly in time!'

Ten years after leaving the Royal Ballet, Robert Irving put his views on de Valois' musicality rather well:

> *In the summer of 1958*
> *I booked a berth on the Mauretania.*
> *They all said, for Heaven's sake wait.*
> *Nothing could possibly be zanier*
> *Than to throw up home and friends and Queen*
> *For the unpredictable Balanchine,*
> *But what can you do when the Sleeping Beauty*

Becomes no more than an irksome duty?
Or when you reflect that by dear Ninette
The message of music is not received yet?

There was nothing wrong in Colin's performance, but because the piano was in the pit, Hilda Gaunt (who played for all the previous rehearsals) knew that some dancers couldn't hear the quiet passages, and so she had played all quiet music very loudly, and at the same time had shouted out the dancers' counts. On the re-run we did likewise.

The Times wrote of Beryl Grey's 'sinister power' in the role of the Black Queen, and it went on:

'Mr Kenneth Alwyn roused his orchestra to a high pitch of excitement, so that the ballet's dramatic climax carried even more than usual of its striking force.'

My very busy season continued with some more 'firsts', most of them without orchestral rehearsal. It got even tougher when the orchestral manager omitted to schedule an hour's brush-up of a ballet which the orchestra hadn't played for over a year: John Cranko's *The Shadow*, set to Ernst von Dohnányi's *Suite in F Sharp Minor*.

I went into the pit to conduct, for the first time, music described as 'a brilliant and attractive essay in orchestration'. It promised to be a very chancy affair, but the orchestra rose to the challenge and, sitting on the edge of their seats, played brilliantly.

But the dangers were not always to do with under-rehearsal. At a mixed-bill evening which included the second act of *Swan Lake*, at the entrance of the Swan Queen, instead of one of our ballerinas, there was a complete stranger. No one had told me that the Queen was to be danced that night by a guest from Paris: the French ballerina, Yvette Chauviré.

The Swan Queen's first step after her leap onto the stage is an *arabesque*. In the Royal Ballet version, the ballerina makes the first move, the conductor starting the music when her toe touches the stage. Not, it seemed, in Paris, where the dancer begins *after* the first note.

I waited for Chauviré. She waited for me. After one of those theatrical silences which seem interminable, for the first time at Covent Garden, the Swan (who, if we believe the words of

Orlando Gibbons, 'living hath no note'), hissed in a voice easily heard by the first ten rows of the stalls: *'Jouez!'*

Possibly the toughest ballet which I ever conducted without rehearsal was Stravinsky's *Agon*. Agon is the Greek word for combat, and Stravinsky's score is an ingenious integration of the combat between twelve-tone music, modal harmony and quasi-medieval counterpoint. Incredibly, they fuse to make one of the most exciting and difficult of all Stravinsky's compositions.

The orchestration includes the mandolin, a romantic instrument not comfortably at home in the halls of ungodly atonalism, and it was said that there was only one mandolin player in London capable of keeping a cool head in this complicated music. The piece had needed a great deal of rehearsal for even our talented band of musicians, and so, as I was escorted through the dark vault under the stage and through the small door into the orchestral pit, I consoled myself with the thought that, provided I made no mistakes, we should get through it together safely.

My greeting applause faded, the light dimmed and I raised my baton and smiled in the relaxed manner required of conductors. But my smile faded when, instead of the famous Hugo d'Alton at the mandolin, a complete stranger smiled encouragingly back, and what is more, a complete stranger with no music. I had no choice but to begin.

So I was more than agreeably surprised when, the next morning, the critic of the *Daily Telegraph*, A. V. Coton wrote:

'*Agon* was danced with less effort and more brilliance than in any previous performance, Kenneth Alwyn investing the score with the same sincere and total confidence apparent in the dancing.'

During the last months of 1958, Fred Ashton began work on a new ballet for Margot, *Undine,* with music by Hans Werner Henze, and I was immensely relieved to discover that Henze (who was to conduct the performances) had made an orchestral recording of the whole score in Switzerland, which we would be able to use for Fred's rehearsals. I allocated a pianist to play not a piano but a reel-to-reel Ferrograph, which we had to buy.

In spite of Madame's doubts about Dr Kingsley's playing for the rehearsal of *Checkmate*, she trusted him and me to make a piano recording of what was to be her last ballet, *The Lady of Shalott*. Her collaborator on *Checkmate*, Sir Arthur Bliss, had written the music, and so one day Dr Kingsley and I went to his house in Hampstead. Sir Arthur was charming, helpful and, unlike my initial experience with Britten, I felt not a trace of anxiety. It was a very pleasant three hours, we played well, and Sir Arthur was delighted with the result. But de Valois was never to create *The Lady of Shalott*. She decided instead that Kenneth MacMillan should make a new ballet, and she gave up her rehearsal time to him.

Our piano recording disappeared without a trace, but Bliss orchestrated his score and recorded it with the BBC Symphony Orchestra. The music was not entirely wasted, for it re-appeared in a stage production at the Haymarket Theatre, Leicester called 'The Girl in the Broken Mirror' with choreography by Mary Hockney and played by the amazingly-skilled Leicester County Schools Orchestra.

The year closed with Decca's release of *1812,* where it was a special feature at the Earls Court Audio Fair. When I enquired of an official where it was being played, he pointed upstairs with a pained look.

'There! There!' he said, desperately.

As I climbed the stairs, the sound of the Franco-Russian war drowned out all other recordings, and I understood his pain. To have to spend the three days of the fair being bombarded by a non-stop performance of possibly the loudest record ever made must have been a dreadful experience.

The year closed with the Royal's pantomime season – *Cinderella* – danced by Margot Fonteyn. From the best seat in the house (the conductor's), I was able to enjoy not only bringing to life Prokofiev's beautiful music but also the mutterings and back-chat (inaudible to the audience) of two of the most outrageously funny female impersonators in the business: Cinderella's ugly sisters, Frederick Ashton and Robert Helpmann.

With Bob's departure for New York, Hugo and I were now the only two Company conductors. As he was increasingly busy with the Birmingham Symphony Orchestra, and I with recordings and the BBC, the search for another conductor began.

CHAPTER 31

MOVING ON

Dame Monica Mason makes her debut

The Royal Opera House leaflet (price one penny) advertised that the Royal Ballet would give thirty-six performances between 19th January and 14th March 1959, but the opera would only give twenty. This confirmed our view that, playing to full houses, the ballet was subsidising the relatively poor attendances on opera nights. It was not until 1988 that, for the first time, an opera performance out-sold the ballet.

The four Opera staff conductors in 1959 included Edward Downes and a man who, after many years at the Royal Opera House, was finally recognised as one of the great Wagnerians: Reginald Goodall. Reg's apparent passion for Adolf Hitler's favourite composer was not inclined to enhance his career when we went to war with Germany. However, being too old for the Army, he redeemed himself by touring with the Wessex Philharmonic, an orchestra which included many Jewish refugees, and giving over eight hundred concerts to a population starved of good music.

Ted Downes, married to one of our dancers, became fed up with losing performances to guest conductors, and he left to become a long-distance lorry driver. As Ted's eyesight was only a tad better than Mr Magoo's, we were all very glad when he'd had enough of feeling his way around Britain and returned to where he rightly belonged: on the rostrum.

In 1959 the Opera's Musical Director was the brilliant and much-liked Rafael Kubelík, but he did not involve himself very much in routine affairs, and David Webster increasingly consulted Ted in the day-to-day matters, casting, rehearsals and all the detailed preparation needed to mount an opera. Not unreasonably, instead of the staff conductors' modest cubby-hole on the first floor, which had no desk and little privacy, Ted took to using the splendid suite high above the clamour of the Covent Garden fruit market, reserved for the Musical Director.

One day Reginald Goodall, hoping for an interview with the elusive Kubelík, mounted the long staircase and knocked at the door of this privileged sanctum.

'Come in!' called not Kubelík but... Downes.

Reg gave him a long look and muttered, 'Shit! Already!'

However, Reg's fear that the thirty-three-year-old Ted might become the next Musical Director (and, at fifty-eight, his boss) was unfounded. In 1961 the Opera House finally got someone who took everything firmly in hand: George Solti.

Nearly fifty years on, Sir Edward Downes still used Room A, as did Goodall, who, with his brilliance finally recognised in his last years, became Sir Reginald.

In that 1959 season, our repertoire included the three-acters *Swan Lake*, *Sleeping Beauty*, *Giselle*, *Coppélia* and *Ondine* and mixed bills of *The Lady and the Fool*, *Petrouchka*, *Checkmate*, *Danses Concertantes*, *La Fête Etrange*, *Harlequin in April* and the frothy *Mam'zelle Angot*.

Of the thirty-six ballet performances (and although Hans Werner Henze conducted his *Ondine*), Hugo and I conducted thirty-one. But Hugo was also Musical Director of the City of Birmingham Symphony Orchestra and so we badly needed another conductor, and preferably one with some experience of the dance.

The possible solution was to use one of the under-worked opera conductors, but ballet is quite a different kettle of fish, for the dancers' physical limitations and the choreography control the music, and without some knowledge of dance steps, the ballet conductor can never bring off a completely successful collaboration. An understanding of this arcane world cannot be learned at music college but only from playing the piano for dance classes and rehearsals. Both Bob Irving and I chose to play for at least one full piano rehearsal of the ballets we were to conduct.

Monia Young, a skilled Opera staff conductor and vocal coach had some previous ballet experience, and he agreed to give it a go. He came to ballet rehearsals but didn't play, and so it was a rather risky business when he was pitched in at the deep end to make his debut with a full-length *Swan Lake*, a ballet with many changes of tempi and stage cues. As I was now in my seventh year in ballet, I put it to Monia that he might like to discuss some of the awkward corners, but he chose to plough his own furrow, and his early performances had one or two uneasy moments. However, he was an excellent musician, a most likeable chap, and he joined the ballet staff.

There were now three of us. Hugo always produced performances with danceable tempi, but his great strength was the excellent *sound* he produced from the orchestra. Even in a theatre orchestra as good as that of the Royal Opera House, the players' principal role is to accompany, and they know that the audience have not come just to listen to them. Hugo would not accept this, and being a very fine violinist himself (and owner of a Stradivarius) he gave special attention to the heart of the orchestra: the strings.

As he was frequently away from London giving concerts at home and in Europe, I always stood by to cover his performances. On one occasion, after conducting the matinée of *Sleeping Beauty*, I was relaxing at home with a gin and tonic when the stage director phoned me to say that Hugo had missed his plane and I had half an hour to change into tails and get back to Covent Garden to conduct the evening performance. By the time I arrived, the audience were all in their seats, and there was just time for me to ask which ballerina was dancing Beauty and to rush straight to the orchestra to begin the second half of my marathon day.

The average symphony concert is usually eighty-five minutes of music. *Sleeping Beauty* has four acts, totalling about a hundred and fifty minutes, and a couple of hundred changes of tempo. To conduct it twice in one day requires the sort of stamina required by an athlete, and leads to the legend of conductors' longevity. I suppose I shouldn't complain, for here I am in my ninetieth year writing about those wonderful years.

Apart from his work with the Royal Ballet and the City of Birmingham Symphony Orchestra, Hugo was clearly getting very busy outside recording and broadcasting, and I sensed the 'treacherous sands' of the Opera House were shifting. It was time to try to establish my future position, and so I asked for a private meeting with Ninette de Valois. She knew a lot about me, and I had a curious intimacy with the way her mind worked, for I'd spent many hours with her and her assistant and old Diaghilev colleague, Ailne ('Babs') Phillips in the staff box which overlooked the orchestra pit, and from where I was able to see how Hugo beat the more complicated bars of unrehearsed ballets.

Whilst I concentrated on the orchestra, de Valois, completely ignoring me, would criticise the dancing and make the occasional spiky and extremely personal comment on individual dancers, which Babs was asked to pass onto them. But Madame came unstuck when she commented that a dancer's breasts had become too big and that Babs should speak to her about a reduction. Babs did, but she brought down on her head the justifiable wrath of the girl's husband. He passed back the message that he was entirely satisfied with his wife's breasts and had no intention of interfering with them.

So when I walked into de Valois' small office, I began with, 'Don't worry Madame, I've not come to ask you for more performances, but this is my seventh year in your Company and this is our first meeting. How am I getting on?'

This brilliant woman – a mother-figure to her dancers, quick-tempered, mercurial, volatile, feared and always totally in command – looked nervous, which was something quite out of character. This was explained to me many years later by Annette Page at the Royal Ballet's 70th Anniversary Party when Annette told me that, whilst not exactly afraid of men (at home she warmed her husband's slippers), de Valois was uneasy with conductors, and there had only ever been one she felt safe with – Constant Lambert.

Our conversation was friendly and reasonably satisfying, and I left her office feeling that, if she had any complaints, she'd had her chance.

The immediate outcome of our meeting was her suggestion that I conduct the first-ever public show by the students of the Royal Ballet School. The young and totally inexperienced dancers were going to need a sympathetic eye in the pit, and she had chosen me. It was the reassurance which I had sought.

On Saturday 21st March 1959, the Royal Ballet School presented a complete performance of *Coppélia*. The principal roles of Franz and Swanilda were danced by two junior members of the main Company. Graham Usher partnered Antoinette Sibley in her first leading role, one which she was to make very much her own during the coming years. The soloists and *corps de ballet* included Deanna Bergsma, whose performance of 'Prayer' marked her out immediately for a great career at the Garden.

This first performance was a great success, and every year since the Royal Ballet School has given a public show.

In May I conducted a Command Performance. The occasion was to celebrate the visit to London of His Imperial Majesty the Shahanshah of Iran and his beautiful Empress, Farah. Weeks previously, I had asked the Iranian Embassy for the orchestral parts and full score, but as the big day approached, it became clear that they were never going to arrive. Instead, they sent a recording of the Shahanshah's very ethnic orchestra playing his tune. There was no indication of which of the three recording speeds available (78rpm, 45rpm or 33rpm) should be used. If they'd recorded it at 45rpm and we played it back at 33rpm, it would be much too slow, and vice-versa. At 78rpm it would sound like a Walt Disney cartoon.

The British home of military music, Kneller Hall, couldn't help, so I took a chance and had it orchestrated to work at 45rpm.

The performance began later than usual because the Shahanshah and his Empress had been to dinner with our Queen and Prince Philip, but, unlike the Franco family, our royals had the good manners to arrive on time. As is customary on these occasions, the audience and orchestra were already seated. I was on the rostrum, awaiting the signal that the four royals were entering the royal box. Standing downstage in front of the monogrammed velvet curtains stood eight magnificently uniformed heralds, each with a banner embroidered in silver and gold, suspended from long shining trumpets. At last came the signal. I cued the heralds, there was a brilliant fanfare and the royals appeared.

I turned back to the orchestra and, as protocol demanded, giving pride of place to the Queen's guests, it played what I hoped to be the Iranian National Anthem and moved quickly into the safer waters of ours. Protocol also required that the presence of an Emperor meant ending the evening with both anthems again, and as I survived the presentation afterwards, and Prince Philip didn't make any comment, my guess must have paid off.

I got that one right, but some years later, on my way to conduct the first night of the Irish National Ballet, the cheery stage manager called, 'Don't forget the Soldiers Song!' 'What's that?' I asked. ''Tis our National Anthem,' he replied. 'Just start the band and they'll carry on,' and to give me the idea of how it went, he sang the opening bars. But as the house lights were already down, and we were in a hurry, he sang them at double speed. The performance by an English conductor of the Irish National Anthem at twice the correct speed was greeted not with howls of rage but (being in Dublin) with cheers and laughter, and with a cry from a Dubliner who'd had a few jars: 'That's the way to do it!'

Act II

Cinderella	SVETLANA BERIOSOVA
The Prince	MICHAEL SOMES
Cinderella's Stepsisters	MOYRA FRASER, MARGARET HILL
Cinderella's Father	FRANKLIN WHITE
Their Suitors	DEREK RENCHER, WILLIAM WILSON
The Jester	ALEXANDER GRANT
The Prince's Friends	DESMOND DOYLE, BRYAN ASHBRIDGE, RONALD HYND, GARY BURNE
A Negro	RITA WILDE
Courtiers	VYVYAN LORRAYNE, MONICA MASON, PATRICIA THOROGOOD, JENNIFER GAY, JACQUELINE DARYL, DOREEN EASTLAKE, MERIEL EVANS, DEIRDRE DIXON, MAURICE METLISS, RICHARD FARLEY, RONALD PLAISTED, KEITH ROSSON, CHRISTOPHER NEWTON, ROBERT de WARREN, GRAHAM USHER, DOUGLAS STEUART
The Fairy Spring	MERLE PARK
Her Pages	JUDITH COLBORNE, PAMELA BOWER
The Fairy Summer	ANTOINETTE SIBLEY
Her Pages	GLYNIS ELLAMS, JUDITH MADEN
The Fairy Autumn	ANNETTE PAGE
Her Pages	KAY SMITH, GLORIA BLUEMEL
The Fairy Winter	ROSEMARY LINDSAY
Her Pages	ROSALIND EYRE, JANET VARLEY
Stars	DOROTHEA ZAYMES, CLOVER ROOPE, ANN HOWARD, DOREEN WELLS, MAVIS OSBORN, HYLDA ZINKIN, DEBRA WAYNE, BRENDA BOLTON, AUDREY HENDERSON, GEORGINA PARKINSON, SHIRLEY GRAHAME, CHRISTINE BECKLEY
Lackeys	KEITH MILLAND, LAMBERT COX, TERRY WESTMORELAND, LAWRENCE RUFFELL
Guests	MYRLEEN HEDLEY, ANN KENWARD, CAROL NEEDHAM, DEANNE BERGSMA, LOUANNE RICHARDS, KENNETH BARLOW, JEFFREY PHILLIPS, BRYAN LAWRENCE

Conductor: KENNETH ALWYN

Cast list of Act II of *Cinderella*
Royal Gala performance, 7th May, 1959

The high spot of the Shah's Royal Gala was the *pas de deux* from Prokofiev's *Cinderella*, danced by Svetlana Beriosova.

But tucked away in Act Three of *Coppélia* in the 'Dance of the Morning Hours' was Hugo Rignold's daughter, Jennifer Gay, and another young dancer who was to become the director of the Royal Ballet: Monica Mason. As a Command Performance, they don't come much better.

So I seemed to have a secure future at the Opera House. But what I didn't know then was that there was a plan to reorganise the whole structure of the ballet and to send the London-based Company to tour the provinces. This all came to light when I came to discuss my next contract with the administrator, John Tooley, who was Sir David Webster's right-hand man at the Royal Opera House. He offered me the job of Touring Musical Director with both companies. But, as they say nowadays, 'Been there, done that'. I'd come to the Garden to get away from five years of touring the provinces, and so I back-pedalled and told him I'd consider his new offer.

Now I had other irons in the fire. After the worldwide success of *1812*, the Managing Director of Decca, Frank Lee, invited me to lunch to discuss Decca's latest move in the recording price war. People were now buying expensive stereophonic equipment, and there was a huge market for these new recordings, which were technically vastly superior to anything in the catalogues at that time. It was Frank's job to keep the price down, and he asked me if I'd be interested in conducting for Decca's new budget label.

The Musicians' Union had placed a twenty-minute limit on the amount of music that could be recorded in a session. The full twenty minutes could be achieved, but only if the music was reasonably straightforward and there were no technical problems. The twelve-inch vinyl long-playing records required a minimum of forty minutes music and so, to be on the safe side, orchestras were booked for three sessions. Frank's idea was to issue budget LPs of no more than forty minutes of music, to be recorded during only two sessions. This way, he could tap into the new market at about two thirds of the full price. Decca would continue to use first-class orchestras under their own names, but, for these low-price recordings, and to protect myself against any criticism, Frank suggested I use an alias. Would I be interested? My reply was quick and to the point.

'Let's make the first one and see how we get on, and if it's good enough for Decca to issue, then it'll be good enough to carry my name.'

And so we had one morning in the Kingsway Hall to make the first two-session stereo LP. The orchestra was the London Philharmonic and our target was two twenty-minute suites: *Swan Lake* and Grieg's *Peer Gynt*.

Two-session recordings allowed no time for me to listen to 'playbacks', so I now had to rely solely on the producer. Although Decca had a crack recording team, it was a close-run thing, and thanks to the skill of the LPO, we finished with a minute to spare.

That recording was re-issued by Decca in 2012.

Frank Lee's two-session recording became the norm for many recording companies, but ours was the first, and my reputation for working quickly led to a great deal of broadcasting with the BBC, where speed is always of the essence.

John Culshaw was trying to find me a job with a symphony orchestra where I could conduct the standard orchestral repertoire, and suggested that I enter the Philharmonia Orchestra's conducting competition. The judges were Sir Adrian Boult, Carlo Maria Guilini and the founder of the orchestra, Walter Legge, but Legge refused my entry, as 'Mr Alwyn is already an established conductor'.

It was just as well, for this trial by television was one of the nastiest things I've ever had to see young conductors endure. Sir Adrian Boult immediately disposed of any who didn't flex their wrists on every single beat, Walter Legge frowned on all of them and Carlo Maria Guilini, who was kinder, told them that he would never conduct any music until he could write out the viola part from memory (he had led the violas in the Orchestra dell'Accademia Nazionale di Santa Cecilia before taking up conducting). It was the X Factor of its day, the only difference being that none of the finalists were ever heard of again.

The door to the symphony world refused to open, and it

became time to seriously consider John Tooley's offer of a new contract. To accept it would have meant an end to this developing relationship with Decca and the BBC, but to give up my regular salary to enter the perilous world of freelance was still a difficult decision, coming just at the time when I was about to propose to the girl who'd become the one sure thing in my life – Mary. Whilst I considered our future, something happened at the Garden in which Margot Fonteyn played a leading role.

After masterminding a failed political coup in Panama, her husband Tito had taken refuge in the Brazilian Embassy there. Margot, although officially on holiday, had gone to Panama to see him, but had promptly been imprisoned herself. As there was nothing against her, except being married to a revolutionary, the Panamanians, anxious to avoid a bad press, decided not to keep this world-famous ballerina in prison. So, after only a day, she was released and flown to New York, and then back to London, from where, on Friday 15th May, she was leaving for Warsaw to dance with the Polish Ballet. She was not scheduled to appear at Covent Garden until later in the season, but Anne Heaton, who was to dance *Giselle* injured her foot and, unannounced, Margot took her place.

The press got to hear of hear it, and her adoring fans filled the theatre to welcome her home from prison. I was the conductor of the evening, and had played the piano for Margot's rehearsals with Karsavina, so I felt quite comfortable with her tempi and the small changes we'd rehearsed. That night Margot danced, as always, beautifully, and she and the music were as one. After her first solo she took four curtain calls, and at the end of the evening, which she described as 'the biggest reception of her career', and holding two-dozen pink roses sent by the still-imprisoned Tito, she received a seven-minute ovation.

The next day, Oleg Korensky, ballet critic of the *Daily Mail* wrote:

'Although in the past Giselle was not always one of Fonteyn's best parts, this performance was supreme – to be compared with Ulanova and the greatest exponents of this classic role.'

He goes on to write of her 'innocent, child-like peasant girl, her unaffected acting and her effortless dancing'. Of her long-term dancing partner, he wrote: 'Michael Somes was, as usual, a perfect partner and acted well as Albrecht.'

It was just as we'd rehearsed with Karsavina, and my curtain call was as warm as ever any ballet conductor expected. Everyone (including de Valois) was delighted, except for a ballet critic of one of the smaller magazines, who wrote that I had 'crippled this great dancer with impossible tempi' and went on to ask 'how much longer at Covent Garden must we put up with conductors who, if they were dancers, wouldn't be good enough to be in the *corps de ballet* of a third-rate company?'

Now, all performers are expected to put up with criticisms which are 'fair comment', but this was not only unfair but also untrue and libellous. It also hurt like hell. On the advice of the Opera House's solicitor Stanley Rubinstein, I sought Counsel's Opinion. In five pages, the barrister concluded that, if I could get Margot to confirm that I had not 'crippled her with impossible tempi', and if a 'musician of repute' stated that I was a competent conductor, then I stood to gain 'substantial damages'.

I was on the horns of a dilemma. If the case went to trial, we would have to put in the witness box Margot, Sir Malcolm Sargent, Sir William Walton (both of whom had been very complimentary about me) or John Culshaw, who'd employed me to conduct Decca's first stereophonic recording – hardly likely if I was as incompetent as was claimed. The case would receive a lot of publicity, and, if the magazine chose to attack me further, I might become the focus of a courtroom discussion of the Royal Ballet's past conducting problems, including Dolly Dullbeat. As to my skills, there are always those who think 'there's no smoke without fire'. I would almost certainly win, but the victory would be pyrrhic.

I dropped the case.

I don't think the negative review had any effect on my position at the Garden, for Tooley's offer was still on the table. But there was a general feeling of insecurity (even amongst the star dancers, some of whom, being frustrated by Madame's insistence on Margot's pre-eminence, left the Company). I decided to make this my last season, take my chances and become completely freelance.

My last appearances with the Company were at the

Alhambra Palace in the gardens of the Generalife, and so, with my first royalty cheque from Decca, I bought a brand new Morris Minor, appropriately christened '1812', and Mary and I set off for the long journey to Granada, where the Company were to share the Festival with the likes of conductor Igor Markevitch, pianist Wilhelm Kempff and the greatest guitarist in the world, Andrés Segovia.

These were the days before the British tourist invasion. Very little English was spoken, and so I was forced to address the Madrid Chamber Orchestra in Spanish. Apparently, it was so good that they replied at a speed, and in accents which quite exceeded anything provided by my teacher, the *Daily Express* 'Teach Yourself Spanish' records. Nevertheless, we managed. Came the first performance and, as before, the dancers were waiting, the orchestra was waiting, and the audience were waiting – this time, not only for Franco's daughter but also for the Generalissimo himself. They arrived a mere half an hour late, but the performance in the open air in the gardens of the Generalife was worth waiting for. It was a beautiful evening, and the cellist played *The Swan* beneath the moon to the distant background of the fountains. Afterwards, we all met in our hotel, the Alhambra Palace, where we were completely ignored by the waiters serving the General and his entourage. He was a dictator and a hidalgo, and we merely entertainers – not only below the salt, but unable to even get a drink.

But our evening ended well amongst the gypsies in the caves of El Sacromonte, who, learning that we were not just ordinary tourists but from a world-famous ballet company, danced flamenco to the sound of guitars, castanets, clapping and high heels on the cave's stone floor as we toasted them with their own Jerez.

The memory of conducting Tchaikovsky under a deep velvet sky in the beautiful moonlit gardens of the Generalife, whilst on stage our stars shone brilliantly, will stay with me always.

The next morning Mary and I climbed aboard the '1812' and left Granada for the long drive back to England, to home and whatever might come our way – together.

CHAPTER 32

TOKYO

Beryl Grey and I meet Harada Daiun Sogaku

My decision to leave the Royal Opera House didn't mean I had finished with ballet, or that ballet had finished with me, for early in 1961, John Tooley telephoned to ask if I'd be free to conduct the long-awaited first visit of the Royal Ballet to Japan. The Japanese had christened the visit 'The East-West Encounter' – a charmingly naive title, given that the last encounter a few years before had given them such a load of grief. The Company was to be led by our two greatest ballerinas, Margot Fonteyn and Beryl Grey, and it included Anya Linden, Lynn Seymour, Michael Somes, Bryan Ashbridge and Brian Shaw. We were certainly putting our very best feet forward to dance *Swan Lake*, *Checkmate*, *Les Sylphides*, *Fête Etrange*, *Les Patineurs*, *Danses Concertantes* and the new production of *Giselle*. The music was to be played by the personal orchestra of the Emperor.

In spite of an exhausting two-day flight, on my arrival in Japan I went straight to a rehearsal, as I was anxious to hear the Emperor's Imperial Philharmonic. Monia Young, who had been sent on ahead, was taking them through *Swan Lake*. When he saw me his relief was palpable. He stopped the music and announced that the number one ('*ichi ban*') conductor had arrived, who was 'a very nice man'! All eighty players came to their feet and bowed low. I bowed back, smiled (they didn't) and, in the manner of our own dear Queen, I said to Monia, 'Do carry on', which he did.

And what a carry-on it was. I beat a hasty retreat from the sound of the oboe, which was actually managing to play wrong notes in what must be one of the most famous of all Tchaikovsky's tunes, the leitmotif of the Swan Queen herself.

'Oh dear,' I thought. 'No wonder Monia was glad to see me!'

The Imperial Philharmonic was a very patchy band. Some of the musicians were excellent, others barely competent. However, Monia and I battled on for the next ten days with our repertoire – all of it unknown to the orchestra – until the music was recognisable and I felt reasonably confident that they would be able to follow my baton for the tricky changes required for *Giselle*, which was to open the season and would be danced by Margot Fonteyn and Michael Somes.

The first night turned out to be a family affair. Although the Imperial Philharmonic was Emperor Hirohito's own orchestra, he didn't come, but instead sent Crown Prince Akihito and Princess Michiko.

The 'East-West Encounter' was a great success with the audience and the Prince and Princess – but not, it seemed, with the ballet critic of the *International Dancing Times*, Cyril Eland.

He described Fonteyn's Giselle as being beyond criticism, but Anya Linden's Queen of the Wilis was 'too warm'. He didn't like Peter Rice's 'drab and uninspired costumes and decor', and he had a go at the production with a rather good quote:

'The departure of the court when Giselle collapses takes place with the indecent haste displayed by eye-witnesses of an accident anxious to avoid police interrogation.'

He was quite kind, if condescending, about the Imperial Philharmonic:

'Their playing, by no means impeccable, never proved an impediment to the dance and – at times – even reached quite a high standard of musicianship.'

How's that for damning with faint praise?!

It's true that, perhaps, the Company was not always at its best, for we played our twelve performances in three different theatres. This involved a hell of a lot of packing up, extra stage rehearsals and travelling about in Kamikaze taxis (Tokyo taxis carried small television sets at which drivers would snatch a glance as they narrowly avoided head-on crashes).

Our visit coincided with a national holiday on 5th May, the 'Day of the Carp', which was a festival dedicated to young Japanese boys. Every building flew giant carp-shaped pink kites, representing the strength of both boy and that great fish. Tokyo was jammed with boys in pink kimonos having the time of their lives, for that day they could do no wrong. But even with *carte blanche*, they were, as ever, polite and disciplined. I felt secure and strangely at home on this far side of the world.

When I spoke of this to the orchestral manager Takahashi San (Mr Highbridge), he smiled and explained that the Japanese and the English have much in common. He said that we both inhabit islands which lie very close to a great land mass but have a different language, and that we are both are protected by great navies (they were immensely proud of how theirs had defeated the Russian Navy in 1905). We both have royal families – theirs divine, ours by divine right – and we both have the good manners, discipline and sense of personal privacy which are vital in our small, overcrowded societies.

'But,' he said, and laughed, 'there is an important difference. We worship foxes and hunt dogs, but you worship dogs and hunt foxes!'

He told me that our two countries even have a special name for the 1960s, ours 'Swinging', theirs 'Golden' – perhaps so named for the beautiful girls in golden kimonos who stood at the department store escalators greeting every customer with a smile and *Ohayou gozaimasu*, and also for the imaginative window displays in the Ginza district. These were Tokyo's showcase to a world beginning to understand that Japan was now in keen and effective competition with Europe and the United States, not only commercially but also in the arts.

War was best forgotten, and to have been a loyal soldier of the 'Son of Heaven' (Emperor Hirohito) was now to be in disgrace. There was an ill-concealed contempt for the old soldiers who'd lost the war. One Tokyo nightclub had a doorman in the uniform of a Japanese General, complete with genuine decorations, who saluted even the lowliest. When I left my hotel each morning, the first thing I saw was four soldiers begging, each missing a limb.

Compared with the beauty of London, I found Tokyo an ugly city architecturally, but the Japanese genius for colour and decoration softened the city's lines. Not understanding the language meant that something which might be a tawdry commercial advertisement in English seemed quite attractive – even artistic – in Kanji (Japan's picture language), and never more so than at night, when many thousands of brilliantly-coloured lights transformed the capital into a fairyland.

I wanted to give Mary a souvenir of my visit, and Margot took me to see Mrs Yashimoto, the leading Tokyo dealer in pearls. Mrs Yashimoto showed us a room where a large table was entirely covered with real pearls of all kinds and colours, even black ones. I chose a lovely necklace which Margot took back to England in the diplomatic bag, being at that time the wife of Tito, the Panamanian Ambassador.

Margot and Michael went up with the Company to Hong Kong. Considering that it was then an enormously wealthy Crown Colony, it had been poorly prepared. There was no orchestra available, and the theatre equipment was in such poor condition that Margot and Michael danced to a piano against a background of black drapes.

I remained in Tokyo and, having left our other halves, Mary and Sven, back home in England, Beryl Grey and I occasionally took meals together. One evening we were joined at dinner by Takahashi San. Realising that we had a great interest in all things Japanese, and particularly the mystical Zen Buddhism, he suggested that we might like to meet the leading Zen master who would, no doubt, answer our questions.

This was a golden opportunity, and so one rainy morning we picked our way through the backstreets of Tokyo to an almost hidden monastery and were ushered into the presence of Harada Daiun Sogaku, an old priest in a black kimono who sat cross-legged gazing at seven stones set in an ornamental pool. The silence was absolute, except for the gentle sound of light rain falling on the water. The Master, without shifting his gaze from the garden, welcomed us in Japanese (duly translated by Takahashi San), and the questions began.

Beryl asked if Buddhists believed that they went to heaven and the Master replied that some did, some didn't. There were other such questions, all requiring double translation by Takahashi. I'd heard of the Zen concept of the 'one-handed clap', but when I asked for an explanation, Takahashi turned to me with a smile and relayed the Master's reply.

'If you were a Zen Buddhist, you wouldn't ask that question.'

Beryl's face fell, for being a very straightforward person, the Master's daft answer perplexed her. But the great teacher had not finished with us yet, for in answer to another question from Beryl (once again translated by Takahashi San), the Master turned to him and in perfect English said, 'No, that's not quite what I meant.'

For the first time, Beryl addressed him directly.

'Why didn't you speak straight to us?'

'Because,' he replied, 'I do not speak your beautiful language well enough'.

We bowed low and left the priest to his seven stones in the rain.

Harada Daiun Sogaku died later that year at the age of ninety and has either gone to heaven or hasn't, depending on what he believed. That, I'm told, is Zen.

The next day, the Company left Tokyo for the Osaka International Festival, where we were to give five performances. The journey was on the Hokkaido Express, the forerunner of the 'Bullet' train for its speeds of over a hundred miles an hour. A loan from the World Bank had enabled the Japanese to develop the first of the world's high speed trains – all part of their 'Golden' 1960s. We had nothing like them in England, where our slam-door rolling stock was still trundling about the country. The 'Brighton Belle', which used to do the journey from Victoria in one hour, now took even longer. Sitting in the luxurious Hokkaido Express, and remembering my tour with the Sadler's Wells Theatre in post-war Germany, where the trains were also new, I realised that, although ours was the military victory, we'd lost the train war.

To keep to schedule, it was necessary for the passengers on the Hokkaido Express to get aboard very quickly. This works well for the Japanese, who travel light, but a ballet company which lives out of suitcases and has to carry extras like shoe-bags and make-up, produced an absolute frenzy of despair amongst the station staff, who ran about blowing whistles, pushing us aboard and trying to shut the doors. Such was the reverence afforded to these high speed trains that those who considered themselves 'unworthy persons' and intended to commit suicide might regain some honour by throwing themselves in front of the fastest train in the world.

The trip to Osaka was extremely comfortable. The train seats all fully reclined, and each headrest contained a small speaker which relayed music and train information in four languages from a central transmitter. Our collection of good-looking youngsters attracted visitors from the other carriages, and one very attractive young Japanese couple – supposedly balletomanes – offered hospitality in their home in Osaka to one of our boys. They gave him a visiting card, on one side of which was their address and on the other a photograph of them smiling at the camera in flagrante delicto. The Japanese are very relaxed and open about sex in all its rich variety.

Unlike in Tokyo, the Osaka Festival was very well organised. The Leipzig Gewandhaus Orchestra had played all nine Beethoven symphonies. Other concerts had been given by the Juilliard Quartet, and both Arthur Grumiaux and Isaac Stern had appeared with Leonard Bernstein. It was heady stuff, but the Company were right up there with the rest of the world-class performers, and on the last night, Beryl's performance of Giselle was described by a critic as 'the best ever seen in Japan'.

The last night of the Festival had a tradition which no one had told me about until just before I went to conduct the final ballet.

'Don't forget *Hotaru no Hikari*,' said the stage manager.

'What the hell is that?' I demanded.

'Oh,' he said, with the ubiquitous smile that the Japanese use to smooth over life's awkward moments. 'Very famous old Japanese song. All people know it,' and he sang the first line of 'Auld Lange Syne'.

I was still completely in the dark. How many verses did they sing? Did they get faster on the repeat? But my questions had to remain unanswered. There was still the last ballet to get through.

Beryl danced like a dream, and at the end I went on stage to take my usual bow, but, unusually, still carrying my baton. Amidst the cheers, to my utter amazement the whole orchestra pit began to rise like a surfacing submarine.

Bryan Ashbridge and Beryl Grey

When it reached stage level, trumpets sounded fanfares from all parts of the theatre, confetti rained down, the timpani player rolled his drums dramatically and all eyes turned to me. I stepped forward made some sort of an upbeat, mouthing the first word ('Should…') and, miraculously, the orchestra, the Company and audience all joined me in this 'famous old Japanese song'!

Curtain call at the Osaka Festival, 1961

I subsequently discovered that 'Hotaru no Hikari' has nothing whatsoever to do with Robbie Burns. It means 'Light of the Firefly' and is a Japanese song, traditionally sung at farewells. The Company were singing 'Auld Lang Syne', the audience were singing a song about fireflies, but everyone was very happy. Another page in the enigma that is Japan.

Our long flight back to England was broken by three performances at the Rizal Theatre in Manila. From comfortable and disciplined Japan, I was pitch-forked into a steamy, unsafe city, where we were warned never to hail a taxi on the street as there was a good chance that we'd be taken downtown and robbed (or worse) in what was then the murder capital of the world. The most dangerous taxis apparently bore the reassuring logo 'Family Cabs'.

Our visit had been organised by Ralph Zulueta, who was the managing director of San Miguel, the best-selling brewery in the United States, and he had paid for the Rizal Theatre to be completely renovated and re-equipped. However, the Manila Symphony Orchestra, which was to play for us, had been forced to disband during the particularly brutal Japanese occupation of the Philippines. When General MacArthur, true to his promise, had returned and had thrown out the Japanese, the musicians

Rehearsing the Manila Symphony Orchestra

had got together again using instruments provided by an American Army band, and for the next few years it was the only symphony orchestra in the Far East.

When I came to rehearse them, I suspected that some of the musicians were still using the old American instruments, for the principal trombone's instrument was patched, and in Manila's sticky heat, all the instruments bore signs of repair.

I narrowly missed being impaled by a screwdriver dropped by a careless stagehand from high above the stage, and when I merely smiled at this, the musicians were very well disposed to me and volunteered for extra unpaid rehearsals. I did my level best for these people, who had been through the hell of an occupation and had been deprived of music. They played very well on the first night, and I was now very comfortably dressed, for the Filipino President had given me a beautifully embroidered and almost transparent cotton shirt, a *Baron Tagalog*, which was very welcome when throwing my arms about in a relative humidity of nearly 100 per cent.

The Company backstage at the Rizal Theatre, Manila, 1961
Left to right: John Field, Anya Linden, Lynn Seymour, Beryl Grey,
Bryan Ashbridge, Desmond Doyle and Peter Franklin White

With Beryl Grey at the Rizal Theatre, Manila

Exciting though the tour had been, most of us now just wanted to get home to England. I was missing Mary and was growing a little weary of the struggle with less-than-average orchestras. We were all very tired and were not feeling very receptive when the few hours of waiting-time between flights in Bangkok was commandeered by the local ballet company. Eager to please their famous guests, they had arranged a bus tour of *The Pagodas*. It would have been a wonderful experience for people if even half-awake, but most of us were asleep, and I believe we offended some of our kind and eager hosts.

The Company boarding a
Constellation at Bangkok

As we took off for the last leg of our journey home, I looked back on the 'East-West Encounter' as a fascinating experience, and I wondered whether I'd ever go back to Japan. Then I remembered the day when the principal cellist of the Imperial Philharmonic, Yoshida San, had, surprisingly, asked me out for a coffee.

After the usual niceties (conducted in French, as he'd studied in Paris), he revealed the secret of his invitation. He spoke in English to make quite certain that I understood his words.

With a smile, he said: 'One day I form the best orchestra in Japan and you be conductor!'

'Mais certainement,' I replied. 'Avec grand plaisir.'

Yoshida's prophecy sounded wonderful – even possible – in Tokyo, but at 30,000 feet, it seemed pie in the sky. So I turned my thoughts to comfortable England and Mary, and went to sleep.

CHAPTER 33

POINTE TO POINTE

Rudolph Nureyev dances without Margot in Bath,
the Royal Ballet dances without costumes in Bordeaux and
Baroness de Rothschild is not amused

'Margot won't be coming this morning,' said Diana Menuhin, leaning over the orchestra rail. 'Tito's been shot.'

'Dead?' I asked.

'She doesn't know. She's speaking to Panama now, but Rudi will be here in a minute.'

I turned to the Bath Festival Orchestra and announced, 'There'll be a delay. Margot Fonteyn's husband has been shot.'

'Dear oh dear,' said the gentle Archie Camden from behind his bassoon. 'What a terrible thing.'

Indeed it was. It was 1964 and I'd just finished rehearsing John Dankworth's *Lysistrata*, written for his wife Cleo Laine, which was being premiered at Yehudi Menuhin's Bath Festival that night. I was waiting to rehearse Margot Fonteyn and Rudolf Nureyev in Nureyev's new version of the *pas de deux* from the second act of the August Bournonville ballet, *La Sylphide*, a ballet completely unknown to me.

If Margot wasn't coming to rehearsal, I would have to accompany her that night without having seen her steps. Not an ideal way of supporting a world-class ballerina and friend.

The Western Theatre Ballet's rehearsals had begun well. The previous day, I'd polished *Lysistrata*; the Festival Orchestra had been joined by three of John Dankworth's jazz musicians; we'd rehearsed Laverne Meyer's ballet *Sextet* to music by Hindemith; John had led his players in the band version of the Beatles songs which Peter Darrell had used for *Mods and Rockers*; and, finally, after the rest of the performers had left, Fonteyn, Nureyev and Menuhin had rehearsed, with Kenneth Macmillan, his ballet set to Bartok's *Divertimento* for solo violin.

I'd stayed on to watch these great artists at work. Menuhin, perched on a fragile-looking dais on the side of the stage, was giving a full performance of the Bartok from memory whilst,

Menuhin, Fonteyn and Nureyev in rehearsal

centre stage, Margot and Rudi were not dancing full out but were 'marking' the choreography (not dancing all the steps). This was possible for the dancers, but not for Menuhin, who still had to play all the notes. When they stopped to make a correction, Menuhin went on playing, and when they re-started, he had to pick up the music again: very difficult, even for a player of his genius.

I could see he was becoming increasingly irritated, until finally he lowered his Stradivarius, looked at the three of them and mumbled, 'I suppose you think this is easy?'

But the rehearsal had finished with smiles all round, and they'd all gone to dinner.

Things had seemed set fair for this morning, but now some trigger-happy hothead in Panama looked like ruining everything.

My musing was interrupted by the sudden arrival on stage of Nureyev. This was our first meeting, but, without any preliminaries, he looked down at me and announced, 'Margot dances tonight. Begin!'

My immediate thought was 'What a rude bastard!' but my second was relief that she was going to dance. So, in an attempt to show that one of us had good manners, I replied, 'Good morning, Mr Nureyev. That is good news.'

'Begin!' he insisted.

'But it says in the score that I have to wait for both of you to be on stage,' I responded.

'Margot is not coming to rehearsal,' he replied.

The orchestra, sensing an approaching crisis, became very attentive.

These early Bournonville ballets (*La Sylphide* dates from 1836) require the conductor to know the choreography, for, like most 'white' classical ballets, the tempi must match not only the choreography but also the differences brought to the role by individual dancers. I have a good memory for choreography, but how on earth could I be sure on this very important occasion of getting it right for Margot, never having seen a step?

'But I don't know Margot's dances at all,' I said.

Back he came with, 'I'll dance them for you.'

Nureyev performed not only his variations and their *pas de deux* but also Margot's solos. As he danced them and I conducted, we called to each other over the footlights. If my speed was danceable he responded 'khorosho' (the Russian equivalent of OK). If not, he'd call 'Not khorosho' and ask me, 'You want again?'

To be on the safe side, I usually said, 'Yes.'

I came away from the rehearsal with a great respect for his professionalism, and a great deal of sympathy for his feet. They had been taking the full weight of his body for a solid hour and where Margot's danced on her toes (*en pointe*) he did the same. But most impressive was the care he took that his partner would be able to dance her best that night.

After hearing the news of the attempted assassination, Margot had managed to get through to Tito's brother in Panama, who told her that Tito was alive and had 'wiggled his toes'. As she couldn't get a flight that day, she decided that the show could go on and passed a message to her husband that she'd see him on Wednesday.

As always, Margot came up trumps and, as the BBC had broadcast the fact that Tito had been shot, the audience applauded with that special warmth that the British show to those artistes whom they love, particularly when they are in trouble.

The evening was a great success, and as I joined the line-up for the curtain calls, I breathed a sigh of relief that I'd managed (with the selfless help of Nureyev) to conduct *La Sylphide* in a danceable way for them both — well enough to be asked if I'd join them on their next tour of Europe. Unfortunately it clashed with some BBC work, and I never again worked with Nureyev.

Margot flew the next day to Panama to find Tito alive, but only just. There was talk of a jealous husband, but the official report stated that the gunman was a young politician who had asked Tito to support him as a candidate in the Panama elections. He was furious that Tito had failed to back him wholeheartedly, and not being a man to take this rejection lightly, in Margot's own words, he '… put a gun in his pocket and drove through town. He saw that Tito's car ahead had stopped at the red light. He got out and shot Tito five times at point blank range. Tito was instantly paralysed.'

He was never to recover.

I was now finding very little time for conducting ballet, but when Dame Beryl Grey asked me to conduct the Festival Ballet's Christmas season of *Casse-Noisette* at the Royal Festival Hall, I found some – not only to please a dear friend and admired dancer with whom I'd worked so often at Covent Garden but also to seize the chance to complete my repertoire of the full-length Tchaikovsky ballets. The dancers were Galina Samsova and John Gilpin and the orchestra was the London Philharmonic, with which I'd often recorded.

The orchestra did full justice to a ballet which, compared with Tchaikovsky's other works, has been called 'a fascinating trifle'. But it's been drawing audiences for over a hundred years to the concert hall and the theatre. Written late in Tchaikovsky's life, he captured the world as seen through the eyes of a child.

Mary brought our daughters to the first matinée, and the effect of this magical ballet on them would have pleased the composer. Timandra, aged four, was so overcome that she removed her dress, and although her older sister Lucina kept her dress on, when I came forward with Galina Samsova for the curtain call, she demanded to know why I was holding the hand of 'that woman'. That afternoon, in just three hours, they both fell in love with ballet and Tchaikovsky.

The dainty, fairy-like Overture, the Christmas presents, the fight between the rats and toy soldiers and the scene when the Christmas tree takes to the air and the young heroine Clara is transported by a handsome prince to the Kingdom of Sweets, where snowflakes waltz to a wordless and invisible chorus… all are pure magic. In the 'Dance of the Sugar Plum Fairy', Russian ballet audiences heard for the first time an instrument that Tchaikovsky had discovered on a visit to Paris: the celeste.

During 1972 I'd been working non-stop: conducting, scripting and introducing *Sound Stage* for the World Service, and presenting *Friday Night is Music Night*, *All Kinds of Music*, *Bring up the Curtain* (my own Radio 2 chat show on Saturday mornings) and *Fanfare*, a live Sunday programme with the BBC Radio Orchestra.

So much of my life was spent in studios that I was missing the buzz of the theatre, and so when the Opera House asked me to conduct a Royal Ballet tour of Europe with Margot Fonteyn, I was delighted. Nureyev had left the Royal Ballet in 1970, and Margot continued to dance with him regularly, but this time her partner was Donald McCleary, who'd come a long way from our days together in the Sadler's Wells Theatre Ballet.

At the end of May I flew to Portugal to rehearse the Gulbenkian Orchestra, which bears the name of its founder, the Armenian oil millionaire. The players came from all parts of the world, including the young violinist with whom I was to share many notable musical occasions when he became leader of the BBC Concert Orchestra, Martin Loveday.

After a couple of performances in Lisbon, I went ahead to Bordeaux to rehearse the orchestra of the Opera House whilst the dancers made their way up by road through Spain and across the border into southern France. Bordeaux was *en fête*, with *tricolore* flags everywhere, and the Opera House was booked solid for our first night, which was to be attended by the French President, Georges Pompidou.

At 10am on the morning of the performance, Gauloises cigarettes extinguished, and everyone tuned to French pitch, the orchestra and I waited to start the dress rehearsal.

But there was a serious problem. Although the Company had arrived, their costumes, sets and ballet shoes had not. These were all still at the Spanish border in our lorries, waiting for Madrid to issue export licences to France. Someone hadn't done the correct paperwork, and even appeals to the Spanish that they were urgently required for a performance attended by the French President had no effect.

Orchestral time was running out and so, hoping for the best, we had to begin our dress rehearsal with the dancers in practice dress, wearing flat shoes and no scenery. Lunchtime arrived and we heard that the lorries were still in Spain.

There was no way we could cancel the performance and so, that night I conducted 'La Marseillaise' and the audience rose. What an audience it was, and what a sight: the ladies in long dresses and white gloves and the gentlemen in tails, wearing those sashes beloved of the French, many of whom were button-holed with the ribbon of the *Légion d'Honneur*. They applauded their President, who wore the *Croix de Guerre* which he had won fighting with the Free French under General de Gaulle.

Under the chandeliers, the auditorium was ablaze with colour, but when the house lights dimmed, the curtain rose to reveal a brick wall, devoid of any set, and dancers wearing a mixture of practice clothes, ordinary skirts, a few opera costumes, and a mixture of *pointe* shoes and slippers borrowed from the local ballet school. We might have got away with it in the first ballet, *Solitaire*, which was a simple tale of a lonely girl and her imaginary friends, but you can imagine the reaction of the audience when, without explanation, the curtain rose after the interval to reveal a flock of off-white swans against the same brick wall. They danced off as the hunting party arrived, carrying not bows and arrows but a variety of weapons, led by Prince Siegfried and his friend Benno in practice tights. An astonished rumble could be heard above the orchestra. Was this a modern version of *Swan Lake*?

In the interval before the last ballet (Noel Coward's *Grand Tour*), an announcement was made, informing the audience and the President that the ballets would be repeated tomorrow with sets and costumes, and that they would all be permitted to come using tonight's tickets.

That evening did little for the *entente cordiale*, and the next night's performance was not attended by M. Pompidou.

Although we were under a cloud for having marred the great day when the President came to town, a few of us were invited to lunch at Chateau Mouton Rothschild. The Baron and Baroness had both been at the first night as guests of the former General Manager of Rothschild Frères, who just happened to be the President himself, so it seemed that all was forgiven.

We were greeted by the head of the vineyard, who took us to a great cellar where there were barrels of wine as far as the eye could see. One of our dancers, who'd lived in France, asked him if it was true that, during the last war when the Chateau was occupied by the Germans, part of the cellar containing the finest wines had been bricked off, and they were not found again until after the war.

'Yes,' said our guide, 'and I'll show you where I did it!'

Then this elderly man, wearing his golden badge of office, showed us where, working secretly at night, he'd built and disguised the wall. After the war, the wall came down and the wines went to Buckingham Palace for the victory celebrations.

Then we moved on to the museum dedicated to wine where, behind bullet-proof glass, the exhibits included a 2nd century mask of the god of wine, Dionysus, a Mogul vase of jade encrusted with emeralds and rubies, and a gold chalice reputed to have been used by Christ at the Last Supper.

A fascinating hour had passed by the time we entered the Chateau, where we were warmly greeted by Baron Philippe and the Baroness and handed Dom Pérignon champagne by white-gloved house-servants. The Baron's English was perfect, as was that of his second wife, who had an American accent. She had been born Pauline Fairfax Potter, reputedly a descendant of Pocahontas. She had been a leading fashion designer and had had much to do with restoring the Chateau to its former glory after the German occupation.

We were about to start lunch when the Baroness discovered that one of our soloists, newly married, had decided to bring her new husband, *uninvited*. This would make us thirteen, and, for a brief moment, her charm failed. But a small table was brought and placed a foot away from ours, so as to break the bad luck associated with that number (perhaps, as the Baron speculated, a hangover from Christ's Last Supper, when he was the thirteenth).

The Baron told us of how, in January 1929, the Ballet Russe gave a season in Bordeaux and Diaghilev lunched at the Chateau with his young lover, Serge Lifar, who had afterwards danced *L'Après-Midi d'Un Faune* on the barrels in the cellar.

He spoke little of his early life as a racing driver, and nor did he mention his *Croix de guerre* won for fighting with General de Gaulle's Free French forces, but he told of how, in 1952, one of his poems dedicated to wine, 'Vendage', inspired Darius Milhaud to write the music for a three-act ballet for the Paris Opera. However, the designs by Salvador Dali were rejected as too erotic.

The conversation was as fascinating as the wine was perfect, for we'd moved to the *filet de boeuf,* and in the manner of a priestly sacrament, it was served with the murmured words '*Mouton Baron Philippe, mille neuf cent soixante-quatre'.* It was a religious moment, but when we moved to *Mouton Rothschild,* drawn from his stock of two hundred bottles of the finest, set aside each year for his own personal use, the waiter's prayer ('*Reserve du Baron') became even more reverential.

The *Reserve du Baron* removed, the cheese chosen, and glorious desserts enjoyed, the lunch ended as it had begun, some two hours before: with champagne.

That night, the sets and costumes having finally arrived, the Company received a wonderful reception from the citizens of Aquitaine – a region that had been English for a hundred years and with which we had once shared a king and, for over eight hundred years, wine for the Royal table.

The next day I flew back to *Melodies for You,* the Light Music Festival at the Royal Festival Hall, and a few days with my Mary and my daughters, before taking the morning flight to my brave little BBC band in Belfast.

A couple of weeks later I flew to Nice to conduct 'The Fonteyn Follies', an ensemble of eight dancers from the Royal Ballet, at the theatre in Monte Carlo where Nijinsky had danced *Spectre de la Rose* with Karsavina, and which, after Diaghilev's death, had become the home of the Ballet Russe de Monte Carlo.

The Théâtre de Monte Carlo is a miniature of the Paris Opera House, only seating around five hundred, which was perfect for 'The Follies', but not for orchestral rehearsals. The room in which I held mine was at the back of the theatre, and the ceiling was so low that I cannot imagine how composers like Bizet and Massenet (both of whom had their works premiered there) could have stood the din of an eighty-piece orchestra. Add to that the fact that half of them were smoking Gauloises Bleues.

It was mid-June and Monte Carlo was warming up nicely, so I was not very surprised when, after about thirty minutes the orchestral *régisseur* called for a break. The musicians poured out onto the beautiful terrace overlooking Monte Carlo's harbour, and gradually the sea brought a welcome change of air, but it wasn't long before the enormous amount of heat and energy (not to mention the Gauloises smoke) made another break essential.

I began to wonder about how we would get the music ready in time, but the *régisseur* assured me, in that superior and slightly off-hand manner which is particular to French officials, that the Monte Carlo Orchestra had never, ever rehearsed for more than forty minutes at a time, and that previous conductors of ballet there (Ernest Ansermet, Pierre Monteux, Antal Doráti *et al*) had all been satisfied.

As, eventually, was I. Although the rehearsals had been fragmented, smoky and not very disciplined, on the first night the orchestra produced an extraordinarily rich sound which matched the beauty of what must be one of the finest small theatres in the world.

It was a night of beauty. In the royal box sat Princess Grace and Prince Rainier with their friends David and Hjördis Niven, a girl that Niven said 'turned his knees to water the first time he saw her'.

Margot danced perfectly, as always, but the show was almost stolen by Deanne Bergsma, who had made such a hit as a student in the school performance of *Coppélia* which I'd conducted fifteen years before.

After a glittering evening, with the stage strewn with flowers, Mary and I walked under the stars to the Hotel de Paris and the after-theatre party hosted by Hitchcock's former star, who was now playing the biggest role of her career. When I thanked her for 'gracing us with your presence', Princess Grace (ever the actress) did a double-take and gave me a quizzical look that might have said 'Is this guy taking the Mickey?'

That was the last time I conducted for Margot – fifteen years after my first *Giselle* with her at Covent Garden.

Margot went on dancing as long as she could, travelling all over the world to earn enough to pay the hospital bills for Tito. She finally quit the stage and returned to Panama to become his devoted wife and nurse. In 1988 she danced for the last time with Nureyev before falling ill with cancer. Nureyev visited her in Panama and paid her hospital bills, for she was penniless. Tito died in 1989 and she followed him just two years later. Thus ended the greatest *prima ballerina assoluta*.

Margot Fonteyn and Michael Somes

I was at a dress rehearsal of the Royal Ballet a few years after Margot's death. Spotting me, Michael Somes, her former partner who had become the Company Ballet Master, told me: 'You were here during the best of times.'

But perhaps we all like to think that!

CODA

A few years ago I was called to the Royal Academy of Music to receive a Fellowship at the Graduation Ceremony, held in Marylebone Parish Church. After a brilliant fanfare by the young Academy brass players, and to the sound of the great organ and Academy Choir, we alumni processed to our places in a church full of young people in the simple red and white of their academic dress. It was a remarkable sight, and the sound of the organ, brass choir and two hundred students singing the National Anthem would have melted even the heart of a Republican.

I sat with Valery Gergiev – the only other conductor to be honoured that day – who received an Honorary degree. The ceremony was linked by John Suchet as the Academy's Orator, in his dual role as a newsreader and Beethoven expert. Afterwards, as Gergiev and I crossed Marylebone Road against the traffic lights (well, it would be a brave motorist who ran down two men in long black cloaks and red sashes), he chatted about how often he'd conducted in London.

Back at the Royal Academy, we lunched together in the refectory which Sir Henry Wood must have used many times, and this great conductor, known to the world as the Musical Director of Russia, surprised me when he announced that the Royal Academy of Music was the finest teaching Academy in the world, and that there was nothing like it in his country.

The refectory was only a few steps from the Duke's Hall where, forty years before, I'd been trained in the 'Timber Wood' method of conducting. I was suddenly struck by how far we had come since the days when Sir Henry first took up the baton, which was at a time when our country was known as 'a land without music', rehearsals were thin on the ground and his concerts might have included Schubert's *Serenade* played by a cornet soloist sporting a monocle, and where the smokers in the audience would be requested not to strike matches during the vocal items.

Now it was the home to the greatest musical festival in the world: the Sir Henry Wood Promenade Concerts.

My father was right about destiny – a word which, as a soldier who'd seen much of death, he must have deliberately substituted for Shakespeare's 'divinity' when he wrote in my autograph book all those years before.

But destiny or divinity, my dream had come true, and I raised my glass to Gergiev as he departed to rehearse at my old home: the Royal Opera House, Covent Garden.

Coming up in Volume II

*BBC Radio 2's
'Friday Night is
Music Night'
and other adventures
at the BBC*

*With Maurice
Cavanagh and the BBC
Northern Ireland
Orchestra*

With Inia Te Wiata
in the West End
premiere of 'The Most
Happy Fella'

At work above on his production of Gilbert & Sullivan's H.M.S. Pinafore
which opened at Her Majesty's Theatre last week is Sir Tyrone Guthrie, whose
production of the partnership's early nautical opera, The Pirates Of
Penzance, opens on Friday. The two operas will be given on alternate weeks
conducted by musical director Kenneth Alwyn, seen behind Sir Tyrone.

With Sir Tyrone
Guthrie in
'H.M.S. Pinafore'
in aid of King George's
Pension Fund for
Actors and Actresses

'Camelot'
with Laurence Harvey
and Elizabeth Larner

*'Charlie Girl'
with Anna Neagle,
Derek Nimmo and
Stuart Damon*

*The Mantovani
Orchestra*

*With the London
Symphony Orchestra
at the Royal Festival
Hall in aid of the RAF
Benevolent Fund*

WESTMINSTER ABBEY

SIR NOËL COWARD

A CELEBRATION

and

UNVEILING OF A MEMORIAL STONE

Wednesday 28 March 1984
11.30 a.m.

*Installation of Noel
Coward in
Poets' Corner,
Westminster Abbey*

*Battle of Britain
50th Anniversary
US Tour
and D-Day
50th Anniversary
Concert*

With Bryn Terfel and the Welsh National Opera recording Samuel Coleridge-Taylor's 'Hiawatha Trilogy'

With Dudley Moore and the BBC Concert Orchestra at the Royal Albert Hall

With the BBC Concert Orchestra at the St George's Day Festival Concert in aid of Imperial Cancer Research Fund

*Recording the film music
of Steiner, Addinsell,
Bax, Arnold,
Waxman and others*

*Gramophone Award for
Best Film Music*

COPYRIGHT NOTICES